Southern Newcomers to Northern Cities

Gene B. Petersen
Laure M. Sharp
Thomas F. Drury

Published in cooperation
with the Bureau of Social
Science Research, Inc.

The Praeger Special Studies program—
utilizing the most modern and efficient book
production techniques and a selective
worldwide distribution network—makes
available to the academic, government, and
business communities significant, timely
research in U.S. and international economic, social, and political development.

Southern Newcomers to Northern Cities
Work and Social Adjustment in Cleveland

PRAEGER SPECIAL STUDIES IN U.S. ECONOMIC, SOCIAL, AND POLITICAL ISSUES

Praeger Publishers   New York   London

Library of Congress Cataloging in Publication Data

Petersen, Gene B
    Southern newcomers to northern cities.

    (Praeger special studies in U.S. economic, social,
and political issues)
    Includes bibliographical references.
    1. Labor and laboring classes—Cleveland. 2. Cleve-
land—Social conditions. 3. Rural-urban migration—
United States—Case studies. I. Sharp, Laure Metzger,
1921-   joint author. II. Drury, Thomas F., joint
author. III. Title.
HD8085.C63P47   301.44'42'0977132   76-24364
ISBN 0-275-24000-2

        The materials on which this book is based were
developed under Contract 82-09-67-54, U.S. Department
of Labor, Manpower Administration. Reproduction in
whole or in part is permitted for any purpose of the
U.S. Government.

PRAEGER PUBLISHERS
200 Park Avenue, New York, N.Y. 10017, U.S.A.

Published in the United States of America in 1977
by Praeger Publishers, Inc.

Printed in the United States of America

ACKNOWLEDGMENTS

This study is based on interviews taken in 1971-72 with 1,044 Cleveland residents who were "survivors" from a cohort, originally interviewed in 1967-68, of 1,299 recent migrants from Southern states to Cleveland and 414 nearby heads of house who had lived in Cleveland for at least ten years. Because of our special interest in the process of occupational and social adjustment of working-class newcomers to major industrial centers, the migrants and their long-term resident neighbors were located through an intensive door-to-door canvass of nearly 68,000 households in Cleveland's poorest neighborhoods. All of these people are most sincerely thanked for answering the brief set of questions that enabled us to locate the recent migrants and their long-term resident neighbors. The migrants and long-term resident respondents deserve our special gratitude for participating in the original interview and the follow-up four years later. Their patient cooperation in both interviews and the willingness with which they provided detailed information on their work and social experiences is deeply appreciated. The Special Surveys Company in Cleveland and in particular Frank Semple, who trained and supervised the interviewers, deserve grateful acknowledgment for the craftsmanlike manner in which they accomplished the fieldwork.

For their continued support, advice, criticism, and encouragement, particular thanks are given to Dr. Howard Rosen, Director, Office of Research and Development in the Manpower Administration, and to Jesse Davis and Beverly Bacheman, who were project monitors for the study.

A study of this scope and duration necessarily engages the efforts of many colleagues and coworkers. All have our gratitude and appreciation. Special credit is due to Dr. Eleanor Godfrey and to Barbara Heller, who made major contributions to the original study design and selection of the study site. Rebecca Krasnegor is thanked for her suggestions and assistance in reviewing the literature, in developing the first round instruments and field procedures, and in guiding the analysis plan. Elaine el-Khawas turned a fresh and critical eye to the data presented in the report on the first round of interviews and drafted the summary of that report. The principal research assistants for the study, Daniel Sharp, Joan Aronson, Marsha Gold, David P. Crews, Claudia Bloom, Alan Carroll, Morris Ledbetter, Robert Wilson, William Stevenson, and Peter de Arcangelis, are thanked for their constant attention to detail and concern for accuracy as well as their willingness to tolerate the frustration inherent in both. Donald Goldstein and Celia Pavis respectively managed the editing and coding crews for the first and second rounds of interviewing. Their patience and conscientiousness assured that the quality of the original interviews was not lost in the translation of the responses to frequencies. For this and their assistance in myriad other ways, they and the now anonymous editors and coders are warmly thanked. In the data processing unit, Richard Jones, Richard Forte, and Fiona Wu Chang managed the data files and our tabulation requests. Their professionalism could always be assumed, but we are still grateful for it and their toleration of persons whose constant refrain seemed to be "could I get just one more table." Preparation of the final typescript for the survey instruments, documents, and working papers and the production of reports was accomplished under the direction of Antonette Simplicio. For their individual efforts in preparing earlier materials and reports, Francys Richardson, Dalia Taube, Beverly Carby, and Annie Liles have our sincere thanks and appreciation. The typescript for this study is the result of the collaboration of Amy Goodman, who typed most of the tables, and Francys Richardson, who typed the text and most of the remaining tables; Jeannie Malenab provided back-up assistance in the stretch. The quality of their work has added materially to the readability of the report and substantially eased the burden on the proofreaders, who were Roberta Rubenstein, Andrea Golden, Paula Freedman, and David Lambert. Karen Howell served as the final reader at the Bureau of Social Science Research and made substantial editorial revisions.

CONTENTS

LIST OF TABLES

LIST OF FIGURES

xxii

The search for jobs and for greater economic opportunity impels our rural population to migrate
to already overburdened, overcrowded cities.
Unfortunately, many of them lack the education
and skills to compete in the technical labor markets where manpower is most in demand. They
are forced then, by economic circumstances, to
live in the slums and ghettos, where they become
the hard core unemployed forced to live at bare
subsistence level.

Senator Fred R. Harris*

Quite apart from either real or perceived benefits,
or added life burdens for individual migrants, the
nature of contact and interaction between either
new arrivals and members of the urban society, or
between different ethnic and racial groups within
urban society, indicates that far-reaching public
consequences of both earlier and latter-day population movements are continuing to be generated.

Lyle W. Shannon and Magdaline Shannon†

---

*U.S. Congress, Senate, Committee on Government Opera-
tions, The Rural to Urban Population Shift: A National Problem,
report of the proceedings of the National Manpower Conference
sponsored by Senate Sub-Committee on Government Research, The
Ford Foundation, and Oklahoma State University. Committee Print,
90th Congress, 2d session. (Washington, D.C.: U.S. Government
Printing Office, 1968), p. 4.
  †"The Assimilation of Migrants to Cities: Anthropological and
Sociological Contributions," in Leo F. Schnore and Henry Fagin,
eds., Urban Research and Policy Planning (Beverly Hills, Calif.:
Sage Publications, 1967).

Much of the recent history of Appalachia has been
marked by a steady stream of people migrating
from the rural hollows of the Appalachian Region
into the urban areas of the North. Many of these
Appalachian migrants have gone into such cities
as Pittsburgh, Cleveland, Cincinnati and Columbus
seeking jobs in the industrial factories--only to
end up on welfare.[1]

In 1947, 25 years before the above words were written, Louis
Bromfield observed, "The migration of Southern hill people into
this rich, literate, hard-working Ohio country has been an almost
total failure."[2] A few pages later, the sage of Malabar Farm makes
it clear that the generalization is doubly applicable to blacks.
Whether the migrants are black or white, hillbillies, miners, or
cotton choppers, whether from urban areas, out of the hollows, or
from rural lanes, there has been a general feeling--despite occa-
sional bits of striking evidence to the contrary--that Southern newcomers to Northern cities are at best misfits, more often than not
becoming a public burden as soon as they can qualify for welfare,
and are disproportionately often found registered on the arrest
blotters of precinct houses. In the popular view, the move north-
ward has traumatic consequences for the migrants from the South,
disastrous ones for the receiving city.

This negative view of the process of migration, fed by the
writing of romanticists like Bromfield and by political and religious
interest groups such as those concerned with the fate of Appalachia,
as well as by the strength and growth of ethnic movements and
ideologies, has persisted in the face of a growing body of empirical
evidence that is basically contradictory to the popular image. This
is not hard to understand.

Against the background of burgeoning urban populations and
problems, absolute declines in rural populations, and regional
shifts in population balance, it is understandable that concern over
the processes and prospects of migration should be continual. But
public consideration of migration and its consequences is seldom
dispassionate. The very term migrant carries with it connotations
of transiency, unreliability, and undesirability. Migrants are
persons who pick peas and cucumbers; responsible citizens who
change their residences are called "newcomers" when they arrive

at their destinations. Characteristically, an either/or logic seems to operate, and the departure or arrival of significant numbers of migrants is seen as an unmitigated gain or liability for the sending or receiving community. The allocative functions or consequences of migration are thereby given implicit recognition in the evaluations, but consideration of the consequences of in- or out-migration rarely stops at objective appraisal of effects on local manpower supplies and the labor market.

In recent years, we have witnessed a renaissance of sentiments and attitudes coupling fears of rural depopulation with the horror of urban sprawl and the crippling effects of urban ghetto residence. But the uneven distribution of opportunities, social as well as economic, continues to stimulate migration. Because of the concern over the ill effects of migration to the largest cities, alternatives are being explored such as the promotion of shorter-distance moves from local areas of economic depression to nearby "regional growth centers" where, it is hoped, employment prospects will be brighter and the detrimental effects of massive urban concentrations fewer.

The positive contributions of internal migration to the economic development of the country and the welfare of its residents have been generally acknowledged by those who adopt a historical perspective. But, despite the volume of migration in the United States and the manifold benefits it holds for individuals and communities, we seem to distrust both the process and its participants. Receiving communities often need additions to their labor forces yet deplore the kinds of migrants that are arriving to seek work; sending communities acknowledge the lack of nearby opportunities yet mourn the departure of the young folks. Simultaneously, migration is praised and condemned, promoted and feared. The migrant's labor is sought, his physical presence and demands for housing and social services resented, especially if he differs in race or ethnicity, but often even in the absence of such differences. As a nation, we seem to have paid more attention to industrial requirements for labor and less to the implicit costs of large-scale in-migration in terms of demands for services and facilities in the new community.

It is our distinct impression that European planners and social observers have given more attention to these consequences of migration. In this regard, it seems worth noting that the European debate over infrastructural costs--as they term these demands for goods and services--has progressed to the point of considering whether migrants (because they are younger, less often married, from cultures of lower standards of living, and so forth), may not make fewer demands than indigenous population groups of the same social class.

DEVELOPMENT OF THE STUDY

When this study was initiated in 1966 there was manifest concern over the inability of Southern migrants to find and hold adequate jobs and to make satisfactory adjustment to life in Northern industrial cities. At the time they were being faulted for disproportionate contributions to welfare rolls and police blotters. While the first round of our fieldwork was in progress, riots in urban ghettos led some, especially local officials, to make the easy but erroneous assumption that the incendiary catalyst had been displaced and unemployed Southern migrants, fairly recent newcomers to the ghetto communities. Systematic studies of the ghetto riots found little to support the view, but it is probably still held to be valid by many. More recently, migrants have been charged with moving solely to gain access to welfare allowances more generous than those available in their home states; and again a popular notion seems to survive in the face of contrary research evidence. Thus, one of our research goals became the development of systematic and objective evidence on these topics.

So far we have mentioned only the public aspects and consequences of migration. But a full assessment of the effects of migration must also consider the personal consequence of migration and explore dimensions such as self-actualization, the realization of expectations, and the fulfillment of aspirations. Because migration and changes in employment are so closely linked, one route to this is through the consideration of work and its consequences.[3]

The jobs workers have depend in part on the kinds of work available to be done by individuals with particular characteristics. The level and structure of economic activity affect the allocation of workers to jobs, as does the exercise by employers of their preferences in worker characteristics. Worker choice is reflected in the decision to enter the labor force or not and to seek employment in some occupations in preference to others. Culture and social structure influence who will work and when. Information processes, whether channeled through the media, employment services, or friendship networks, make knowledge about some kinds of job opportunities more likely than is awareness of others. Once on the job, the consequences of particular choices are equally abundant. Since most occupations have both tangible and intangible reward systems, one's style of life and physical as well as psychological well-being are also affected. The social structure of employment (or unemployment) has broad effects in the choice of friends, in the development of interests, and in the pursuit of personal activities. To the extent that one is dependent upon the tangible rewards of work for support, choice of job constrains the scope of choice of residence, thus influencing the quality of education and social behavior of children in the household--to say nothing of personal safety. Similarly, choice of occupation also entails exposure to on-the-job health hazards and thus influences the kinds of illnesses one is likely to have, how acute and prolonged the episodes will be, indeed, length of life and probable cause of death.

In 1965, when concern about recent Southern migrants and the problems they were bringing to the cities of the North and West was at its height, the U.S. Department of Labor, through the Manpower Administration's Office of Research and Development, provided a grant for the Bureau of Social Science Research, Inc., to explore the feasibility of conducting a large-scale study of work adaptation and social adjustment of recent Southern migrants to low-income neighborhoods of a Northern city. Following the feasibility study, funds were provided to conduct a survey of migrants from Southern states who had lived in Cleveland less than five years and of a smaller comparison group of neighbors with at least ten years of Cleveland residence. All were members of the labor force as usually defined, except that persons who were not working or looking for work because of a personal belief that no work was available for them--now called "discouraged workers"--were also included. So were female heads of house, whatever their labor force status, because of the concern about the contribution of migrants to burgeoning urban welfare rolls.*

The survey migrants and their long-term resident counterparts were located through an intensive door-to-door canvass in Cleveland's lowest-income neighborhoods. In all, about 68,000 households were contacted to locate the migrants with whom detailed personal interviews were conducted first in the fall and winter of 1967 and spring of 1968 and again approximately four years later. This report contains the major findings from the interviews with 745 migrants and 299 long-term Cleveland residents who were interviewed during both field work periods.†

An indication of the depth of federal concern about the outmigration of Southerners is provided by the fact that more than a half dozen studies focused on various aspects of the "problem" were

---

*Full details on the survey methodology and definition of criteria for selection of respondents will be found in the Appendix.

†Most of the material and data presented in this study are made available here for the first time. Where appropriate, as in Chapter 1, we have also included material from prior reports and working papers developed during the course of the study.

funded by federal agencies, mainly the Manpower Administration of the U.S. Department of Labor, the Office of Economic Opportunity, and the National Institute of Health, around the time the fieldwork for this study was being done. All are important departures from traditional approaches to the study of migration, which are usually dependent upon analysis of available data, generally from censuses, or case studies of the lives of a small number of migrants. Some of this research has been reported; results of other inquiries are still emerging. But throughout the period of the study there has been a fair amount of exchange of points of view, study designs, instruments, and approaches among the investigators, which was partially stimulated by the opportunity to discuss each other's work at several small research conferences.

The breadth of the analytical task is illustrated by the variety of approaches investigators have used recently in trying to describe and understand the process of migration and the adjustment of migrants. Consideration of some of the differences in study design with respect to major variables also helps place the Cleveland project in relationship to other work on migration and on migrants being done at about the same time. For example, a design decision as to whether the subject of the study shall be migration or migrants is fundamental. In the Cleveland study we took migration as a given, and limited exploration of reasons behind the move to a single broad-gauged question. Others--for example, John Lansing[4] and Abt Associates[5]--have directed their attention to the factors that lead to migration, without concerning themselves with problems that occur farther down the road. The Tracor group[6] set as their central problem an exploration of the economic benefits of migration and contrasted the situation of persons in sending communities with those of migrants in major destination cities. Similarly, Morgan[7] and his associates at the University of Kentucky studied the economic costs and benefits incurred by migrants who moved from rural Kentucky to various urban destinations. At the time our investigation began, the individual benefits of migration seemed less important than major welfare and unemployment problems in Northern cities that were being attributed to the massive influx of poor Southerners. Thus, we chose to restrict our study population to residents of the city's poorest neighborhoods who, presumably, would be making the largest contribution to the problems of the community.

The problem of locating migrants in their new localities is also a vexing one and serves to further differentiate these studies. The use of school records tends to bias samples by excluding younger, older, and childless migrants. Other public registers are similarly incomplete; for example, records of motor vehicles bureaus exclude those without cars registered in the state or without current driver's licenses, while welfare lists and police blotters exclude those who have not yet run afoul of the law or applied for welfare assistance. Where migrant communities are well established and have developed their own institutions, heads of organizations and membership lists can sometimes be used as a sampling frame, a method utilized by Choldin and Trout.[8] This, however, tends to produce a sample of subjects who are well known to one another and tied to the community by an organizational bond, hardly the kind of persons likely to be contributing to urban problems as a result of failure and isolation in a complex and assumedly hostile environment. Similar objections pertain to the use of chaining techniques, in which migrants nominate others they know. Occasionally one can take advantage of the coverage of some other survey, such as a decennial census, and use its questions to locate appropriate subjects; but that depends on fortuitous timing and the cooperation of other researchers. Lacking an appropriate sampling frame, but assured that migrants existed in great numbers in the city, we mounted a door-to-door canvass in the city's poorest neighborhoods. Of all the census tracts entered in the search for migrants, only one ranked above the third family income decile in the Cleveland area. The Abt group subsequently used the same technique to locate respondents in their destination cities.

Another fundamental design choice, often channeled by the major study objectives, is in the selection of appropriate comparison groups. The Lansing and Parnes[9] studies both set as their research goal generalizations about major segments of the national population and both relied on national samples, selected to best reflect their particular interests. Lansing, concerned about the mobility of workers, focused the data collection effort on heads of families and supplemented the national sample with a special sample drawn from redevelopment areas to provide additional information about the mobility of persons in economically distressed areas. Parnes, looking at labor force behavior at crucial turning points in the life cycle, sampled men and women under 25, women 30-44 years of age, and men 45 to 59 years old, specifically contrasting the different experiences of white and black citizens. The Abt and Tracor groups each contrasted people in sending areas in the Southern black, white Appalachian, and Mexican-American migratory streams with newcomers in destination cities in order to better understand poor people's mobility or lack of it and the economic benefits of migration. The Shannons[10] started their investigation of assimilation into a single North Central city with an analysis of the experience of Mexican-Americans but broadened their study population to include Southern blacks and local "Anglos" as well. In their study of the process of moving from agricultural to nonagricultural employment,

Choldin and Trout, working out of a state university of the Northern
end of the Texas-based migratory farm worker stream, attempted
a statewide sample of Mexican-American migratory farm workers
but ultimately drew in nonagricultural migrants and native-born
persons of Mexican-American descent. When they make comparisons
with other elements of the population of their state, the data are
generally drawn from a public data file or publication. The Cleveland study compares the experience of adult black and white newcomers with that of established residents from the same neighborhoods. Because there were so few members of other nonwhite
ethnic groups in the Cleveland population, they were excluded from
the outset in our study.

Some decision is also necessary on the amount of attention to
be given to contextual factors, such as community organization. In
the assimilation studies of the Shannons and of Choldin and Trout,
community organization and peer or small group relationships are
given major importance in the analysis. In the Cleveland study,
family networks and the circle of friends emerge as potent forces in
the lives of the migrants but no attempt was made to address these
except as they influence the settling in of the newcomers and their
search for employment. Our study also does not treat Cleveland as
a community. For us the city merely constitutes the milieu within
which residence and jobs were sought. Fascinated as we personally
became with the public details of Cleveland's political and economic
life at the end of the 1960s, the city was for us a representative of
Northern industrial cities chosen because of the several factors that
made it a more promising locale for conduct of the research. Rather
than looking to community organization, we have given attention to
the contrast in level of economic activity during the first round of
interviewing in 1967 and 1968 and the second round of interviews
that were completed in 1972.

Finally, in addition to deciding how and from whom the data
are to be collected, study designers must also give some consideration to the number of observations that will be sought for each subject. Of the studies with which the Cleveland investigation has here
been compared, only two others attempted repeated interviews with
the same subjects. Where the other studies introduce time as a factor, it is done either through recall or by the use of prospective
questioning. The essence of the Shannons' work is based on two
sets of interviews taken about a year apart at the beginning of the
1960s. The Parnes group outlined five rounds of interviews with
their subjects; when this was written, reports were available on
only the first two yearly cycles or waves. The Cleveland study is
based on data collected in two rounds of interviews taken about four
years apart. Data from the migrants collected in the first round of

interviewing are augmented by retrospective information on aspects
of their lives that had taken place before the move to Cleveland.

While the retention of the interest of subjects, investigators,
and funders over the life of a panel study is difficult, it is possible;
and some definite benefits occur. Generally a broader variety of
information can be obtained and errors of recall, particularly with
respect to attitudinal or evaluative variables, are reduced. Unlike
sequential cross-sectional studies, in panel studies differences
over time can be described not only for aggregate groups but also
for individuals, by which means compensatory shifts may be uncov-
ered. Moreover, one can also have increased confidence that similarities observed are not accidents and that differences do not arise
from having made observations on substantially different populations.
The drawbacks are also obvious. The commitment of individuals to
the study must be obtained and maintained. Further, final results
are delayed until after the final round of interviewing is completed
(though, in the Cleveland study, as in most other panel designs,
interim reports provide early leads to data trends and tendencies).
For example, in the Cleveland study, in addition to periodic progress
reports that provided substantive feedback to the sponsor, two substantive working papers, a report on highlights from the first round
of interviews, and a detailed report and analysis of the first round of
interviews were prepared.

ANALYTIC APPROACH

The design of the study and the organization of this report are
centered on two classes of variables. The characteristics of the
migrants and members of the comparison group of long-term Cleveland residents are considered first. These input variables define
the characteristics of the human resources made available to employers or prospective employers by the movement of these migrants from their Southern homes to their new homes in Cleveland's
low-income neighborhoods. These variables are of varying degrees
of objectivity, for we consider not only the usual dimensions such as
sex, race, age, and prior experience but also attitudinal dimensions
indicative of the commitment to work or enter the labor force as
well as to remain in Cleveland or move elsewhere. As outcome
variables we consider the rewards or return on the investment of
moving to Cleveland and living in an inner-city neighborhood: labor
force status, occupation, wages, poverty status, dependence
upon public assistance, and some evaluative dimensions such as

satisfaction with the move and individual appraisals of progress toward self-defined ideal life states or goals.*

The study is organized around the temporal sequence of events, starting with a discussion of socialization and work experiences before the move. While our main focus is on work and labor force participation, these also become points of departure for considering other aspects of the adjustment of the migrants to living in Cleveland, including their evaluations of their life situation and hopes for the future.

Ideally, one would have liked to follow a natural cohort through its entire settling-in period to help answer the question of whether there are discernible stages or patterns in the process of adaptation to life in a Northern industrial city. Such a design would not only require a greater span of years than was actually used on this study, but would also require a greater number of repeated observations of the same individuals (say, a first observation during the first two weeks of Cleveland residence, another at about the end of the third month, still another at the end of the first year, followed by less frequent observations until the effects of newness in the community are no longer discernible). The design actually adopted for this study involved the use of a synthetic cohort, assembled by interviewing a spectrum of Southern newcomers to low-income neighborhoods of the city, including some who had arrived within the past few days and others who, initially, had lived in the city as long as five years. Except in the sections dealing with premigration experiences, the migrants are regularly compared with a group of neighbors, persons generally chosen from the same block who had lived in Cleveland at least ten years.

A couple of drawbacks to this design are immediately apparent. The long-term residents, who had lived in Cleveland ten years or more, tended to be a bit older, on the average about ten years older than the migrants. Hence the members of the comparison group are at a different point in their life cycle. Most of the migrants came to the city as young marrieds, many with preschool children or elementary school enrollees. The long-termers were further along in the family cycle. They had older children, who were facing high school and the personal events beyond school, and were

---

*Obviously, interaction can be assumed among some variables, particularly between outcome variables such as labor force status, occupation and wages, and attitudinal dimensions. The order adopted here is primarily for convenience in presentation and discussion.

more settled into the community. They also tended to have greater amounts of work experience and more years of service with their employers. In a sense, as a comparison group, the long-termers were not Clevelanders similar to the migrants in most ways except for their greater experience in the community, but were more nearly what the migrants might come to be in the future.

Even that comparison, however, is confounded by other factors. The original populations were located by means of a house-to-house canvass in inner city neighborhoods. But the reasons for residing in a poor inner-city neighborhood are undoubtedly different for newcomers and for people with rather lengthy experience in the community; they are also quite different for whites and blacks.

For the migrants, the poor neighborhoods seem to be a point of entry; a place for persons without much money to get oriented to a new environment, find a job, and begin to make their way, perhaps to a better house and neighborhood. (See the Appendix for the criteria by which neighborhoods were defined as "poor" and selected for inclusion in the study.) For the long-term residents, living in the areas on which the study was based may be more clearly a manifestation of failure. In the same fashion, black respondents lacking available housing outside the Hough area and nearby ghetto districts are constrained in their choice of residence. Whites have more options, though some successful long-term residents might choose not to exercise them because of personal, ethnic, or occupational ties to the neighborhood.

Our analytic approach relies heavily on the three basic variables--race, sex, and duration of residence--that were used initially to classify the study population. Three duration-of-residence categories were distinguished: latecomers (migrants who had lived in the city less than two full years when first interviewed), early arrivals (newcomers who had lived in the city for more than two but fewer than five full years), and long-term residents (sometimes called long-termers), persons who had lived in Cleveland at least ten years when first interviewed. This classification serves as a rough control for the amount of experience members in each group had in coming to terms with the city.

Even if the intervals of residence had been divided more finely, we would still obtain only a crude measure of experience in coping with or adapting to Cleveland, if only because participants in the life of any community are drawn differentially into its affairs both with regard to the domains within which they move and the intensity or frequency of their interaction with others within those domains. Finer measurement and conceptualization could have important consequences for the interpretation of data on adjustment and adaptation. For example, it seems plausible that workers whose jobs bring them into contact with a wide variety of other workers (say, workers like relief men in factories or coin-operated vending machine routemen) are in a position to acquire more knowledge about employment opportunities than workers with more limited patterns of work interaction (say, punch press operators, production workers, or typists) and consequently are able to be more effective change agents in promoting mobility for themselves and others (within their realms of specialized knowledge and interaction).

Race was an obvious candidate for inclusion as a primary analytic variable.* The study was planned and initiated as one of the early investigations sponsored under the Manpower Development and Training Act at a time when it was hoped that the then nascent war on poverty would have dramatic effects on the lives of poor people, black and white. The burgeoning civil rights movement also gave hope that race would lose some of its castelike qualities and that the life chances of black citizens might begin to improve markedly. Indeed, the changes in language surrounding these events was so rapid that we found ourselves in the midst of a small editorial conundrum. When the study was being formulated it was conventional to refer in print to persons with darker skins as Negroes. As the fieldwork progressed, it became fashionable and then policy to refer to the same group as blacks (though the vexing problem of appropriate capitalization remained).

Nevertheless, at the time of the study, more so than now, race was a factor in the marketplace[11] and in the community.[12] It was also a factor in which the Manpower Administration had a strong interest. Changes in the relative position of members of the two racial groups would constitute strategic information for planning and policy decisions at the federal level.

At the time this study was initiated, equality of opportunity for women did not enjoy the same official priority status as equality for blacks; the women's rights movement had not yet exploded. Given the current high interest in this topic, and especially the

_____

*Though it had not always been so; at various times in the planning stages, the suggestion was made to limit the study population to whites only or to blacks only. Members of other ethnic or racial groups (for example, American Indians or Spanish-speaking persons) were excluded from the outset in the belief that the number of migrants from these groups in inner-city neighborhoods in Cleveland would be too small for fruitful analysis. The availability of comparative data for whites and blacks of both sexes and for persons of various durations of local residence is one of the strong points of the Cleveland study.

increasing awareness of the disadvantaged situation of black females in the labor force, our decision to include women, although it greatly complicated definitional and analytic tasks, is especially fortunate. Sex was included as a primary analytic variable not only because of longstanding differences in labor force participation of men and women, but also because of the growing concern about the adaptive styles of female heads of house who were included in the study population irrespective of their labor force status. (See the Appendix for criteria used to select study population.) Because of its correlation with other indicators, sex, like race, is a potent variable. Taken alone it stands not only for physiological differences, of which some are of importance to employers, but also for differences in socialization, including culturally derived expectations concerning appropriate social roles for men and women that help set the expectations of workers and employers on such topics as occupations, industry, work hours and conditions, and levels of pay.

Taken in combination, these primary analytic variables form 12 comparison groups: two sex groups, two race groups, and three duration-of-residence groups. Generally, measures concerning activities in Cleveland, including attitudes and expectations, were obtained in both rounds of interviewing. Thus, for most indicators we have two sets of observations, separated by about four years and based on interviews with the same individuals. During the first round of interviewing, in the fall and winter of 1967 and the spring of 1968, the job market was relatively good. When the second round of interviews was conducted, between July 1971 and May 1972, jobs were considerably scarcer. For example, the Index of Help Wanted Advertisements, prepared by the National Industrial Conference Board and issued in their Conference Board Statistical Bulletin, showed the volume of help-wanted advertisements to be about 90 percent greater during the first period of interviewing than during the reference years (1957-59). But there were just over three-fifths as many ads being inserted in the Cleveland papers during the second period of interviewing as in the first. While the volume of want ads is a better indicator of the demand for professional, technical, and managerial personnel and for clerical and sales workers than for other occupations, it does provide a convenient indication of the degree to which the number of job openings had fallen off between the two fieldwork periods.

Differences in levels of business activity may have important consequences for the relative position of groups of cohorts that are hired or fired at different rates.[13] In a tight labor market the differentially hired groups are closer together (for example, in occupations or earnings) than they are when the labor market is slack, largely because the labor shortage does not permit the development of highly differentiated queues. In a loose labor market such as one undergoing a recession, if the groups are retained or fired at differential rates they move apart (again, in occupations or earnings). The first-round data for the Cleveland study were gathered under tight labor market conditions; the second-round data were collected when the demand for workers was far less. Thus, under these assumptions, the intervening events had worked against the anticipated convergence in the position of workers in the two race groups. Business conditions favored less differentiation between members of the two races at the time of the first interviews than at the time of the second interviews.

In looking at the data, the first search was generally within sex and race categories to isolate indications that the migrants were moving into positions approximating those held by long-term residents. This does not necessarily involve an assumption of improvement. Generally two opposing hypothetical models are presented in the literature on adjustment and adaptation of migrants. The assimilation model posits the gradual remolding of the newcomers into something approximating actors with greater amounts of experience in the life of the group or society. In contrast is a second model that emphasizes resistance to change and capitalization upon initial differences such as descriptions attributing the success of newcomers to greater motivation or drive or the willingness to tolerate lower standards of living.

The next comparison made was generally between races within sex categories. Finally, we searched for race and sex convergences and differences. With the accumulation of the data from the second round of interviews, this perspective was broadened to observe the changes that had accrued over time.

ORGANIZATION OF THE STUDY

The characteristics of the migrants and some aspects of the host city are explored in Chapter 1. The background data describe the kinds of persons the migrants were when they entered the city, something about the nature of the receiving milieu, and some indication of what the migrant's hopes and aspirations were. Chapter 2 examines labor force participation and the movement in and out of jobs. The divergent occupational experiences of the men and women are described separately in Chapters 3 and 4 respectively. Wages, family income, and relative economic position are considered in Chapter 5. In the final data chapter, attitudinal and nonwork aspects of the adjustment of the Southern newcomers are explored.

As we reviewed the data we were impressed by the amount of change indicated. Partly, of course, this is a reflection of our own anticipation and the expectations of the sponsors of the study. There is, however, abundant indication that the change was not uniform. It has become commonplace to observe that social mobility (presumably, but not necessarily, upward) is often a consequence of geographic mobility. There is little in our data to the contrary. But the path of mobility experienced by the migrants is not always upward or even on a plane. Indeed, there is more than a suggestion in the data that the skills, qualifications, and experience brought by the migrants often count for little in landing their first job.

From the first round of interviews, where advantage could be imputed, it generally favored whites, males, and persons who had been in the city for longer durations of time. More directly, from the first set of data, the proverbial visitor from outer space could have inferred that the social structure of the Cleveland poverty area consisted of four distinct populations; white men, black men, white women, and black women. On the basis of the second round of interviews, held just four years after the first, he would be more likely to posit a simpler structure: a man's world and a woman's world. At the most general level, the second-round data suggest that, for the migrants who remain in the city, the initial advantage held by whites and those with longer durations of residence has vanished, or at least become less significant. The relative position of men and women, however, has not changed.

NOTES

1. "Appalachia on Cleveland's East Side," Appalachia: A Journal of the Appalachian Regional Commission 5, no. 7 (July-August 1972): 50.

2. Louis Bromfield, Malabar Farm (New York: Harper and Row, 1947), p. 111.

3. A similar interest in the consequences of work is displayed in Work in America, the report of a special task force to the Secretary of Health, Education, and Welfare (Cambridge, Mass.: MIT Press, 1973).

4. John B. Lansing and Eva Mueller, The Geographic Mobility of Labor (Ann Arbor, Mich.: Institute for Social Research, 1967).

5. Abt Associates, Inc., The Causes of Rural to Urban Migration among the Poor (Cambridge, Mass.: Abt Associates, Inc., 1970).

6. Sociometric Research, A Study of Economic Consequences of Rural to Urban Migration (Austin, Tex.: Tracor, 1969).

7. Larry C. Morgan, "An Economic Analysis of Out-migration from a Depressed Rural Area" (Ph.D. dissertation, University of Kentucky, 1973).

8. Harvey M. Choldin and Grafton D. Trout, Mexican Americans in Transition: Migration and Employment in Michigan Cities (East Lansing, Mich.: Rural Manpower Center, Michigan State University, 1969).

9. Herbert S. Parnes, John R. Shea, Ruth S. Spitz, Frederick A. Zeller, and Associates, Dual Careers: A Longitudinal Study of Labor Market Experience of Women, Vol. 1 (Columbus, Ohio: The Ohio State University, Center for Human Resource Research, 1970).

10. Lyle Shannon and Magdaline Shannon, Minority Migrants in the Urban Community: Mexican-American and Negro Adjustment to Industrial Society (Beverly Hills, Calif.: Sage Publications, 1972).

11. See Otis Dudley Duncan, David L. Featherman, and Beverly Duncan, Socioeconomic Background and Achievement (New York: Seminar Press, 1972), pp. 55-62.

12. See Karl E. Taeuber and Alma F. Taeuber, Negroes in Cities: Residential Segregation and Neighborhood Change (New York: Aldine Publishing, 1965).

13. Avril V. Adams and Gilbert Nestel, "Interregional Migration, Education, and Poverty in the Urban Ghetto: Another Look at Black White Earnings Differentials," unpublished paper prepared for the Manpower Administration.

Southern Newcomers to Northern Cities

1

MIGRANTS, MIGRATION, AND
THE CITY OF CLEVELAND

The Southern migrants in Cleveland are no part of a "dust bowl" exodus, though changes in man's relation to his environment were basic to the impetus to move. Nor is their migration the thrust of pioneers seeking new lives in a wilderness which, though highly urbanized, is for them uncharted; the greater share of these migrants had been preceded by others who, as we will see, often urged them to follow. Instead, we are looking at the results of a "free" migration,* largely unsponsored and unaided, but also unfettered by political authority either at the source or the destination, stemming mainly from the aspirations of the individuals concerned; stimulated both by changes in local economies and by broader social conditions, channeled in part by the routes of rapid overland transportation and in part by information--firsthand or hearsay--of opportunities for making it. On the whole, these migrants are less uprooted than transplanted.

There seems to be a tendency to think of the South-to-North migrant stream as being mainly composed of rural Southerners moving to Northern urban places. However, census data and other previous research indicate that the stream includes sizable proportions of urban Southerners and that for those of rural origin the migration

---

*While the present study focuses on the experiences of migrants from one area to another, it is not otherwise concerned with the process of migration, except insofar as being a newcomer from a culture and social order somewhat dissimilar to that of a Northern industrial city affects labor force participation, choice and exercise of an occupation, earnings, and the settling-in process of broader social adjustment to a new environment.[1]

often takes place in stages, with an intervening residence in an urban Southern place. While we assumed that urban residential experience would facilitate adjustment to living in Cleveland, it did not seem feasible to control for that experience at the time the respondents were chosen for the study. At the outset, however, the migrant study population was restricted to persons who had not lived in any other Northern place or places for as many as six months in the aggregate. While this provided the assurance that the subjects had had little opportunity to effect a prior adjustment to living in a Northern city, it provided no control for the advantage that might be gained through living in Southern urban or industrial milieus.

To some extent, the existence of substantial differences between Southern and Northern places, as well as between Southern and Northern persons, was implied in the initial study design. Policy issues rather than sociological theory determined the main elements of the study design. Obviously one could argue that a dominant culture overrides regional variants, that the remaining disparities between Southern and Northern culture and social organization are less real than imagined, and that the differences are further reduced through such mechanisms as contact with returned migrants or exposure to the mass media.

Three indicators, size of home town, location of residence within the home community (as urban, farm, or rural nonfarm), and size of largest community ever lived in, were used to provide data on urban residential experience or exposure as proxy measures for a personality dimension--sophistication or urbanity--that would have been extremely difficult to capture retrospectively.

In addition, we accumulated information on the patterns of migration prior to moving to Cleveland to determine whether movement out of the South involved prior socialization for living in a large industrial city. Staging--moving from a smaller community to a larger one before moving to Cleveland--or prior residence in or near a large Southern city could substantially reduce the kind and severity of difficulties the newcomers would encounter. Here again it is easy to overstate the discontinuity in culture and social organization encountered by newcomers. Participants in social systems seldom confront the entire system. Urban working-class residents have been shown to establish segmental networks centering on neighborhood and workplace that effectively reduce the complexity of the systems for the participants and provide some of the stability and familiarity said to be properties of smaller communities. In this regard, it is important to note that the strangeness of the receiving community is probably also reduced through the orientation and assistance provided by hosts or sponsors in the new city.

One could also argue that "home town" and all it stands for
may help account for differences in primary socialization of the sort
that is said to establish basic value orientations and goals. Appalachians, for example, have been noted to have value orientations that
do not include metropolitan living and factory work as elements of
an ideal life style. To an unknown degree, their preferences in social relationships at the workplace, time schedules, workplace characteristics, and a host of other values may be fundamental ingredients
in their presumed dissatisfaction with the city. It is important to
note, however, that the social support provided by earlier migrants
may prevent these sources of dissatisfaction from developing into
severe problems.[2]

ORIGINS

The Southern migrant streams coming to Cleveland were pre-
dominantly from two sources. Whites came overwhelmingly from
West Virginia and bordering states, that is, from Appalachia. Blacks
came mainly from Alabama and the adjacent states in the Deep South.
Among whites, three-quarters or more of the migrants in each category came from West Virginia. The heavy concentration of West
Virginians in the study population seems likely to be more typical of
Ohio than other states. In a paper prepared for a conference on
Appalachians in urban areas (held in March 1974 under the cosponsor-
ship of the Academy for Contemporary Problems and the Urban Appalachian Council), James S. Brown and Clyde B. McCoy note that the
1960 and 1970 censuses both show West Virginians to predominate
among Appalachian migrants to Ohio; this was not the case in the
streams to Indiana, Illinois, or Michigan. Fewer than 5 percent in
any category came from any of the states outside the Northern tier
of Southern states.* Native Clevelanders predominated among all
four groups of long-term residents. Aside from the Clevelanders,
very few other Ohioans were found in this group. Other long-term
residents came from the areas contributing the greatest share of
migrants in the same race and sex category.

---

*States in the Northern Tier, as the term is used here, are
Delaware, Maryland, District of Columbia, Virginia, West Virginia,
North Carolina, Kentucky, and Tennessee. Deep South states are
South Carolina, Georgia, Florida, Alabama, Mississippi, Arkansas,
Oklahoma, Louisiana, and Texas.

HOME TOWNS--SIZE OF PLACE AND
LOCATION OF RESIDENCE

Although they did not come from farm backgrounds, the migrants were overwhelmingly drawn from the countryside, both in terms of the location of their family residence within the community and with regard to the size of their home towns. Ninety percent of the white males and over 80 percent of the white females, but just under two-thirds of the black migrants, named a place of fewer than 25,000 inhabitants as their home town. (Home towns were categorized in terms of their 1960 city-proper populations; that is, without making allowances for fringe or suburban populations in the case of large cities and without assigning satellite or suburban communities to metropolitan areas.) The remaining white migrants were more likely to have grown up in medium-sized cities than in places of over 100,000 population. Black migrants, both men and women, who did not come from small towns were more likely to have come from metropolitan centers; between 20 and 30 percent of the black migrants were raised in large cities.

EXPOSURE TO URBAN LIVING

By the time of their move to Cleveland a substantial portion of all migrants had gained some experience with living in large cities. In this respect black migrants were better prepared than whites for the life they would encounter in Cleveland. Between two- and three-fifths of the black and roughly one-fifth of the white migrants had lived in a city of at least 100,000 inhabitants before moving to Cleveland. But for roughly half of the white and about two-thirds of the black migrants, the largest place ever lived in before moving to Cleveland was their home town. Among those who had moved to larger places, the move was far more often to a city in their home state than to a city in another state. For four-fifths of the migrants, whites and blacks alike, the largest place ever lived in before the move to Cleveland was either their home town or another place in their home state. Black migrants, both male and female, were more likely than whites to have spent their Southern residence entirely within the boundaries of their home state. Because of the way the study population was defined, few had lived in any state outside the South other than Ohio. Migrants who had lived in non-Southern places other than Cleveland for six months or more were excluded from the study population. (See the Appendix.)

AGE

The age distribution of the respondents at the time of the first
interview reflects both the general youthfulness of migrant populations and the age limitations imposed on the study population (18
through 50). The most recent arrivals were the youngest; their
median ages ranged from 23 to 25 years (Table 1.1). Earlier arrivals, who had been in the city longer, tended to be slightly older,
and long-term residents were the oldest (with median ages running
between 33 and 36 years). The age data are, of course, proxy indicators for a host of age-related phenomena. As a group, the study
population consists of youthful workers or those just moving into
mature years. Among the migrants, the youthfulness stands for
physical stamina, relative inexperience, and, as they have demonstrated by their own migration, flexibility. The age of the long-term
residents places them further along in their careers, at a juncture
where they not only have more experience in the city but also greater
maturity. Their greater years placed them on the average about half
a generation beyond the migrants. As such they were largely established in the labor force when the early years of the war-related
build-up of industrial activity began. At the same time, their presence in poorer inner-city neighborhoods was an indication that they
had not made it as far as lower-middle-class suburbia.

EDUCATIONAL PREPARATION

To the extent that number of years of school indicates educational preparation, the black migrants, both men and women, were
considerably better educated than other respondents. The apparent
educational advantage of the black migrants is consistent with the
Taeubers' observation from 1960 census data that black urban migrants moving from metropolitan areas are generally of higher educational (and occupational) status than nonmigrants or migrants from
nonmetropolitan areas.[3] Within race groups, greater proportions
of women than men had completed the twelfth grade. Within race
and sex groups, migrants were generally more likely than long-term
residents of the city to have completed high school. Just over half
of the black male and three-fifths of the black female migrants had
finished high school. For white migrants the proportion of high
school graduates ranged from 27 to 51 percent. By comparison,
between 31 and 40 percent of the long-term Cleveland residents of
both races had finished high school.

TABLE 1.1

Age at First Interview, by Race, Sex, and
Duration of Cleveland Residence
(percentages)

Duration of Cleveland Residence	Male		Female	
	White	Black	White	Black
Latecomers				
19 or under	18	14	29	22
20–24	33	41	18	37
25–29	20	16	16	18
30–34	8	15	6	11
35–50	20	14	31	13
Total	100	100	100	100
Median years	24.8	24.4	25.9	25.3
(N)	(117)	(80)	(49)	(95)
Early arrivals				
19 or under	6	9	15	3
20–24	34	35	31	49
25–29	34	33	12	25
30–34	12	14	15	13
35–50	14	9	26	11
Total	100	100	100	100
Median years	26.5	25.9	26.7	24.8
(N)	(145)	(78)	(72)	(109)
Long-termers				
19 or under	3	3	9	8
20–24	15	7	25	9
25–29	20	18	2	16
30–34	8	21	19	24
35–50	54	51	45	44
Total	100	100	100	100
Median years	36.1	35.3	33.7	33.5
(N)	(105)	(61)	(53)	(80)

Note: Unless otherwise noted, all tables in this study have
been compiled by the authors.

We asked the respondents to compare themselves with average high school graduates insofar as their abilities in reading and mathematics were concerned. This was done to obtain a subjective appraisal of the quality of their schooling and also as a measure of self-confidence in these two basic marketplace skills.

Women and blacks, who had more often finished high school, were more confident than men or whites of their own reading abilities. Between 70 to 80 percent of the women and 50 to 70 percent of the men claimed that they read and wrote as well as the average high school graduate. While earlier migrants were slightly more generous than later migrants in their appraisals of their language skills, comparison with the ratings of long-termers shows no consistent pattern. In all cases, the self-ratings for reading show considerable percentage gains over the proportion in the same race-sex-duration-of-residence group who had finished high school. Similar ratings for arithmetic abilities also showed gains over the proportion of high school graduates, but these were modest for all except white male migrants. Though there are exceptions, within sex and duration-of-residence groups, blacks tended to regard their arithmetic abilities more favorably than did whites. Within race and duration-of-residence groups no clearly claimed superiority was apparent for either men or women.

LABOR FORCE EXPERIENCES

Considering the youthfulness of the study population, the premigration labor force participation rates are rather high. Upwards of four-fifths of the male migrants and nearly as many of the black female migrants, but fewer of the white females, had worked at some time prior to coming to Cleveland. Information on employment just prior to moving to Cleveland is congruent with the reasons migrants gave for moving. Nearly half of the white men but only a third of the black men were without work just prior to moving to Cleveland. Among women, whose premigration labor force participation rates were generally lower than those for men, greater proportions of the more recent and earlier black migrants (43 and 50 percent) than of white migrants (39 and 15 percent) were working just before moving.

Premigration employment centered on operative occupations for men and service occupations for women. Among men, whites were next most often found in nonfarm laboring occupations while service occupations were the second most common type of work for black males. Though the migrant women had most often found work in one of the service occupations, for white women food service employment predominated, and black women had been most often employed

as private household workers. (Premigration occupations and wages
are discussed here to provide a brief description of the migrants.
Further details are provided in subsequent chapters.)

PREMIGRATION WAGES

Wages before coming to Cleveland exhibit the expected differentials across sex, race, and duration-of-residence categories.
Earlier migrants, at least among the men, earned less than the recent migrants, who came at a time when inflation and the rising wage
levels in the world had left their mark. Women, irrespective of
race, were far more likely than men to have earned less than the
then current minimum wage (at least two out of five women had
earned less than $1.40 per hour as their top wage before moving);
black workers earned less than whites. Among males there was a
difference of roughly ten percentage points between whites and blacks
across the duration-of-residence categories in those working below
current minimum wages prior to migration (28 percent of the most
recent white migrants and 38 percent of those who came earlier
earned less than $1.40 per hour). At the other end of the pay scale,
at $2.50 an hour or above, the gradient is reversed. Just under 20
percent of the white male migrants had achieved this top pay level before moving, as had 10 percent of the black male migrants and 5 percent of those who migrated earlier. Among women, whether white
or black, such rates of pay were rarely reported.
        The predominant reason given for moving to Cleveland by all
groups except the black women was economic, a matter of jobs and
wages. This motive was mentioned to the greatest extent by white
male migrants: (82 percent of the recent migrants, 92 percent of
those who had come earlier). Jobs and wages were less often named
as predominant motives for moving to Cleveland by white females
and by black migrants of either sex. A fifth or more in each of these
groups gave the desire to join family, relatives, or friends as the
main reason for making the move. Surprisingly, only five black migrants, all members of the group that had been in Cleveland longest,
gave reasons related to social conditions or relationships in the South.
Yet no more than 5 percent of the black migrants, as opposed to as
many as a fifth of the white migrants, had returned to the South to live.

THE JOURNEY TO CLEVELAND

Although the range of patterns of migration was restricted by
screening out migrants who had lived in Northern places other than
Cleveland for as many as six months, there is still some evidence

of stage migration or movement from home town to some other place
prior to coming to Cleveland. But the most common pattern of movement was one that ruled out the possibility of prior adaptation to
Northern urban living, a direct move from home town to Cleveland.
Upwards of 60 percent of the black migrants made the move directly;
those who did not tended to have staged the move by first living in
another Southern place. Whites were less likely than black migrants
to make a direct move to Cleveland, though that was still the predominant form of migration for them (experienced by 47 percent
overall, slightly more often by earlier migrants, slightly less often
by those who came later). White migrants who did not make the
move directly were also most likely to have made an intermediate
stop in a Southern city (as 28 percent did). Shuttling, or recurrent
migration between home towns and Cleveland, was seldom reported
by blacks, but had been practiced by 15 percent of the white migrants.

Although the general tendency was for the migrants to relate
moving with the intention of living permanently in Cleveland, sizable
minorities viewed the move as temporary or conditional on the way
their lives worked out, or had no particular plans regarding the
permanence of their residence. Upwards of two-thirds of the black
female migrants planned to remain permanently; in other groups the
proportions with similar intent ranged between 45 and 59 percent.

Black and white migrants also differed in the means used to
make the journey to Cleveland. Whites, making the relatively short
trip from Appalachia, were more likely than black migrants to use
automobiles. They were, therefore, less in need of sizable amounts
of cash to pay for tickets and in a better position than the black migrants to reduce the cost of the move for individuals by sharing the
same conveyance. Thus, the white migrants probably initially in-
vested less than the blacks in the move, but they also came in a way
that made the move less irreversible. The black migrants had made
a greater commitment by investing in public transportation fares (for
a much longer trip). To return home would require an equally large
investment.

In making the trip to Cleveland, white migrants were also more
likely than blacks to have the support and companionship of others
traveling with them. But for all except the black male migrants, of
whom just under half came alone, the move was more likely to be
made in the company of others than as an isolated individual. When
the move was made in a group, the other members were considerably more likely to be members of the migrant's family or other kin
than to be unrelated friends. Thus, the social support for the move
tended to be within the network of one's own family and kin. Blacks of
both sexes, however, were more likely than whites of the same sex
to have made the journey alone, perhaps another indication of the
greater financial as well as social cost of their journey.

As we have seen, economic motives tended to predominate as reasons for moving to Cleveland. To gauge the relative urgency of finding jobs, or the amount of dependency on others, we asked the migrants how much money they had when they came to Cleveland (interviewers were instructed to amplify this to include all available funds, not just those in hand). Unfortunately for our purposes, the codes we provided in the questionnaire had "under $50" as the lowest category. Between half and three-fifths of all migrants except the black men, who were only slightly better off, claimed they had less than $50 to meet their immediate needs. Overall, only one in six migrants had as much as $200 available to fund his settling in.

THE RECEIVING CITY

What kind of city is Cleveland? Partly the answer depends on who is asked. Those who call it "the mistake by the lake" probably took even greater delight the day the river burned. Others, whose interest is in ghetto uprisings, would probably respond in terms of the Hough, the scene of the first urban riot of the 1960s, or the shoot-out of 1968. Boosters take pride in the city location, "the best in the nation," and in its cultural amenities. Mention of the symphony orchestra is sure to be followed by reference to the collections of fine arts and industrial museums, by mention of a major-league football team, or, in good years, reference to a tribe of baseball players. Others point with pride to the election of the country's first black mayor in a city noted for its hospitality to ethnic minorities (some say that the number of members on the city council, 33, represents the allocation of one to each major ethnic group). In 1960, 29 percent of the city's population was nonwhite. The 1970 census showed the total population within the city limits to have fallen by 21 percent over the decade; the proportion of black residents had risen to 41 percent. Of the population five years of age or older, 3.5 percent of the blacks and 2.3 percent of the nonblacks had been living in the South five years earlier.

Cleveland is easily labeled one of the monarchs of American industry. The importance of its manufacturing and commerce is clearly evident in the plants and factories throughout the city and in the solid red-brick office buildings downtown. Long a major port city, it is connected via the Great Lakes and the St. Lawrence Seaway with the deepwater ports of the world. Yet the predominant impression conveyed by the city and by statistics on economic activity is of a place whose main growth period is over and whose relative position is declining. Once the country's fourth largest city and the home of the then nascent automobile and aviation industries, it now

ranks twelfth among the cities of the nation (tenth among metropolitan areas) and is still a city of major automobile and steel plants.
Among aviation buffs, the executive airport, within walking distance
from downtown, is known as the site of the historic Cleveland Air
Races. Once a major rail center, the city recently lost all rail
passenger service and then regained service on a severely curtailed
schedule. Union Terminal remains the dominant feature of the urban
skyline, but its vaulted interior has been converted to indoor tennis
courts. Nearly two-fifths of the workers are employed in manufacturing; yet, in family income, the city ranks 585 in the nation's 840
places of 25,000 or more inhabitants. Nestled on the shoulder of the
city above the university, connected with the city square by a private
streetcar line, lies Shaker Heights where family incomes rank sixth
among the nation's cities. In the city itself there is abundant evidence of the emergent problems of major American cities. In coming to Cleveland, the migrants moved not to a boom town but to an
aging city struggling against decline. Its resources are far from
exhausted but also far from unlimited.

THE RECEIVING COMMUNITY: FRIENDS AND KINFOLK

If friends and the bonds of kinship serve to cushion individuals
against the shocks and strains of moving into strange environments,
the migrants were well protected. More than nine out of ten in every
race, sex, and duration-of-residence group reported that they had
relatives or friends living in Cleveland before they themselves made
the move. Roughly 60 percent or more reported that they had been
urged by relatives or friends to come to Cleveland. Three-quarters
or more in each group spent their first night in Cleveland with relatives or friends. Fewer than 10 percent took commercial accommo-
dations in motels, hotels, or rooming houses.

SUMMING UP

It is evident that this is a group of young and poor migrants,
with a great amount of schooling and work experience, coming from
a predominantly rural Southern environment to seek work in Cleveland. The receiving city is far from being a center of growth, but
its powerful industrial plant is still a major national producer and
employer. The migrants have friends and kin in the city; they are
eager to find work, and, in the long run, to improve their lives. The
balance of the study is devoted to what actually happened to them,
their jobs, their incomes, and their hopes and expectations during
their early years in Cleveland.

NOTES

1. For a helpful categorization of types of migration and discussion of differences between them, see William Petersen, Population, 2d ed. rev. (Toronto: Macmillan Company, 1969), pp. 289-301; or the same author's earlier article, "A General Typology of Migration," American Sociological Review 23, no. 3 (June 1958): 256-66.

2. See Harry K. Schwarzweller, James S. Brown, and J. J. Mangalam, Mountain Families in Transition: A Case Study of Appalachian Migration (University Park: The Pennsylvania State University Press, 1971), especially pp. 161-64.

3. See Karl E. Taeuber and Alma F. Taeuber, Negroes in Cities (Chicago: Aldine Publishing Co., 1965), pp. 134-35.

2

**LABOR FORCE
PARTICIPATION**

In relation to the labor force, migration--like education, kinship, and norms governing sex roles--functions socially as an allocative mechanism, differing from the others in that human resources
are shifted from one geographic area, often characterized by a relatively restricted range of opportunities, to other areas in which
opportunities are or are thought to be greater. For individuals,
migration may be an adaptive mechanism resulting in a net gain in
rewards, but one in which the broader consequences are not all necessarily equal or even in the same direction within or across behavioral fields. To take a mundane example, workers may abandon
the security of established social networks and life patterns in the
hope of gaining higher money returns in different occupations in
other areas, but in so doing lose considerable autonomy over such
matters as hours, days, pace of work, and choice of work partners.
Evidence from a variety of national and local sample surveys indicates that migration generally has beneficial effects on the occupational achievement of migrants.[1]

Because it is an allocative mechanism, migration invariably
poses a correlative problem both for the migrant and for the receiving community: that of integration into new patterns of social relationships. But, unlike the more gradual processes of integration
that surround many other status changes, the integrative problem
generated by migration arises more or less abruptly.

We say "more or less" because much seems to depend on
differences and similaries between the new environment and the old.
In this regard we are not ignoring the mediating influence that may
be exercised by others who have preceded the migrant from his home
community. On the other hand, we would wish to argue that the
effect these "sponsors" in the receiving community have on the

integration of the migrants is problematical. The point is not
whether or not they facilitate integration, but the locus at which the
newcomer is integrated and what the consequences of that are. The
emergence of "Chinatowns" and other ethnic communities in major
American cities is one obvious example. In a more dramatic case
involving the creation of a new nation state, Israeli sociologists
have abundantly documented the differential effects resulting from
the nature of the integrating communities.

In the world of work, the immediate integrative task is to put
migrants and jobs together, for there is no necessary correspondence
between the specific labor force needs in a community and the number and kinds of human resources it attracts or recruits, unless
special efforts are made at the source to recruit or attract persons
with the specific skills needed. Traditionally, the migrants are
faulted, and attention is drawn to their intractability, poor training,
or general unsuitability for employment in the occupations for which
workers are being sought. At times they are criticized for the
"mistakes" they make, deriving from factors such as ignorance of
the range and location of opportunities, lack of a keen sense of the
conditions at various potential destinations, errors in judgment, or
the priority of concerns unrelated to the exercise of judgments
(such as the desire to migrate to rejoin kinsmen). More recently,
attention has been directed to similar "errors" generated in receiving communities by factors such as licensing requirements, preju-
dicial hiring practices, and reliance on internal labor markets.
Needless to say, when the migration is unsponsored and unregulated
by employers or their agents, the likelihood of an exact or even
reasonably good fit between the number and kinds of worker candi-
dates entering the new community and the number and kinds of jobs
available there becomes problematical, hinging at least in part on
the willingness of workers to reassess the perspectives by which
they evaluate openings and the willingness of employers to relax
hiring criteria. Generally, in times of tight labor markets the tip
of the balance is toward easing entry requirements; when workers
are plentiful employers adhere to more rigid standards.

If the receiving community is unable to satisfy its manpower
needs completely by recruiting workers possessing specific skills
in the numbers needed, other options must be considered. Among
these are job restructuring, technological innovations, relaxation of
standards, and training programs ranging from formal sessions in
institutional settings to casual instruction by more experienced
workers at the work station. To some degree, several of these options may be exercised simultaneously. Many operative occupations, for example, have emerged from the fragmentation of more
complicated operations into simpler repetitive tasks, easily

communicated to new workers by others only slightly more experienced. When new workers enter the labor force in the lower ranges of skills hierarchies, requirements for prior experience, training, or education are relaxed, and the integrative task eased. Since the demands are less rigorous, the qualifications needed by the candidate are fewer; generally a demonstrated willingness to work (that is, some sort of stable work history) and indication of an ability to do the work to be done (for example, satisfactory health and prior experience in some remotely similar work) or an indication of latent ability such as that implied by the acquisition of a high school diploma or equivalency certificate.

For the migrants, the latter mode of integration into the Cleveland work force was by far the most common. As we shall see, most of the newcomers surveyed entered the Cleveland work force in middle- or low-skill-level occupations. Four out of five migrants said they had learned the skills for the work they were doing while in Cleveland; two-thirds had picked up the skills by themselves or were taught by foremen or coworkers at work.

ENTERING THE CLEVELAND WORK FORCE

Except for the female heads of house, who were eligible to be participants in the study whatever their labor force status, the selection criteria emphasized attachment to the labor force. And, indeed, in all but two groups of females virtually everyone had worked in Cleveland at some time prior to the first interview (Table 2.1). Among the women of both races, the more recently arrived migrants and the long-term residents were less likely than others ever to have worked in Cleveland. For these two groups, the proportion of blacks with prior local work experience was somewhat lower than that of whites. For the long-termers, this may be the result of a pattern of earlier childbearing among the blacks than among the white women. The higher-than-usual proportion of women with work experience among the early arrivals is consonant with the "better life" theme most often given as a reason for migrating. In time, one would expect the rate for migrants who had entered the city more recently to rise to a similar level. The inclusion in the study population of female heads of house who were not in the labor force or who could be classified as "discouraged workers" creates problems for comparisons across sex groups. See the Introduction for a general description of the criteria used to select the study population and the Appendix for a more exact definition of the basic terms in the criteria.

TABLE 2.1

Cleveland Employment History at the Time of the
First Interview: Percentage Who Had Ever
Worked in Cleveland

Race	Type of Respondent		
	Latecomers	Early Arrivals	Long-Termers
Male			
Whites	99	100	99
	(117)	(145)	(105)
Blacks	98	99	100
	(80)	(78)	(61)
Female			
Whites	84	99	85
	(49)	(72)	(53)
Blacks	70	97	71
	(95)	(109)	(80)

For the migrants, the time needed to get going on a job in Cleveland differed considerably among the comparison groups. No more than a quarter in any group had a job already lined up in Cleveland so they could start work immediately on arrival. White men were slightly more likely than black men to have prearranged employment; such arrangements were more often made by men than by women; and they were made more often by white women than by black women. The order of movement into jobs within seven days after arrival in Cleveland was much the same. About two-thirds of the white male recent arrivals and slightly fewer of those who had come earlier had begun work in Cleveland within a week of their arrival. Among the black males, the more recent migrants enjoyed a similar advantage over those who had come earlier. The greater ease with which recent arrivals had moved into jobs within a week after their arrival probably reflects the tightening of the labor market during the Vietnam buildup.

Women were far less likely than men to have moved so directly to employment in Cleveland (a quarter at most started within their first week of residence) and white women were more apt than blacks to have started work within a week. The lower rate of employment of black women than white women, discussed above, and the higher proportion of white women beginning work within a week are perplexing. White women were less inclined than black women to

indicate that they had expected to work in Cleveland when they migrated; hence one would expect them to show slower rates of entry
into the Cleveland work force. Inequalities in employment opportunities undoubtedly lie behind some of the delay that blacks experience
in getting employment in Cleveland, but it is also likely that black
migrants had greater difficulty than whites in acquiring information
about acceptable jobs that were available to them. Differences in
access to information about job openings may also account for the
state employment service getting higher marks as a means for finding employment from black than from white respondents.

TRENDS IN LABOR FORCE STATUS

Male Labor Force Participation

Only nine male migrants and four male long-term residents
(in each case 2 percent of those interviewed) were outside the labor
force at the time of the first interview.* Of that number only one
male, a migrant, fit the discouraged worker concept (that is, was
available for work but had abandoned the search for work out of a
belief that no work was available). At the time of the second round
of interviews, 18 migrants and 10 long-term residents had dropped
out of the labor force (respectively, 4 and 6 percent of the male

-----

*The labor force definition used here follows the revisions to
the concept made in 1967. As in the Census and Bureau of Labor
Statistics usages, persons not working or looking for work because
of a belief that no work existed for them are classed as being outside the labor force. Our own definition is also less precise than
the Federal definition because of limitation on the length of our survey instrument. As a result, we are unable to distinguish between
temporary illness and permanent disability as reasons for being out
of the labor force. Under the procedure used to construct the variable, "out of labor force" is a residual category including all cases
for which information was missing on any required component of the
definition. While it would have been preferable to have added one
more category in the constructed variable to hold all cases for which
information was missing, the logic for the construction of the variable would have been considerably more complicated. A check on
the maximum amount of error that may have been introduced by the
procedure actually used showed that not more than 1 percent of the
migrants could have been erroneously assigned to the nonlabor-force
category on the basis of missing information.

respondents in each group). Again, discouraged workers were
scarce despite the general downward turn in the economy. Only one
respondent, this time a long-term Cleveland resident, stated that
he was available for work but that no work was available for him.
Six other male respondents were able and willing to work but were
not working or looking for work for other reasons. At both times,
the major reason for males being outside the labor force was sick-
ness or disability. At the time of the first interview there was no
difference in labor force participation between black and white males;
at the time of the reinterview, four years later, nonparticipation in
the labor force for white males had trebled to 6 and 9 percent for
migrants and long-termers respectively, while the rates for black
males remained unchanged (Figure 2.1).

Female Labor Force Participation

As was guaranteed by the screening procedures and rules governing eligibility for inclusion in the study population, at the time of
the first interview female labor force participation was lower than
that of the men (because female heads of house were included, whatever their labor force status), with white women being more likely
than black women in each comparison group to be in the labor force.
(These differences between black and white women stem from the
ways in which the criteria for inclusion applied to the two populations. White women were less likely than black women to have been
found to be heads of house in the screening process; therefore, a
larger proportion of white than black women were included because
they were working or looking for work.)
For the second interview no labor force restrictions were imposed. All who had been interviewed during the first phase of the
fieldwork were sought for reinterview. The second interview showed
larger numbers of white than black women who had dropped from the
labor force, with the result that labor force participation rates in the
two groups were then almost identical.
The composition of the segment of the female population that
was out of the labor force at each time is of some interest. There
were no discouraged workers at either time among the female long-
term residents; among the migrants the number had risen from four
to nine (that is, from 1 to 2 percent of the female migrant population). Next farther away from the boundaries of the labor force are
persons who are able and willing to work but who are neither working
nor seeking work, for reasons other than a belief in the unavailability
of work. This group can perhaps best be described as female heads
of house who are potential workers; their entry into the labor market

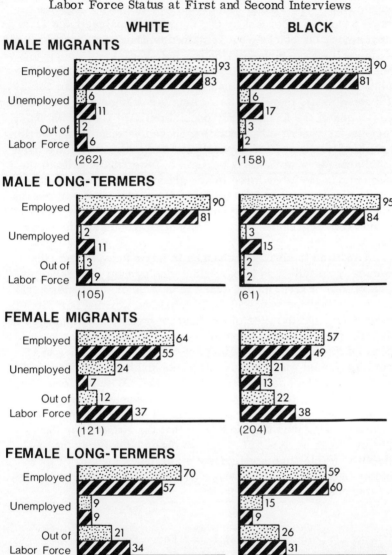

FIGURE 2.1

Labor Force Status at First and Second Interviews

WHITE   **BLACK**

MALE MIGRANTS

Employed — 93 / 83 (WHITE); 90 / 81 (BLACK)
Unemployed — 6 / 11 (WHITE); 6 / 17 (BLACK)
Out of Labor Force — 2 / 6 (WHITE); 3 / 2 (BLACK)
(262)   (158)

MALE LONG-TERMERS

Employed — 90 / 81 (WHITE); 95 / 84 (BLACK)
Unemployed — 2 / 11 (WHITE); 3 / 15 (BLACK)
Out of Labor Force — 3 / 9 (WHITE); 2 / 2 (BLACK)
(105)   (61)

FEMALE MIGRANTS

Employed — 64 / 55 (WHITE); 57 / 49 (BLACK)
Unemployed — 24 / 7 (WHITE); 21 / 13 (BLACK)
Out of Labor Force — 12 / 37 (WHITE); 22 / 38 (BLACK)
(121)   (204)

FEMALE LONG-TERMERS

Employed — 70 / 57 (WHITE); 59 / 60 (BLACK)
Unemployed — 9 / 9 (WHITE); 15 / 9 (BLACK)
Out of Labor Force — 21 / 34 (WHITE); 26 / 31 (BLACK)
(53)   (80)   Figures in Percent

First Interview   Second Interview

19

depends on a constellation of factors including total family income
and need, availability of attractive or convenient jobs, and child care
arrangements. The size of this group rose slightly among the mi-
grants--from 4 to 6 percent among the white females, from 11 to 15
percent among the blacks--but remained unchanged at roughly 6 percent among the long-term residents. But, because of the larger
numbers of women who had dropped from the labor force for other
reasons (for example, to become full-time homemakers or for
health conditions), they constituted smaller segments of the nonlabor-
force portion of the female study population. We restate the point
for emphasis: among this population chosen because it was working,
was seeking work, or had responsibility for a household, the number of discouraged workers is negligible; fewer than a fifth of the
women outside the labor force in any group at either time defined
themselves as even remotely available for work. But, for reasons
we shall see later, one should not infer that the women in this study
included large aggregates permanently situated outside the labor
force.

In addition to clear-cut changes in labor force status, the
movement from full-time to part-time employment also deserves
consideration. Except among black female labor force members,
there were slight increases in the proportions working part time in
all categories. At the time of the first interview, black females had
the highest proportions of part-time workers (12 to 14 percent). By
the time of the second interview, part-time work had risen to 17
percent for recent white female migrants and had fallen to only 5
percent among black female recent migrants. With this one exception, at the second interview as at the first, women were more
likely than men to be working part time. Roughly half of the women
who were working part time indicated that the reasons for their
short work week were not of their own choosing. Thus, the unavailability of full-time employment emerges as another of the
problems in attaining satisfactory work positions that these women
in low-income neighborhoods faced.

Net Changes in Labor Force Status

The broad outlines of the major changes in labor force positions at the time of the first and second interviews are already apparent in the histogram. Among all groups except black female
long-term residents there was a decline in the proportion who were
employed (Table 2.2). Among all groups of men, the proportion
who were unemployed increased. In each group of women the proportion outside the labor force increased and, in three of the four

female comparison groups, the unemployed proportion declined.
This cross-sex ripple suggests that, as economic activity was cut
back during the later stages of the war in Indochina, men tended to
move from employment to being unemployed, while women in the
study moved from active labor force positions and unemployed states
out of the labor force altogether. The magnitude of the change in
the proportion who were unemployed among the men, ranging between 5 and 12 percentage points, would once have been regarded as
spectacular; though the movement of the women from labor force
positions might have been more easily interpreted as normal ac-
commodations to labor market conditions and to changes in marital
and parental status.

TABLE 2.2

Net Changes in Labor Force Status from
First to Second Interview
(percentages)

| Labor Force Status | Type of Respondent | | | |
| | White | | Black | |
	Migrant	Long-Term Resident	Migrant	Long-Term Resident
Males				
Employed	-10	-15	-10	-12
Unemployed	5	10	11	12
Out of labor force	4	6	-1	--
(N)	(262)	(105)	(158)	(61)
Females				
Employed	-8	-13	-8	1
Unemployed	-16	--	-8	-6
Out of labor force	(25)	13	16	5
(N)	(121)	(53)	(204)	(80)

Data on the individual occupational shifts for women suggest that these women, drawn originally from the city's poorer neighborhoods, provide part of the labor force reserve needed to accommodate changes in labor force demands. If this is indeed the case, the discouraged worker concept may be less appropriate than another concept, such as "poor job market," that conveys the notion of generally unattractive employment prospects based on low wages, unfavorable working conditions, or occupations to be performed only as a last resort.

It is also far from certain that movement out of the labor force inevitably implies a decline in personal position for women. Furthermore, movement out of the labor force may tend to signal substantially different social and economic events and conditions for black than for white women living in inner-city low-income neighborhoods. More attention is given to this topic in Chapter 4, "Women and Their Occupations."

CHANGES IN LABOR FORCE STATUS

Up to this point, we have considered only aggregate data that show the composition or structure of the various comparison groups at the time of their first and second interviews in 1968 and 1972. In this section, the data derived from reinterviewing the same persons are used to examine the fate of individuals and to explore the likelihood of changes in their labor force status.

Although the panel data give insight into the individual dynamics of change in ways that aggregate cross-sectional data cannot, they are not continuous observations of the various states, aspects, or attitudes measured, but are based here on a series of measures taken roughly four years apart. In particular, one cannot infer from the observation that some of the respondents were engaged in the same activity or held the same attitude at the time of each of the interviews that they were continuously in that state. Similarly, where change is observed, we know little of its recency or the number of other changes that may have occurred in the interval between the observations. Because experience with unemployment was of special interest for this study, that subject was probed retrospectively in the second interview and will be discussed later in this chapter.

Stability of Labor Force Position

The data on the stability of labor force positions clearly show the different labor force routes followed by the men and the women.

The men demonstrated a relatively high degree of stability in labor force position that centered on being employed; just over three-quarters of the men in each of the study groups were employed at the time of both interviews (Table 2.3). The labor force statuses of the women were less stable, and far fewer than among the men were employed at both times.

The rising proportions of unemployed men and the sizable share of women who were unemployed in the first and second rounds of interviewing, shown in the cross-sectional data, suggest the existence of hard-core unemployed or unemployables. This would be consistent with popular stereotypes. But comparison of the individual labor force states for each of the two time periods shows this interpretation of the cross-sectional data to be entirely misleading. Black females (both migrants and long-term residents) were most likely to be unemployed at the time of both interviews, as 4 percent in each group were. But, on the other hand, no male long-term resident was unemployed at both times and only 2 percent of the white migrants, male and female, and 3 percent of the male black migrants were unemployed at both times. Even more important is the finding that, among these women chosen from Cleveland's poorest neighborhoods to include female heads of house as well as labor force participants, no more than a fifth in any group were outside the labor force at the time of both interviews.

Differing Directions and Rates of Mobility

The differing rates of change from each of the earlier labor force positions consistently reflect the greater participation of the men than the women in the labor force. (In Tables 2.4 and 2.5, labor force position at the time of the first interview is controlled, and change from that position is the dependent variable.) If employed, men who changed their status were more likely to become unemployed than to leave the labor force (Table 2.4). Unemployed men were also more likely to become employed than to move out of the labor force (the small number who were outside the labor force when first interviewed were more often found to be employed than unemployed when reinterviewed). For the males who were employed at the time of the first interview there was virtually no difference across the comparison groups in the likelihood of being employed four years later. But among those who had stopped working, white males were more likely than black males to move out of the labor force. Nonlabor-force statuses are consistently more prevalent for women who changed their labor force status following the first interview (Table 2.5). But the experience of those who were outside the

TABLE 2.3

Stability of Labor Force Position: Position at Second Interview
Compared with Position at First Interview
(percentages)

| | Type of Respondent | | | |
| | White | | Black | |
Labor Force Position	Migrant	Long-Termer	Migrant	Long-Termer
Males				
In same position both times	81	77	80	79
Employed at both times	79	77	76	79
Unemployed at both times	2	--	3	--
Out of labor force at both times	--	--	1	--
In different positions at the two times	19	23	20	21
Total	100	100	100	100
(N)	(262)	(105)	(158)	(61)
Females				
In same position both times	45	68	51	72
Employed at both times	39	49	35	49
Unemployed at both times	2	2	4	4
Out of labor force at both times	4	17	12	19
In different positions at the two times	55	32	49	28
Total	100	100	100	100
(N)	(121)	(53)	(204)	(80)

TABLE 2.4

Changes in Labor Force Status for Men: Labor Force Position at Second Interview by Labor Force Position at First Interview (percentages)

Labor Force Status at First Interview	Labor Force Status at Second Interview				
	Employed	Unemployed	Not in Labor Force	Total	(N)
White male migrants					
Employed	85	9	5	100	(243)
Unemployed	60	33	7	100	(15)
Out of labor force*	50	25	25	100	(4)
White male long-termers					
Employed	81	11	8	100	(100)
Unemployed	50	--	50	100	(2)
Out of labor force*	67	33	--	100	(3)
Black male migrants					
Employed	84	15	1	100	(143)
Unemployed	50	50	--	100	(10)
Out of labor force*	60	20	20	100	(5)
Black male long-termers					
Employed	83	16	2	100	(58)
Unemployed	100	--	--	100	(2)
Out of labor force*	100	--	--	100	(1)

*With the exception of one migrant, who was classed as a "discouraged worker," men outside the labor force at the time of the first interview were included in the study population only as a result of having moved from the labor force after being located in the screening process and having been designated as eligible subjects for the study.

TABLE 2.5

Changes in Labor Force Status for Women: Labor Force Position at Second Interview by Labor Force Position at First Interview

(percentages)

Labor Force Status at First Interview	Labor Force Status at Second Interview				
	Employed	Unemployed	Not in Labor Force	Total	(N)
White female migrants					
Employed	61	9	30	100	(77)
Unemployed	34	7	59	100	(29)
Not in labor force	67	--	33	100	(15)
White female long-termers					
Employed	70	11	19	100	(37)
Unemployed	40	20	40	100	(5)
Not in labor force	18	--	82	100	(11)
Black female migrants					
Employed	61	10	28	100	(116)
Unemployed	35	19	46	100	(43)
Not in labor force	31	16	53	100	(45)
Black female long-termers					
Employed	83	4	13	100	(47)
Unemployed	42	25	33	100	(12)
Not in labor force	19	10	71	100	(21)

labor force during the first interview deserves special comment.
They were unlike the men in that they were generally more likely to
remain outside the labor force than to enter it; but, like the men,
those who had entered the labor force were more often found to be
employed than unemployed.

In large part this is because "unemployed" as customarily used
refers to a condition that is usually in a change state. The Bureau
of Labor Statistics definition implies an expectation of change precisely because to be classified as unemployed the individuals must
be in one state (without work) and be engaged in an activity expected
to result in a change from that state (actively seeking employment).

Locations of Change

As would be expected from the differences in the initial labor
force distributions and from the differences in stability we have observed, men and women in the study also differed in the location of
their mobility within the labor force. For men, the main centers of
movement were into or out of the employed or unemployed states
(Table 2.6).* For women the main centers of change were into or
out of employment and between being in or out of the labor force
altogether. For both, but particularly for the women, the magnitude
of the swings in labor force position was considerable. Between
one- and two-fifths in each group of women had changed labor force
positions entirely by either entering or leaving the labor force.
Movement around the employed state was equally large. Among the

---

*The data on which this and the following paragraphs are based,
like those used in the preceding section, were derived from cross-
tabulation of labor force status at time of second interview by labor
force status at time of first interview. But the arithmetic is changed
a bit.

In the preceding paragraphs, the data were percentaged separately for each earlier labor force status. This, of course, facili-
tates comparison of the likelihood of various groups changing their
labor force position by eliminating the effect of different sized
groups. In the process, however, one loses sight of the relative
contribution of each to changes in the whole population or subpopu-
lation. The bases for the percentages used here are the entire relevant population in the race-sex-duration-of-resident category. Using
the population subgroup N as a percentage base permits easy comparison across groups yet allows us to observe changes in the structure of the labor force within groups.

TABLE 2.6

Location of Labor Force Mobility: Amount of Mobility into or out of Labor Force Statuses (Comparing Position at First Interview with Position at Second Interview) (percentages)

Labor Force Position	Type of Respondent			
	White		Black	
	Migrant	Long-Termer	Migrant	Long-Termer
Males				
Employed	18	21	20	21
In	4	3	5	5
Out	14	18	15	16
Unemployed	13	13	17	18
In	9	11	14	16
Out	4	2	3	3
Out of labor force	6	12	3	4
In	5	9	1	2
Out	1	3	2	2
(N)	(262)	(105)	(158)	(61)
Females				
Employed	41	29	36	21
In	16	8	14	11
Out	25	21	22	10
Unemployed	28	16	26	16
In	6	8	9	5
Out	22	8	17	11
Out of labor force	41	21	36	20
In	33	17	26	12
Out	8	4	10	8
(N)	(121)	(53)	(204)	(80)

Note: Due to rounding, totals are not always equal to the sum of the components.

men, the relative lack of movement into or out of the labor force
altogether may be viewed as an expression of the limited number of
options working-class males have in principal life activities. If not
working, most may be found looking for work. The resulting differences between the sexes are undoubtedly a blend of societal expectations, opportunities, and options that differ greatly for men and
women. Preferential treatment in hiring and firing, the pressure
from competing statuses (as in the constellation centered on the
home and traditional women's roles), and differences in the options
for making a living that are open to the two sexes all play a part.

Patterns of Change

In one respect, the net changes in labor force position between
first and second interviews for men and women were similar; in
both groups there was a general movement out of employment (except among the black female long-term residents among whom the
proportion employed was virtually stable). But for the men this
movement was toward the ranks of the unemployed, and in each instance was larger than the growth in the size of the nonlabor-force
group (Table 2.7). For the women the net movement tended to be
out of the labor force altogether from having been employed or unemployed.

If one is willing to assume for the purposes of argument that
labor force positions form a hierarchy, at least for working-age
males, then the data on net exchanges among labor force positions
show some common and important patterns of movement. No group
of males made any substantial improvement in labor force position
over that held at the time of their first interview. Gains in the
proportion employed among black female long-termers were so
small as to be virtually negligible and smaller yet among both groups
of female migrants. As among the males, the level of labor force
participation among the women tended to be deteriorating. In broad
outline, somewhere between about 10 and 15 percent of the males in
each group had left employment. Except among the black female
long-term residents, between one in eight and one in four of the
women had moved from a position in the labor force to one outside.

UNEMPLOYMENT

Among the labor force participants, unemployment at the time
of the first interview was considerably higher for women than for
men and was also generally associated with duration of residence in

TABLE 2.7

Net Exchanges Between Labor Force Positions at Time of First and Second Interviews
(percentages)

	Labor Force Position at Second Interview					
	Migrants			Long–Term Residents		
	Employed	Unemployed	Out of Labor Force	Employed	Unemployed	Out of Labor Force
White male						
Employed		5.3	4.2		9.5	5.7
Unemployed	-5.3		0.0	-9.5		0.0
Out of labor force	-4.2	0.0		-5.7	0.0	
Total	-9.5	5.3	4.2	-15.2	9.5	5.7
	(N = 262)			(N = 105)		
Black male						
Employed		10.1	-0.6		11.5	0.0
Unemployed	-10.1		-0.6	-11.5		0.0
Out of labor force	0.6	0.6		0.0	0.0	
Total	-9.5	10.8	-1.3	-11.5	11.5	0.0
	(N = 158)			(N = 61)		
White female						
Employed		-2.5	10.7		3.8	9.4
Unemployed	2.5		14.0	-3.8		3.8
Out of labor force	-10.7	-14.0		-9.4	-3.8	
Total	-8.3	-16.5	24.8	-13.2	0.0	13.2
	(N = 121)			(N = 53)		
Black female						
Employed		-1.5	9.3		-3.7	2.5
Unemployed	1.5		6.4	3.7		2.5
Out of labor force	-9.3	-6.4		-2.5	-2.5	
Total	-7.8	-7.8	15.7	1.2	-6.2	5.0
	(N = 204)			(N = 80)		

A Note on the Matrices in Chapter 2

A note on reading the matrices may be helpful. The data are the result of subtracting the percentage of persons in the group who left a given labor force position from the percentage of the total group who were recruited to the same labor force position. The signed result of this simple bit of arithmetic is a description, in percentages, of the net result of the exchange between the two labor force positions and describes the amount of change in the total labor force structure for the group that is due to the interchange. In the form that the matrices are presented for this study, the last figure in each column represents the total change occurring to each category from the earlier time to the subsequent time, with minuses indicating a decrease in the percentage of the group in the relevant category and unsigned nonzero numerals indicating growth in the category. Whether seen from position a or from position b, the amount of the flow between categories must be identical and opposite in sign. While one-half of the data displayed are therefore redundant, because they differ only in sign from the data displayed on the other side of the major diagonal, we have retained both the upper and lower portions of the matrices so that columns may be read to show signed gains and losses.

As an illustration, let us consider the data for white migrant females shown in Table 2.7. The third column of that portion of the table shows the net change in the proportion out of the labor force (24.8 percent, the largest change in any stratum among all the comparison groups). Reading down the column we find that this change is a result of net gains from women who had been unemployed when first interviewed (14.0 percent) and from women who had then been employed (10.7 percent). Across the major diagonal, in the next to the last row of the first two columns, we find figures of identical magnitude, but opposite in sign, indicating that there had been net losses from the ranks of the employed and unemployed into the group outside the labor force altogether. Thus, reading down the columns, as the data are displayed here, positive entries answer the question, "Where did the net growth in this category come from ?" Negatively signed entries answer the question, "To which categories did the net losses from this category go ?"

the city; long-term residents tended to have lower rates of unemployment than earlier migrants and these, in turn, had lower rates than recent migrants (Table 2.8). At the time of the first interview, unemployment rates among the men ranged from 1 to 9 percent of the labor force participants; among the women unemployment ranged from 12 to 36 percent. Again, no clear-cut racial differential was apparent. Unemployment rates were higher at the time of the second interview than at the first for all groups of male labor force members and lower for women. The higher unemployment rates for males were expected in the wake of the economic downtrend at the close of the Vietnam conflict, but the lower rates for women were unexpected.

TABLE 2.8

Unemployment Among Labor Force Participants
(percentages)

Population Group	First Interview	Reinterview	(Ns)*
White males			
Latecomers	4	8	(115)
Early arrivals	5	13	(143)
Long-termers	1	12	(96)
Black males			
Latecomers	9	16	(78)
Early arrivals	3	14	(75)
Long-termers	3	13	(98)
White females			
Latecomers	31	17	(42)
Early arrivals	17	8	(64)
Long-termers	12	11	(66)
Black females			
Latecomers	36	24	(78)
Early arrivals	16	14	(81)
Long-termers	19	13	(69)

*Because of the procedure used to construct the labor force variable for the Cleveland data, the percentage base for each time is the same.

The finding that larger proportions of the women were found outside the labor force during the second round of interviews than during the initial interviews suggests that at least part of the decline in unemployment may be an artifactual consequence of the study procedures. To be eligible for inclusion in the study population, migrants and long-term residents had either to be members of the labor force, discouraged workers, or female heads of house. During the second round of interviews no such restrictions were imposed. We will subsequently argue that much of the elasticity in the labor force necessary to meet changing demands is primarily provided by women and, furthermore, that the working careers of working-class women probably include a much larger number of movements into and out of the labor force than is the case for men, whose careers are more apt to be characterized by movements within the labor force. If our interpretation is correct, the criteria related to labor force participation loaded the first round interviews with the cases of women who would subsequently withdraw to positions outside the labor force. On the other hand, we lack parallel information from women, other than female heads of house, who were originally outside the labor force. As a result of the opposite trends in the unemployment rates for the sexes, at the time of the second interview the differences by sex were less than first observed. With only two exceptions, the most recent arrivals among the migrants had higher unemployment rates at both times than other groups, suggesting both the greater difficulty of getting established on a steady job and the vulnerability of the last through the hiring gate.

In comparison with national rates, the unemployment rates for males in the Cleveland study at the time of the first interviews were not markedly high (national rates were averaging 2.1 per 100 labor force members for white males and 4.3 for nonwhite males during the months of the first round of interviewing).* But the unemployment rates of women in the Cleveland study ranged from more than three times to more than eight times the national rates during the same period (the national rates were 3.7 for white women and 7.4 for nonwhite women). For the second round of interviews, the unemployment rates for all groups of males in the Cleveland study were substantially higher than the national rates. National unemployment rates during the months of the second round of interviews averaged 3.9 for white males and 7.4 for nonwhite males. Rates for the women had moved closer to the national rates (which at that time were 5.1

*National data are unweighted averages of the seasonally adjusted national unemployment rates for the months during which the fieldwork was being conducted.

for white women and 8.7 per 100 labor force members for nonwhite
women) than at the time of the first interviews but were still roughly
twice as high as in the national population. Blacks in every comparison group had unemployment rates at least as high as those of
the comparable groups of white workers and generally considerably
higher. But, for all, the absolute level of unemployment in the
study population signaled a problem of major importance.

                FREQUENCY AND DURATION OF UNEMPLOYMENT

        The high unemployment rates and the absence of any sizable
hard-core segment among the unemployed strongly suggest that this
population experiences considerable amounts of sporadic unemployment. Certainly unemployment is a relatively common experience.
The number who had been out of work but looking for employment at
any time during the two years preceding their second interview ranged
from one in eight persons to more than one in every three (Table 2.9).
Incidences of this magnitude convert unemployment from a remote
statistical probability to a phenomenon having personal immediacy,
making it something one is likely to experience directly or through
the lives of friends and neighbors. No pattern related to sex, race,
or duration of residence appears in the data, other than the tendency
for black female migrants to have slightly greater experience with
unemployment than white female migrants.
        Unemployment was a relatively frequent as well as common
personal experience; roughly half of those respondents in each group
who had been unemployed reported having experienced two or more
episodes of unemployment, times when they were without jobs and
were actively looking for work (Table 2.10). The median number of
unemployment episodes tended to be slightly higher for the migrants
who had arrived most recently in Cleveland, suggesting a "last
hired, first fired" pattern. However, except for the generally higher
number of unemployment episodes experienced by white female migrants, there was little difference in the frequency of unemployment
in the study group; but there was a strong difference in the severity
of the episodes. It is noteworthy that three of the four long-term
resident groups reported the highest median duration of any single
episode of unemployment and the highest duration of total time lost
through unemployment (Table 2.10). These data on duration of unemployment deserve emphasis. In each group, half or more of the
respondents who had experienced any unemployment had experienced
at least one unemployment episode that had lasted as long as three
weeks. In three of the four long-term resident groups, half or more
had experienced at least one unemployment episode lasting about 20

weeks, or roughly one-fifth of the two-year time period they were asked about. Medians for the total time of unemployment were a month or more for all groups and were more than two months for 9 of the 12 comparison groups.

TABLE 2.9

Percentage of Respondents Who Had Experienced Any
Unemployment in the Two Years Preceding
the Second Interview*

| | Type of Respondent | | |
	Latecomers	Early Arrivals	Long-Termers
Males			
Whites	20	30	25
	(117)	(145)	(104)
Blacks	29	30	20
	(80)	(77)	(61)
Females			
Whites	20	14	25
	(49)	(72)	(52)
Blacks	36	27	13
	(95)	(109)	(76)

*Persons with unemployment experience are those reporting at least one episode during preceding two years in which they had been without work and were actively engaged in the search for employment.

JOB TENURE

From the data on the frequency and duration of periods of unemployment, it would be easy to draw the conclusion that the negative portrayals of Southern migrants are reasonably accurate, that they are indeed a shiftless lot. Yet the data on job tenure seem to run in the opposite direction. In analyzing data on job tenure from a national sample of workers taken in 1968, O'Boyle found age to be a highly important correlate of continuity of work with the same employer.[2] Partition of the Cleveland data by five-year age groups as well as race and sex (to match O'Boyle's data) and migration status reduces the number of cases in each group to a point where comparison with other data is at best approximate. Nonetheless, out of

TABLE 2.10

Severity of Unemployment Episodes During Two Years
Preceding Second Interview: Respondents with
Unemployment Experience Only
(percentages)

Type of Respondent	Number of Unemployment Episodes (Medians)	Longest Period of Unemployment (Median Weeks)	Total Weeks Unemployed (Medians)
White males			
Latecomers	2.3	3.0	4.0
	(24)	(22)	(22)
Early arrivals	1.9	3.4	6.0
	(44)	(42)	(42)
Long-termers	1.8	19.3	27.9
	(25)	(25)	(25)
Black males			
Latecomers	2.0	4.0	5.4
	(23)	(20)	(20)
Early arrivals	2.1	3.5	8.6
	(23)	(19)	(20)
Long-termers	1.9	22.0	24.0
	(12)	(11)	(11)
White females			
Latecomers	3.2	6.0	10.0
	(10)	(8)	(8)
Early arrivals	2.8	14.0	19.0
	(10)	(9)	(9)
Long-termers	1.6	6.0	9.0
	(13)	(12)	(11)
Black females			
Latecomers	1.9	6.6	9.0
	(34)	(29)	(29)
Early arrivals	1.8	13.5	15.4
	(29)	(26)	(26)
Long-termers	1.6	21.0	33.5
	(10)	(11)	(11)

36 possible comparisons with the national data, we found the median number of months worked with the same employer to be higher for the Cleveland respondents in 24 instances and lower or approximately tied (that is, within three months of the national data) in 6 cases each.* Black migrants, both male and female, were decidedly more likely to have held onto their jobs longer than workers of similar age in the national sample (out of five possible comparisons, the medians for black males in this study were higher in four instances and tied in one; all five medians for black women in the study were higher than in the national sample).

Out of six possible comparisons, medians for white migrant males were higher than the national sample in three instances and lower in three others; in seven possible comparisons with women in the national sample, median months of employment with the same employer were higher for white migrant females in three instances, lower in three instances, and tied in one place.

Compared with the national sample, long-term residents fell into a position intermediate between that of the black and white migrants. Where sufficient data were available for comparison with the national sample, the long-termers uniformly had higher median months of employment with the same employer. In fact, the greater tenacity of the workers in the national sample becomes evident only at age 40 and beyond. Below that age, in all but one instance in which comparisons were possible, the Cleveland respondents had worked for their employers as long as or longer than the workers in the national sample.

The absolute level of the medians for months employed by the same employer suggests that the workers and their employers find one another, work assignments and conditions, performances and rewards at least minimally satisfactory. Medians for all groups of men were over three years at the time of the second interview, with long-term residents (who had been in town longer and were thereby able to work longer for the same employer) showing longer periods with the same employer than migrants (Table 2.11).† The women,

---

*Arbitrarily, we set the lower limit of the base for computing median months with same employer at 6 cases. As a result, we have no data for 20 groups, half of them long-term resident groups, most in groups aged 40 or beyond.

†For phenomena such as these, which depend on performance over protracted periods of time, cross-sectional measures are grossly inadequate. Job tenure, like completed fertility, is a behavior that can be adequately measured only at the close of the period of risk. When currently employed workers are queried about the

who, as we have seen, move in and out of the labor force with greater frequency than the men, had shorter medians. But in all instances, at least half of the women in each group who had had employment had worked at least two years for the same employer.

SHIFT WORK

Among the barriers that obstruct ease of movement into employment opportunities is the inability of some workers to meet employer requirements concerning work hours. As one might expect given the predominance of manufacturing for the employment of the Cleveland study population, jobs requiring shift work were fairly prevalent. About two-fifths of the employed men and a third of the employed women were on jobs that actually required them to work odd schedules (Table 2.12). The lower proportions of women, and in particular black women, who were working on jobs requiring shift work is readily explained by the proportions who reported that they were unable to work other than standard daytime hours. For women, who more often than men are encumbered by traditional home responsibilities, the inability to work odd hours seems to exert a channeling effect that eliminates some potential sources of employment. Among the workers who were employed on jobs not requiring shift work, the women far more often than the men reported that they were unable to accept employment requiring shift work (Table 2.13). Firm comparison of the availability to do shift work among those seeking work is precluded by the small number of cases in each group. But, as one would expect, men were generally more likely than women to be able and willing to work odd hours.

SUPPLEMENTARY EMPLOYMENT

Fewer than a fifth of the employed respondents in any of the comparison groups were holding down two jobs at either interview. At both times men were more likely than the women to have more than one job, but they were also less likely to be constrained in their mobility than the women since they were more likely to have driver's licenses and the use of a car or truck and are traditionally less hampered by diurnal parental obligations. During the first interviews

---

length of time they have been on their jobs, those who will ultimately receive a gold watch are indistinguishable from those who will quit or be laid off tomorrow.

TABLE 2.11

Median Months with Current Employer and on
Current Job at Time of Second Interview
(percentages)

Type of Respondent	Median Months with Current Employer	Median Months on Current Job
White males		
Latecomers	53	42
	(98)	(98)
Early arrivals	60	39
	(120)	(120)
Long-termers	74	61
	(83)	(83)
Black males		
Latecomers	49	44
	(64)	(64)
Early arrivals	54	43
	(62)	(61)
Long-termers	74	67
	(51)	(51)
White females		
Latecomers	33	24
	(24)	(24)
Early arrivals	32	29
	(43)	(43)
Long-termers	72	42
	(30)	(30)
Black females		
Latecomers	38	34
	(42)	(42)
Early arrivals	45	42
	(58)	(58)
Long-termers	46	42
	(48)	(48)

TABLE 2.12

Job Requires Shift Work: Currently Employed Respondents Only
(percentages)

| | Type of Respondent | | |
	Latecomers	Early Arrivals	Long-Termers
Males			
Whites	39	48	37
	(98)	(120)	(84)
Blacks	41	37	43
	(64)	(62)	(51)
Females			
Whites	33	35	37
	(24)	(43)	(30)
Blacks	20	34	31
	(41)	(58)	(48)

TABLE 2.13.

Not Able to Do Shift Work: Currently Employed in Nonshift Work Only
(percentages)

| | Type of Respondent | | |
	Latecomers	Early Arrivals	Long-Termers
Males			
Whites	4	13	2
	(57)	(60)	(51)
Blacks	6	3	7
	(36)	(37)	(27)
Females			
Whites	53	29	16
	(15)	(24)	(19)
Blacks	30	47	33
	(30)	(36)	(30)

black men were more likely to be moonlighting, but by the time of
the second interviews this difference had disappeared.

SUMMARY

The data on labor force participation show the comparison
groups to be quite differently located in relation to the labor force,
with the line of differentiation lying more clearly between the sexes
than between blacks and whites. Male newcomers moved more
quickly than women into jobs in Cleveland, but more of them had in-
tended to work before making the move. For both men and women,
labor force positions tended to have deteriorated over the time between the first and second interviews, with men experiencing rising
rates of unemployment while larger proportions of women were found
outside the labor force at the time of the second interview than at the
first. Men were more stable in their labor force position, and that
stability centered on being employed; they were also more likely
than the women to be working full time as well as to have some sort
of second job. When men changed their labor force position, it was
more likely to be a change between being employed and unemployed
than a movement into or out of the labor force. Women, on the
other hand, were found more likely to shift position between being in
or out of the labor force than between being on a job or unemployed.
Unemployment rates for all groups of men rose over the time between the two interviews with rates at the time of the second interview frequently more than double what they had been at the time of
the first. But, among labor force participants, the unemployment
rates for women in the study had shaded downward. Looking backward
over the two years preceding the second interview, we see that unemployment had been a rather widespread experience affecting between
one in eight and more than a third in the various comparison groups
(but without any discernible pattern between the race/sex groups).
Unemployment was not only a relatively common experience among
the study participants, it was also a rather frequent one, with the
median number of episodes of unemployment among those who had
been out of work running roughly two or more. The episodes tended
to be severe, with median weeks of the longest period of unemployment ranging upward from three to more than 20 weeks and
with the median cumulative length of unemployment ranging from
about a month to more than seven months. Nonetheless, age for
age, within race and sex groups, the participants in the study reported durations of employment with the same employer that tended
to exceed the medians reported for a national sample of workers.
Finally, we found shift work to be a rather common employment

requirement for men and women but with women more often than men reporting themselves to be unavailable to work odd hours and non-daytime shifts.

In general, the data reported here seem consistent with a notion that has gained greater currency in the years since the Cleveland Southern Migrant Study was started. In the main, difficulties in the workplace tend to fall more on women than on men. Contrary to our general expectations on starting the study, there is no clear and consistent line of demarcation between migrants, whether recently arrived or of greater sojourn in the city, and their long-term resident neighbors. But, in the next two chapters, in which we examine the occupational experiences of the men and women in the study, differences between the races become evident.

NOTES

1. See Otis Dudley Duncan, David L. Featherman, and Beverly Duncan, Sociometric Background and Achievement (New York: Seminar Press, 1972).

2. Edward J. O'Boyle, "Job Tenure: How It Relates to Race and Age," Monthly Labor Review 92, no. 9 (September 1969): 16-23.

CHAPTER

3

MEN AND THEIR
OCCUPATIONS

Information on occupations supplements the data on labor force participation by providing some indication of the tasks involved in the work performed and the social composition of work groups. It likewise leads to a discussion of hours and the range of workplaces and rewards, including the relative security of continued employment. Insofar as occupation is an indicator of the kinds and levels of skill needed to perform the work tasks, it is a crude proxy measure for the relative development of human resources. Comparing information on occupations among groups and over time, we are able to get a more refined, though still rough, idea of the relative social position of the individuals in the study population and to gauge the relative amounts of mobility, to better or worse positions, as the migrants settle into Cleveland. From another perspective, the occupational data are indicative of the relative contribution of the study subjects to Cleveland's manpower supply.

Although throughout this study we hope that readers will keep in mind the time frame within which the study was conducted and the survey methodology and population definitions, it seems especially important at the beginning of this section to call attention to these matters. As was discussed in greater detail in the introduction,

As we have shown, the labor force paths for the men and women in the study diverge sharply. In order to simplify presentation of the data and to make more explicit the ways in which their involvement in the Cleveland work force differs, the occupational movement of men and women is discussed in separate chapters. Underlying both chapters, however, is a common rationale, methodology, mode of data presentation, and structure of the discussion.

the two rounds of interviews were conducted in very different economic climates in Cleveland; for the population under study, this
may or may not have been offset by the fact that migrants had had
between four and nine years of experience in Cleveland and opportunity for promotion and relocation by the time of the second interview. Most important, perhaps, the original study sample was
drawn in low-income white and black areas; we feel that this decision
may have led to the inclusion of a number of well-qualified black migrants whose white counterparts would initially have moved to better
areas outside the ghetto at a time when such alternatives did not exist for blacks. Thus comparisons across racial groups, which are
often made in this section, may tend to overstate the progress of
blacks as compared to that of whites, since the two groups may not
initially have been fully comparable although both lived in low-
income areas.

      In tracing the work patterns of newcomers to Cleveland and
judging the contributions and progress they did or did not make, it
is also essential to assess briefly whether structural changes in the
Cleveland labor market over the period covered by the panel study
were such that their effects might have been overwhelming in relation to our data. This was not the case, however. As shown in
Table 3.1, the Cleveland male labor force grew moderately between
1960 and 1970, with larger growth rates for blacks than for whites
(35 percent versus 15 percent). But the occupational distributions
were basically static, with only a slight growth in professional-
technical occupations and minor declines in other occupational groups,
primarily in the operative and sales categories for whites, and in
laborer jobs for blacks. The latter shift is of some importance in
understanding the unemployment picture among the group of male
black migrants.

      In our study, data on occupations were acquired for six time
periods. The respondents were asked their father's occupation when
he was about their age, their own usual premigration occupation,
their occupation on the first job they held after arriving in Cleveland, their occupation at the time of the first interview, and again
at the time of the second interview, about four years later. They
were also asked what kind of work they would be doing if their life
were to work out in the best imaginable way.

      The data on father's occupation provides an indication of
social origins and, in comparison with the respondents' own occupations, of intergenerational social mobility. Usual premigration
occupation specifies in part the kinds of credentials and experience
the migrants bring with them to place before potential employers
in Cleveland. This, in turn, is related to the kinds of jobs they get

TABLE 3.1

Occupation of Employed Males by Race, Cleveland SMSA,
1960 and 1970 Censuses
(percentages)

Occupation	White Males		Black Males	
	1960[a]	1970[b]	1960[a]	1970[b]
Professional, technical, managerial	25	28	6	9
Craftsmen and foremen	24	23	14	16
Operatives	23	21	35	36
Clerical and sales	18	16	10	12
Service	5	6	14	13
Farm workers	--	1	--	--
Nonfarm laborers	5	5	21	13
Total percent	100	100	100	100
(N)	392,727	452,528	49,631	66,336

[a]U.S. Bureau of the Census, U.S. Census of Population: 1960 General Social and Economic Characteristics, Ohio. Final Report PC(1)-37C, Table 74, p. 37-288 and Table 78, p. 37-335.

[b]U.S. Bureau of the Census, U.S. Census of Population: 1970 General Social and Economic Characteristics. Final Report PC(1)-C37 Ohio, Table 86, p. 37-433 and Table 93, p. 37-517.

Note: Data base for both years is number of employed males. 1960 data for black males include other nonwhite males. 1970 data for white males includes other nonblack males. Persons without reported occupations are excluded from the 1960 data.

on arrival.* These measures are all retrospective. Information on occupations at the time of first and second interviews is fuller, because the recall problem is largely eliminated, and presents a more detailed picture of movement in the Cleveland labor force. Remote as it is from reality, the information on ideal occupation provides

---

*The data sets for the long-term residents do not include pre-migration occupations, or occupations on first Cleveland job, since so many were native Clevelanders. Thus, comparison between the migrants and the long-term residents for these earlier times is not possible.

some indication of where the respondents place themselves under the most optimistic personal conditions; as such, the information on ideal occupations permits a comparison between work life as it is and what it might be like in the best of all possible worlds.

In addition to being displayed in the customary occupational groupings, * data on occupations were retabulated in two other ways. No new information is presented, but each of the retabulations does emphasize different and salient information. The first, which we call type of work activity, is a recombination of the occupational data to permit comparison between white- and blue-collar jobs and service occupations. This reclassification links the occupational data with other observations on social stratification and emphasizes the differences in mobility opportunities for white- and blue-collar workers.† Movement between type of work activity categories is also a crude indicator of the extent to which previously acquired skills are set aside and new ones acquired. Again, however, the dissimilarity in the content of occupational skills is probably greater between blue- and white-collar occupations than between either of these and service occupations. For example, health service occupa-

---

*While standard U.S. Census Bureau occupational groupings were used as the point of departure for classifying occupations for this study, several important changes in the groupings seemed advisable. In particular, clerical and sales occupations were grouped together as were all farm occupations. We also found it necessary to combine the category for professional, technical, and kindred occupations with that for occupations of proprietors, managers, and officials. For convenience this last combination is labeled "professional-managerial" and "professional, technical, or managerial" in this study. Though the number of cases in this category is generally small, technical and managerial occupations tend to outnumber occupations in other categories (except in choice of ideal occupation where the status of owner or proprietor was more likely to be designated). The occupational categories used in this study also differ from usual presentations in the inclusion of the category "no occupation." In addition to labor force participants who were unemployed, that category also includes those who have left the labor force for whatever reason.

†Because of the heterogeneity of the occupations in the service category, the mobility opportunities for that group of workers are more difficult to assess. Some service occupations border on white-collar occupations, some are more similar to blue-collar occupations, and the activities of others (such as policemen and detectives) have elements of both kinds of work.

tions have skills contents that border on technical, managerial, and professional occupations in the same field.

The other form of retabulation, which we call skill level, is into three categories roughly indicative of the level of skill represented by the occupations in each group. Again, no new information is presented that is not implicit in the source occupational distributions, but this retabulation directs attention to skills hierarchies and is particularly useful in examining mobility. Occupational groups forming these three skill levels are the following: high (professional, technical, and managerial occupations, foremen, and craftsmen); medium (operatives, and clerical or sales workers); and low (service occupations and laborers). Farm operators, including tenant farmers, were placed in the top skill level; all other farm occupations were relegated to the lowest level.

The aggregate data are displayed as three histograms showing the changes in occupational distribution across time, differences in the type of work activity of this segment of the work force, and changes in skill level (see Figures 3.1–3.3). In the following section of the chapter, the occupational data are reexamined to note the effect of earlier occupational positions on subsequent ones. In the final section exchanges between pairs of occupations are examined.

TRENDS IN OCCUPATIONS

The aggregate data tell much of the story of what happened to each of the groups (Figures 3.1 to 3.3).* In each data set, comparison of the positions held by the white and black respondents emphasizes the differences in occupational movement for these two groups. Initially the black males enter the Cleveland work force in less favorable positions than those obtained by white male migrants; compared to all blacks employed in Cleveland, migrants also hold fewer jobs in the industrial categories (Table 3.2). Over time some of the initial disadvantage is overcome. Between the first and

---

*The aggregate descriptions are typical of the kinds of observations that can be made from subsequent surveys using independent samples. But a panel study has obvious advantages over such surveys. Because the observations used here are for the same individuals, we can be sure that the differences we observe are not due to initial differences in the composition of the samples. Reinterviewing the same individuals also avoids the problems associated with recall error in retrospective questions and permits firmer analysis of the effect of earlier positions on subsequent mobility.

FIGURE 3.1

Occupational Distributions for Male Migrants and Long-Term Residents

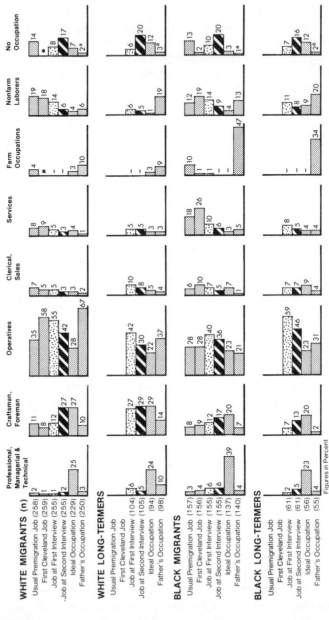

*0.5 percent or less.

Note: "a" category includes respondents without a father or father surrogate as well as respondents whose father or father surrogate was unemployed when he was the respondent's age.

48

FIGURE 3.2

Distribution of Type of Work Activities for Male Migrants and Long-Term Residents

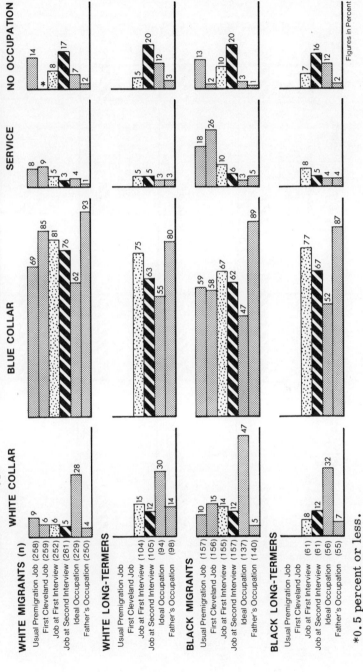

Figures in Percent

*0. 5 percent or less.

49

FIGURE 3.3

Skill Level Distributions for Male Migrants and Long-Term Residents

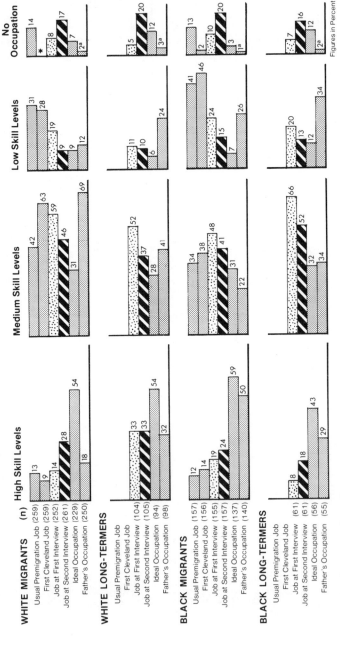

*0.5 percent or less.

Note: "a" category includes respondents without a father or father surrogate as well as respondents whose father or father surrogate was unemployed when he was the respondent's age.

TABLE 3.2

Occupational Distribution: Comparison of Census Data (1960 and 1970) and Migrant Survey Data (First Jobs and Occupation at Second Interview): Males (percentages)

| | White Males | | | | Black Males | | | |
| | Census | | Migrants | | Census | | Migrants | |
Category	1960[a]	1970[b]	First Cleveland Job	Second Interview	1960[a]	1970[b]	First Cleveland Job	Second Interview
Professional, technical, and managerial	25	28	1	2	6	9	5	8
Craftsmen and foremen	24	23	8	32	14	16	9	21
Operatives	23	21	58	51	35	36	29	45
Clerical and sales	18	16	5	4	10	12	10	6
Service	5	6	9	3	14	13	26	8
Farm workers	--	1	--	--	--	1	1	--
Nonfarm laborers	5	5	19	8	21	13	20	11
Total percent	100	100	100	100	100	100	100	100
(N)	392,727	452,528	(258)	(217)	49,631	66,636	(153)	(217)

[a]U.S. Bureau of the Census, U.S. Census of Population: 1960 General Social and Economic Characteristics, Ohio, Final Report PC(1)-37C, Table 74, p. 37-288 and Table 78, p. 37-335.

[b]U.S. Bureau of the Census, U.S. Census of Population: 1970 General Social and Economic Characteristics. Final Report PC(1)-C37, Ohio, Table 86, p. 37-433 and Table 93, p. 37-517.

Note: Data base for both years is number of employed males. 1960 data for black males include other nonwhite males. 1970 data for white males include other nonblack males. Persons without reported occupations are excluded from the 1960 data.

51

second interviews the males of both races had moved into occupations more closely resembling those held by long-term Cleveland residents who lived in low-income areas; in fact, the blacks did at least as well as or even slightly better than all employed black males in Cleveland in 1970. If the individuals interviewed could manage to realize the life ideals they expressed, black male migrants would have occupational positions superior to each of the other comparison groups.

When the same data are regrouped according to type of work activity, the predominance of blue-collar activities for all groups of males in the study is evident. Over four-fifths of the males were drawn from blue-collar backgrounds; only for the ideal occupations of black male migrants does any other type of work activity approach blue-collar work in prevalence.

Over time, the movement in skill level has two focuses. For the migrants, there is the initial movement into middle and low skill level jobs, with the black males ranking below the white males. Subsequently, the skill level distributions for males of both races show movement into the ranks of men without jobs and slight movement into jobs in the highest skill level. Viewed in terms of the skill component, the level of aspiration of the males is clear; in all but one of the comparison groups over half of the males named an occupation classed as being high in skill content. The skill level data for fathers show the black migrants to have had some advantage over the white male migrants, largely because all farm operators were classed in the highest skill level group, along with foremen and craftsmen, professionals, technicians, managers, officials, and proprietors.

Overview of Occupational Distributions

Usual Premigration Occupation

More than four-fifths of the males, both black and white, had worked prior to migration, both most often in one of the operative occupations. Employment as an operative was, however, more common among white migrants than among the black men. The next most common occupation for white males was as nonfarm laborers; for black males it was employment in a service occupation. Fewer than 10 percent in either group were accustomed to working in higher skill level jobs, as craftsmen or foremen or as professionals, technicians, or managerial workers. As one would expect from the neighborhoods canvassed to obtain the study population, the men were solidly working-class in their backgrounds, with the majority having most of their experience in lower-level blue-collar occupations.

First Cleveland Occupation

White male migrants overwhelmingly began work in Cleveland
as operatives; black males were more evenly divided between those
who began work in Cleveland as operatives and those who found service jobs. For both groups the next most common start in Cleveland
was as a nonfarm laborer. Detailed tabulations, not presented here,
show that the white male migrants had greater access than black
male migrants to jobs on assembly lines and closely related operative tasks. White male migrants were about three times as likely as
the black males to have begun work in Cleveland as assemblers,
sorters, or machine operators.

The entry advantages of the white male migrants over the black
males show up clearly in the histograms for type of work activity and
for skill level. Black males were less likely than whites to enter
blue-collar occupations and more likely than whites to get jobs in
service occupations. As a result the black male migrants were
more likely than the whites to have entered the Cleveland work force
in a low skill level job.

Occupation at First Interview

The most striking change in the occupational distributions,
relative to entry jobs in Cleveland, was in the increase in the proportion of men without work. *

In other respects, the occupational distributions at the time of
the first interview continue to show the dominance of blue-collar jobs
in the Cleveland area. Operative occupations remain at the top of
the distribution and had increased among the black migrants. More
male black long-term residents than any other group of males were
employed as operatives. Next to working as operatives, white male
long-term residents were most often employed as craftsmen or foremen; among all other groups of men, employment as nonfarm laborers followed jobs as operatives. Relative to first Cleveland occupations, the proportion in service occupations had declined for both

---

*Of course, this is partially the effect of a change in the inter-
val of measurement. First Cleveland job and usual premigration occupation are referenced on a longer time interval, as long as necessary to encompass anyone who ever held a job in Cleveland or to include the period during which a customary premigration occupation
was exercised. The present measure (and the one for occupation at
time of the second interview) is an instantaneous measure centered
on the time of the actual interview.

white and black males. The proportion employed as craftsmen and
foremen was approximately the same for whites as before moving to
Cleveland and was higher than before migration for black males.
For the first time in this series of observations, the skill level distributions for the black males begin to resemble those for the white
males.

Occupation at Second Interview

The ramifications of the general downturn in economic activity
in the early 1970s are abundantly apparent in the occupational distributions for the second round of interviews. In each of the four male
comparison groups at least twice as many as at the first interview
were without jobs. In no group were fewer than 15 percent without
work. As at the first interview, the largest proportion in every
group were working as operatives. For whites the next most common positions in the occupational structure were as craftsmen and
foremen and being without work. Black males were second most
often found without work and had employment as craftsmen or foremen as a third most likely occupational status.

Most of the loss in the movement into the group without jobs
occurred at middle and low skill levels. Despite the uniform rise in
the proportion without work, the number having high skill level jobs
held steady or increased. Viewed in terms of type of work activities,
the data show most of the loss to the group without work to have occurred to the pool of blue-collar workers, with the white-collar and
service groups shading downward only slightly.

Occupational Aspirations

Data on occupational aspirations were obtained in the second-
round interviews when the respondents were asked to describe what
their lives would be like under the best possible set of conditions.
If they did not mention practicing an occupation they were asked the
direct question, "What kind of work would you be doing then?" While
the question does not proscribe a "no work" answer, it does suggest
strongly that reply in terms of some particular kind of work would
be preferable. The "no work" response is taken here as indicative
of a desire for withdrawal from the labor force rather than unemployment. As an indicator of the number of people who would probably opt for a nonwork status, if they had the chance, the measure
is probably conservative.

A number of unrealities enter into the consideration of data on
occupational aspirations. The meaning of the data themselves is
ambiguous. Simultaneously, they may be interpreted as indications

of satisfaction with present occupation (those contented with their statuses less often choose to change) as well as indications of the shape things might be in if ideal conditions were realized. From the point of view of the respondent other ambiguities are added by the unreality of the basic question. For instance, we do not know how many respondents, in defining an ideal state, set aside rather immutable constraints such as age, ability, and customary sex roles.

While the responses for all four groups of male respondents were remarkably similar, the distributions do show some differences. In all four groups there were at least one-fifth in each of the three most commonly mentioned occupational groups (professional, technical, and managerial; crafts and foremen; and operatives). Black migrants were far more likely to designate a professional-managerial occupation (39 percent, mainly proprietors) than any other group and were least likely to opt out of the working force. While very small percentages of the whites named farming occupations, no black male respondent chose farming as a basis for his ideal life. White males were also more likely than the black males to envision themselves as craftsmen or foremen (mainly as mechanics).

Father's Occupation

The occupational heritage of the respondents was diverse. The greatest homogeneity in father's occupation occurred among white male migrants (two-thirds of them had fathers who had been operatives). Consideration of type of work activity, however, shows the comparison groups to be markedly similar; four-fifths or more of the males in each group were from blue-collar backgrounds. Classification of the farm operators in the high-skill-level group resulted in the black migrants having a slight apparent advantage in skill level over white migrants. Among the long-term residents, the white respondents tended to be from higher skill level backgrounds than the blacks.

Net Changes in the Composition
of the Groups

While the histograms are useful in giving an overall impression of the net changes in the aggregate composition of the groups, for detailed analysis it is more convenient to look at the data in tabular form (see Tables 3.3 to 3.5).* Starting with the comparison between

---

*Slight differences in the amount of change described in these tables and shown in the cross-sectional distributions in Figures 3.1,

usual premigration occupation and first Cleveland occupation, it is clear that white and black male migrants had different destinies. Roughly a quarter of the white male study population was added to the group of operatives as they entered the work force in Cleveland. Among the black male migrants, the destinations and the recruitment from other occupational categories were more diffuse (in this case, no category gained as many as 10 percent of the group's members and only one lost that many). This pattern is still evident at the time of the first interview, when occupations held at that time are compared with usual premigration occupations.

As a result of job changes subsequent to entry into the Cleveland work force, however, the advantage of the white male migrants over the black male migrants was less pronounced by the time of the first interview than it had been at the time of first Cleveland employment. For both races the stream continued to flow toward operative occupations. Between the first and second interviews, as the level of economic activity slumped during the closing days of the Vietnam war, the general pattern of movement was into a higher-ranked occupation or into a nonwork status. Still, as a group the white male migrants continued to enjoy a more advantageous position than the black male migrants; more of the white than the black male migrants moved to higher-ranked occupational categories.

Looking toward the ideal future from the vantage point of the occupational position held at the time of the second interview, the males expressed a common preference. Generally, the choice of work expressed in the description of ideal life states implied a movement out of the group without work and out of operative occupations and implied sizable increases in the proportion of persons with top-level white-collar occupations.

Viewed in terms of type of work activity, the data show movements from being without work into blue-collar occupations for white male migrants, and into white-collar and service occupations for black male migrants. Job shifts in Cleveland prior to the first interview lessened the initial advantage whites had in blue-collar occupations but also reduced the amount of movement out of the nonwork

---

3.2, and 3.3 are due to tabulation procedures. The histograms are based on the total number of cases for which information was obtained at each time period. The net change information is derived from turnover tables that excluded cases lacking occupational information for either or both of the times under comparison. The amount of net change shown in these tables, therefore, differs slightly from that shown in the histograms as does the number of cases on which the change tabulations are based.

TABLE 3.3

Net Changes in the Occupational Structure for Males (percentages)[a]

Occupational Category	White Migrants	White Long-Termers	Black Migrants	Black Long-Termers
Time Period: Premigration to First Cleveland Job				
Professional, technical, or managerial	-1		1	
Craftsmen or foremen	-3		1	
Operatives	24		1	
Clerical or sales	-2		4	
Services	*[b]		7	
Farm workers	-4		-9	
Nonfarm laborers	-*[b]		6	
Not working	-14		-11	
(N)	(255)		(155)	
Premigration to First Interview				
Professional, technical, or managerial	-1		3	
Craftsmen or foremen	2		3	
Operatives	19		13	
Clerical or sales	-1		1	
Services	-4		-9	
Farm workers	-4		-10	
Nonfarm laborers	-4		2	
Not working	-6		-3	
(N)	(252)		(155)	
First Interview to Second Interview				
Professional, technical, or managerial	*[b]	-1	--	3
Craftsmen or foremen	14	1	6	7
Operatives	-13	-12	-4	-13
Clerical or sales	-3	-2	-2	--
Services	-2	--	-4	-3
Farm workers	--	--	-1	--
Nonfarm laborers	-7	-1	-5	-3
Not working	9	15	10	10
(N)	(255)	(104)	(155)	(61)
Second Interview to Ideal Occupation				
Professional, technical, or managerial	23	19	33	18
Craftsmen or foremen	-1	-1	2	7
Operatives	-14	-5	-13	-23
Clerical or sales	-1	-2	2	4
Services	*[b]	-2	--	-2
Farm workers	3	3	--	--
Nonfarm laborers	-3	-3	-4	--
Not working	-7	-8	-19	-4
(N)	(229)	(94)	(136)	(56)

[a]Percentage bases are total number of males in each race and duration-of-residence category excluding cases for which occupational information was lacking for either of the times being compared.

[b]"*" = 0.5 percent or less.

57

TABLE 3.4

Net Changes in Structure of Type of Work Activity for Males
(percentages)

Type of Respondent

First group of columns:

Type of Work Activity	White Migrants	White Long-Termers	Black Migrants	Black Long-Termers
Premigration to First Cleveland Job				
White collar	-3		5	
Blue collar	16		-1	
Service	*b		7	
Not working	-14		-11	
(N)	(255)		(155)	
First Interview to Second Interview				
White collar	-2	-3	-2	3
Blue collar	-6	-12	-4	-10
Service	-2	--	-4	-3
Not working	9	15	10	10
(N)	(255)	(104)	(155)	(61)

Second group of columns:

Type of Work Activity	White Migrants	White Long-Termers	Black Migrants	Black Long-Termers
Premigration to First Interview				
White collar	-2		4	
Blue collar	12		8	
Service	-4		-9	
Not working	-6		-3	
(N)	(252)		(155)	
Second Interview to Ideal Occupation				
White collar	22	17	35	21
Blue collar	-15	-6	-15	-16
Service	*b	-2	--	-2
Not working	-7	-8	-19	-4
(N)	(229)	(94)	(136)	(56)

Time Period

aPercentage bases are total number of males in each race and duration-of-residence category excluding cases for which occupational information was lacking for either of the times being compared.

b"*" = 0.5 percent or less.

TABLE 3.5

Net Changes in Structure of Skill Levels for Males
(percentages)*

Type of Respondent

Skill Level	White Migrants	White Long-Termers	Black Migrants	Black Long-Termers
Time Period: Premigration to First Cleveland Job				
High	-4		3	
Medium	22		4	
Low	-4		4	
Not working	-14		-11	
(N)	(255)		(155)	
Time Period: First Interview to Second Interview				
High	15	--	5	10
Medium	-15	-14	-6	-13
Low	-9	-1	-9	-7
Not working	9	15	10	10
(N)	(255)	(104)	(155)	(61)
Time Period: Premigration to First Interview				
High	1		7	
Medium	18		14	
Low	-13		-17	
Not working	-6		-3	
(N)	(252)		(155)	
Time Period: Second Interview to Ideal Occupation				
High	24	19	35	25
Medium	-15	-7	-12	-20
Low	-1	-3	-4	-2
Not working	-7	-8	-19	-4
(N)	(229)	(94)	(136)	(56)

*Percentage bases are total number of males in each race and duration-of-residence category excluding cases for which occupational information was lacking for either of the times being compared.

59

status. Except among male black long-term residents, the changes
between first and second interviews in every case resulted in a decrease in each division of type of work activity and an increase in
the proportion without work. Realization of aspirations would reverse that trend and result in a substantial increase in each group
of the number of white-collar workers with decreases in the number
in each of the other categories, including the nonwork status.

Changes in occupation resulted in an initial increase in the proportion of male migrants, larger for whites than blacks, who held
middle-skill-level jobs. Between the first and second interviews,
the middle-skill-level group decreased in size while the proportion
in high-skill-level jobs increased among all but white male long-
term residents. The number without work, as we have noted above,
increased in all groups. In comparison with the skill-level positions
occupied at the second interview, realization of occupational aspirations would substantially increase the number of persons in high-
skill-level jobs in all groups. The data presented so far point in
several clear directions. White men have faster and better access
to factory jobs in Cleveland; from the data we have on the job search
we are convinced that this initial advantage is largely due to the op-
eration of friendship and kinship networks, which are abundantly used
in integrating newcomers into the world of work. However, the
blacks' initial disadvantage is gradually overcome with length of
residence. Judging from our data and from the broad census data
available, much of this narrowing in opportunity differentials was
due to the black migrants' familiarization with Cleveland and its job
market, rather than to a change in the opportunity structure associated with progress in the equal opportunity area. Most of the
progress was made between time of arrival in Cleveland and first
interview; between the times of the first and second interviews,
there was little progress for migrants, for long-term inner-city
residents, or for all black males in Cleveland (as measured by 1960-
70 trend data). The greatest impediment to progress and mobility
for the males in our study during the period under observation was
apparently the lack of suitable jobs, resulting in a gradual increase
in the number of people without occupation at each interview. This
may be due to an actual reduction in the number of unskilled jobs or,
possibly, to the unwillingness of black males to accept this type of
employment. Aspirations for mobility, for higher-level jobs than
the one currently held, were most marked among blacks. Their
clear preference is for work, preferably at a high skill level. Whites
seem more inclined to find their current work situation congruent with
their long-term aspirations.

In the remainder of this chapter, these and other findings will
be further refined and developed by introducing measures of occupational stability and gross and net occupational turnover. Essentially,

we will now shift from an aggregate or cross-section analysis to an examination of individual mobility. * For example, we will examine details on individual movement such as the effect of earlier occupational positions on subsequent mobility, the weight of the total or gross mobility centered on each of the major occupational categories, and the net exchanges behind the changes in structure just described.

Although it is felt that these analyses at the level of the individual greatly strengthen and clarify the data presented so far, readers interested only in the general transformations in working life encountered by the migrants as they moved into Cleveland may wish to turn to Chapter 4.

CHANGING OCCUPATIONS

Occupational Stability

While the preceding section focused attention on changes in the aggregate distribution of occupations among the males in the study, the present section extends the analysis by looking at the data on the movement of the individuals. The previous discussion emphasized outcomes, changes in the composition of the groups. This section discusses the process of change, the extent to which individuals remain in the same occupational category over time or move into other sectors of the work force. Then attention is directed to the drawing power of other occupational groups. This form of analysis, feasible only with longitudinal data, extends our understanding of the mobility process by exploring the effect on subsequent mobility of one's original position in the occupational structure. While the same data are being reworked, the information derived from these tabulations is quite different from that discussed above. For example, except for those without an established occupation, from the shape of the histograms one might be tempted to infer that the transition from premigration jobs to work in Cleveland consisted mainly of persons moving into lines of work similar to those they had followed at home. However,

---

*Panel analysis, the analysis of data for the same population at two or more different points in time, can be approached in many ways. The least complex is via comparison of data for the total group at the two time points. The "aggregate analysis" has been presented in this chapter up to this point. More complex are various types of analyses that examine the position of the same individual at the two points in time and examine the data in relation to the new groupings that are created through this approach. These are the analyses presented in the balance of this chapter.

the data on occupational stability discussed in the next paragraphs, which are based on a comparison of the position each individual occupied at an earlier time with the position held by the same individual at a later time, show that for roughly two-thirds of the male migrants the move to Cleveland involved a shift between major occupational groups.

Occupational mobility, of so great a degree as to be represented as a change between major occupational categories, was more common than occupational stability among the males. Over time, generally about a third or more of the males in each group were found in the same major occupational category in which they had been located earlier (Table 3.6). Higher rates of stability within race groups were observed for long-term residents who, being older, had had a longer period of time to become established in their occupations. Long-termers were also less likely than migrant males to name an ideal occupation that was outside the occupational arena in which they were found at the time of their second interview. With the exception of the comparison between occupation at second interview and ideal occupation for the black male migrants, over the entire series of comparisons it is evident that the major source of occupational stability stems from prior employment in operative occupations (sometimes supplemented substantially by the stability of workers in crafts and foremen's positions).

While there was substantial movement between occupational categories, there was considerable stability in type of work activities (Table 3.7), with whites being slightly more likely than black males to remain either in white-collar or blue-collar work. This is largely due to the fact that, albeit at various levels, blue-collar occupations predominate for this population, and the principal avenue of occupational mobility for this group of workers is from one blue-collar occupation to another. However, realization of one's occupational ideal would shift about half of the men in each group out of the type of work activity they were in at the time of the second interview, most often, of course, out of blue-collar work.

Skill levels show more stability than was the case for occupations, but less than was found in type of work activity, reflecting the mobility across skill level lines within blue-collar activities (Table 3.8). With only one exception (white long-term residents), roughly half of the males or fewer remained at the same skill level over time. Movement into ideal occupation implies about the same level of mobility.

TABLE 3.6

Stability of Occupational Status: Males
(percentages)[a]

Type of Respondent — Time Period

Premigration to First Cleveland Job

Occupational Category	White Migrants	White Long-Termers	Black Migrants	Black Long-Termers
Professional, technical, or managerial	--		2	
Craftsmen or foremen	2		3	
Operatives	23		12	
Clerical or sales	1		1	
Services	2		7	
Farm workers	--		1	
Nonfarm laborers	4		3	
Not working	--		1	
Total	32		30	
(N)	(255)		(155)	

Premigration to First Interview

Occupational Category	White Migrants	White Long-Termers	Black Migrants	Black Long-Termers
Professional, technical, or managerial	--		2	
Craftsmen or foremen	4		4	
Operatives	22		14	
Clerical or sales	1		1	
Services	--		4	
Farm workers	--		--	
Nonfarm laborers	3		4	
Not working	2		3	
Total	32		33	
(N)	(252)		(155)	

First Interview to Second Interview

Occupational Category	White Migrants	White Long-Termers	Black Migrants	Black Long-Termers
Professional, technical, or managerial	*b	2	3	--
Craftsmen or foremen	6	19	3	2
Operatives	28	22	18	34
Clerical or sales	2	5	--	--
Services	1	3	3	3
Farm workers	--	--	--	--
Nonfarm laborers	1	1	3	2
Not working	3	2	4	--
Total	40	54	34	41
(N)	(255)	(104)	(155)	(61)

Second Interview to Ideal Occupation

Occupational Category	White Migrants	White Long-Termers	Black Migrants	Black Long-Termers
Professional, technical, or managerial	1	5	6	4
Craftsmen or foremen	11	19	9	9
Operatives	18	11	2	18
Clerical or sales	2	4	3	4
Services	1	1	3	2
Farm workers	--	--	--	--
Nonfarm laborers	2	1	2	4
Not working	*b	2	--	2
Total	36	43	32	43
(N)	(229)	(94)	(136)	(56)

[a]Percentage bases are total number of males in each race and duration-of-residence category excluding cases for which occupational information was lacking for either of the times being compared.

[b]"*" = 0.5 percent or less.

63

TABLE 3.7

Stability of Position in Type of Work Activity: Males (percentages)[a]

Type of Work Activity	White		Black		White		Black	
	Migrants	Long-Termers	Migrants	Long-Termers	Migrants	Long-Termers	Migrants	Long-Termers
	Premigration to First Cleveland Job				**Premigration to First Interview**			
White collar	2	7	4	--	2	11	3	7
Blue collar	60	54	39	56	58	40	43	41
Service	2	3	7	3	--	1	4	4
Not working	--	2	1	--	2	2	3	2
Total	64	65	50	59	61	54	54	54
(N)	(255)	(104)	(155)	(61)	(252)	(94)	(155)	(56)
	First Interview to Second Interview				**Second Interview to Ideal Occupation**			
White collar	2	7	6	--	4	11	12	7
Blue collar	64	54	47	56	48	40	34	41
Service	1	3	3	3	1	1	--	4
Not working	3	2	4	--	*[b]	2	--	2
Total	70	65	60	59	52	54	46	54
(N)	(255)	(104)	(155)	(61)	(229)	(94)	(136)	(56)

[a]Percentage bases are total number of males in each race and duration-of-residence category excluding cases for which occupational information was lacking for either of the times being compared.

[b]"*" = 0.5 percent or less.

TABLE 3.8

Stability of Skill Level Position: Males
(percentages)[a]

Premigration to First Cleveland Job

Skill Level	White Migrants	White Long-Termers	Black Migrants	Black Long-Termers
High	3	26	6	3
Medium	28	30	16	43
Low	10	5	21	7
Not working	--	2	1	--
Total	41	62	44	52
(N)	(255)	(104)	(155)	(61)

Premigration to First Interview

Skill Level	White Migrants	White Long-Termers	Black Migrants	Black Long-Termers
High	4	30	6	16
Medium	26	17	21	25
Low	6	3	15	7
Not working	2	2	3	2
Total	39	52	44	50
(N)	(252)	(94)	(155)	(56)

First Interview to Second Interview

Skill Level	White Migrants	White Long-Termers	Black Migrants	Black Long-Termers
High	7	26	8	3
Medium	32	30	23	43
Low	2	5	6	7
Not working	3	2	4	--
Total	44	62	42	52
(N)	(255)	(104)	(155)	(61)

Second Interview to Ideal Occupation

Skill Level	White Migrants	White Long-Termers	Black Migrants	Black Long-Termers
High	23	30	19	16
Medium	21	17	18	25
Low	3	3	2	7
Not working	*[b]	2	--	2
Total	47	52	39	50
(N)	(229)	(94)	(136)	(56)

[a]Percentage bases are total number of males in each race and duration-of-residence category excluding cases for which occupational information was lacking for either of the times being compared.

[b]"*" = 0.5 percent or less.

The Differential Attractiveness of Occupations

The kinds of work found, of course, are partly a reflection of the kinds of work available and partly a reflection of the kinds of qualifications presented by the job seekers. Examination of the 1960 and 1970 census data shows blue-collar occupations to be of major importance for men working in the Cleveland metropolitan area (Table 3.1). About half of the white employed males in the Standard Metropolitan Statistical Area (SMSA) and about two-thirds of the employed black males worked in one of the blue-collar trades. For the whites, employment as a craftsman or foreman or as an operative is about equally likely. Among working black males, employment as operatives predominates and the 1970 census data show opportunities for employment as craftsmen and foremen to narrowly outweigh employment as laborers. Indeed, except for the far greater intercensal increase in the number of employed black males as compared to the increase in the number of employed white males, the decline in the proportion of black males working as nonfarm laborers is the only major change evident in a comparison of the occupational distributions from the 1960 and 1970 censuses. While these figures are not a precise measure of the structure of occupational opportunities for newcomers, they do provide a vivid demonstration both of the difference in occupations held by white and black men and of the minute amount of change in the structure of the area's male work force. (One would hazard a guess that adjustment for undercounts separately by race would show greater growth in the number of employed black males but less change in their occupational distribution.)

First Cleveland Occupation

The relative increase in the number of operatives among white males is accounted for by the fact that, with the exception of farm workers (who most often began work in Cleveland as nonfarm laborers), white males from all other occupational backgrounds were more likely to start work in Cleveland as operatives than in any other occupation (Table 3.9). Even so, a third of the white males with experience in one of the operative occupations moved into some other major occupational category, mainly to begin work as nonfarm laborers. For the black males, employment as operatives was the most likely starting job in Cleveland only for those who had worked as operatives before migration and for those who had had jobs as farm workers (nonfarm laborers were about equally divided among those who started as operatives, service workers, or nonfarm laborers).

Viewed in terms of type of work activities, the greater pull of blue-collar work for white than for black males is even more evident (Table 3.10). Larger proportions of white than black men from all origins entered (or stayed in) blue-collar occupations. The only group of black men with an entry rate into blue-collar occupations even similar to that of the white males is the group already working in blue-collar occupations.

The pattern of movement revealed by tabulation in terms of skill level also differs for white and black male migrants (Table 3.11). White males, pulled strongly into operative positions, show high percentages in middle-level occupations. Once again, from all skill-level origins, a distinct majority of the white males moved into middle-skill-level occupations. Black male migrants were most likely to be found in middle-skill-level jobs only if they had done that sort of work before the move. Black workers with experience in high-skill-level occupations tended to remain at that level. Workers without premigration occupational experience and those who had worked at jobs requiring little skill tended to enter the Cleveland work force near the bottom of the skills hierarchy.

Occupation at First Interview

Relative to their usual premigration position, white male migrants continued to show strong movement toward operative occupations, with work as an operative being the most likely destination for white males from every premigration occupational category (Table 3.12). Black male migrants also began to show a strong convergence on operative occupations (with that destination being most likely for five of the eight occupational categories). But, as shown in Table 3.12, recruitment to operative positions from "lower-level" jobs (laborers) or among persons with no previous experience occurred much more frequently among whites than among blacks.

It would seem that experience and opportunity played quite different roles in the occupational lives of the black and the white male migrants. For all prior occupational backgrounds, employment as an operative was the most likely destination for male white migrants. Among the black males, operative occupations were also important, but less so. Moreover, black migrant males who had been employed as operatives before the move were less likely than white male migrants with similar experience to be found in an operative occupation at the time of the first interview. Otherwise, black males were generally more likely than whites to be found in the same general occupational category as before the move. For better or worse, geographical mobility failed to produce the same kinds of occupational

TABLE 3.9

Changes in Occupation for Male Migrants: Usual Premigration Occupation to First Cleveland Occupation
(percentages)

Usual Premigration Occupation	First Cleveland Occupation								Total Percent	(N)
	Professional, Technical, or Managerial	Craftsmen or Foremen	Operatives	Clerical or Sales	Services	Farm Workers	Nonfarm Laborers	Not Working		
White										
Professional, technical, or managerial	--	17	67	17	--	--	--	--	100	(6)
Craftsmen or foremen	--	21	54	7	11	--	7	--	100	(28)
Operatives	1	2	66	3	7	1	19	--	100	(88)
Clerical or sales	6	6	47	18	6	--	18	--	100	(17)
Services	--	14	50	9	23	--	4	--	100	(22)
Farm workers	--	9	27	--	18	--	46	--	100	(11)
Nonfarm laborers	2	4	66	--	2	--	23	2	100	(47)
Not working	--	11	50	6	14	--	19	--	100	(36)
Black										
Professional, technical, or managerial	60	40	--	--	--	--	--	--	100	(5)
Craftsmen or foremen	--	38	8	8	23	--	23	--	100	(13)
Operatives	2	7	42	7	23	--	16	2	100	(43)
Clerical or sales	10	--	20	20	30	--	20	--	100	(10)
Services	--	3	28	17	38	--	14	--	100	(29)
Farm workers	6	--	38	6	19	6	25	--	100	(16)
Nonfarm laborers	--	5	26	5	26	5	26	5	100	(19)
Not working	5	10	20	15	25	--	20	5	100	(20)

A Note on the Change-of-Occupation Tables in Chapter 3

Data comparing earlier with subsequent occupational positions are presented as conventional turnover tables. The earlier position for each individual is shown in the categories at the left side of the table. The subsequent positions are shown in the categories at the top of the table. The percentages, running across the rows, show the movement of each occupational origin to a subsequent destination. Thus, the percentage base in each row is the number of persons in that occupational category at the earlier time. Due to pairwise exclusion of cases for which information is missing at either time, the percentage bases for the tables vary slightly and differ in some cases from the bases shown in the histograms. Three items of information are contained in the tables. The percentages representing the probability of being found in the same occupational category at a later time as at an earlier time are displayed along the major diagonal, running from the upper left corner to lower right hand corner of the table. Subtracting that percentage from 100 gives the probability of moving. The percentages in each cell off the major diagonal are the probabilities of moving from the original occupation to each of the other possible subsequent locations.

TABLE 3.10

Changes in Types of Work Activity for Male Migrants: Usual
Premigration Occupation to First Cleveland Occupation
(percentages)

Usual Premigration Occupation	First Cleveland Occupation				Total	
	White Collar	Blue Collar	Service	Not Working	Percent	(N)
White						
White collar	22	74	4	--	100	(23)
Blue collar	4	88	7	1	100	(174)
Service	9	68	23	--	100	(22)
Not working	6	81	14	--	100	(36)
Black						
White collar	40	40	20	--	100	(15)
Blue collar	9	66	23	2	100	(91)
Service	17	45	38	--	100	(29)
Not working	20	50	25	5	100	(20)

TABLE 3.11

Changes in Skill Level for Male Migrants: Usual Premigration
Occupation to First Cleveland Occupation
(percentages)

Usual Premigration Occupation	First Cleveland Occupation				Total	
	High	Medium	Low	Not Working	Percent	(N)
White						
High	21	65	15	--	100	(34)
Medium	5	69	27	--	100	(105)
Low	9	59	31	1	100	(80)
Not working	11	56	33	--	100	(36)
Black						
High	56	11	33	--	100	(18)
Medium	9	47	42	2	100	(53)
Low	6	41	52	2	100	(64)
Not working	15	35	45	5	100	(20)

TABLE 3.12

Changes in Occupation for Male Migrants: Usual Premigration Occupation to Occupation at First Interview (percentages)

| Usual Premigration Occupation | Occupation at First Interview | | | | | | | | Total | |
	Professional, Technical, or Managerial	Craftsmen or Foremen	Operatives	Clerical or Sales	Services	Farm Workers	Nonfarm Laborers	Not Working	Percent	(N)
White										
Professional, technical, or managerial	17	17	50	17	--	--	--	--	100	(6)
Craftsmen or foremen	--	33	44	4	--	--	15	4	100	(27)
Operatives	1	4	63	2	8	--	14	8	100	(89)
Clerical or sales	--	20	40	13	13	--	7	7	100	(15)
Services	--	32	32	14	--	--	9	14	100	(22)
Farm workers	--	18	36	--	9	--	27	9	100	(11)
Nonfarm laborers	2	2	65	4	2	--	17	6	100	(46)
Not working	--	14	53	6	3	--	14	11	100	(36)
Black										
Professional, technical, or managerial	60	--	20	20	--	--	--	--	100	(5)
Craftsmen or foremen	--	46	31	--	8	--	15	--	100	(13)
Operatives	5	7	51	9	2	--	12	14	100	(43)
Clerical or sales	--	20	60	10	--	--	10	--	100	(10)
Services	3	7	38	10	24	--	7	10	100	(29)
Farm workers	12	--	44	6	12	--	25	--	100	(16)
Nonfarm laborers	--	10	26	5	10	5	32	10	100	(19)
Not working	10	15	35	--	10	--	10	20	100	(20)

mobility for blacks as for whites. Being without work experience
was also more detrimental for black than for white males. Eleven
percent of the whites but 20 percent of the blacks without any premigration work experience were not working when first interviewed in
Cleveland. On the other hand, among the blacks, the professional,
technical, and managerial workers and the craftsmen and foremen
were slightly more likely than whites to be working in the same occupation in Cleveland (in each instance, however, the percentage bases
are very small).

Job changes subsequent to entry into the Cleveland work force
resulted in a convergence of black males on blue-collar occupations
(Table 3.13). Though black male migrants (except for those whose
premigration experience had been in white-collar work) were still
less likely than white male migrants to be found in blue-collar jobs,
the gap in the rate of movement toward blue-collar positions had narrowed. With the exception of the black workers who remained in
high-skill-level occupations, the same convergence on the pattern of
movement shown by white males is apparent in the tabulation for
levels of skill (Table 3.14).

TABLE 3.13

Changes in Type of Work Activity for Male Migrants:
Usual Premigration Occupation to Occupation
at First Interview
(percentages)

Usual Premigration Occupation	Occupation at First Interview				Total	
	White Collar	Blue Collar	Service	Not Working	Percent	(N)
White						
White collar	19	67	10	5	100	(21)
Blue collar	4	84	5	7	100	(173)
Service	14	73	--	14	100	(22)
Not working	6	81	3	11	100	(36)
Black						
White collar	33	67	--	--	100	(15)
Blue collar	11	74	7	9	100	(91)
Service	14	52	24	10	100	(29)
Not working	10	60	10	20	100	(20)

TABLE 3.14

Changes in Skill Level for Male Migrants: Usual Premigration
Occupation to Occupation at First Interview
(percentages)

Usual Premigration Occupation	Occupation at First Interview					
	High	Medium	Low	Not Working	Total Percent	(N)
White						
High	33	52	12	3	100	(33)
Medium	8	64	21	8	100	(104)
Low	14	58	19	9	100	(79)
Not working	14	58	17	11	100	(36)
Black						
High	50	33	17	--	100	(18)
Medium	13	62	13	11	100	(53)
Low	12	44	36	8	100	(64)
Not working	25	35	20	20	100	(20)

Second Interview

With the acquisition of information on occupations at second
interview, some comparison between the differences in occupational
movement between migrants and long-term residents becomes possible. Starting with the migrants, for whom the number of cases is
somewhat larger than for the long-termers, it is apparent that the
patterns of movement for white and black males were no longer con-
verging, though some similarities remain. In both groups of men,
for example, those without work at the time of the first interview
were most likely to be found without work at the time of the second
interview four years later (Table 3.15).

Being without work at the time of both interviews does not, of
course, imply that the respondents had been without work over the
entire time period. Nonetheless, the high probability of being without work at the time of the second interview for those who were in a
similar condition at the time of their first interview points toward
the problem of the "hard-core" unemployed. Here, however, the
group without work includes all persons who were not actively exer-
cising an occupation for whatever reason. Readers interested in the

TABLE 3.15

Changes in Occupation for Male Migrants: Occupation at First Interview to Occupation at Second Interview (percentages)

Occupation at First Interview	Occupation at Second Interview								Total	
	Professional, Technical, or Managerial	Craftsmen or Foremen	Operatives	Clerical or Sales	Services	Farm Workers	Nonfarm Laborers	Not Working	Percent	(N)
White										
Professional, technical, or managerial	33	67	--	--	--	--	--	--	100	(3)
Craftsmen or foremen	--	47	25	--	3	--	3	22	100	(32)
Operatives	2	21	51	2	1	--	9	14	100	(140)
Clerical or sales	--	38	23	31	--	--	--	8	100	(13)
Services	--	33	42	--	17	--	--	8	100	(12)
Farm workers	--	--	--	--	--	--	--	--	--	--
Nonfarm laborers	--	29	37	--	6	--	6	23	100	(35)
Not working	--	15	30	5	5	--	5	40	100	(20)
Black										
Professional, technical, or managerial	50	10	--	10	--	--	10	20	100	(10)
Craftsmen or foremen	--	28	50	--	--	--	--	22	100	(18)
Operatives	2	23	45	6	6	--	6	11	100	(62)
Clerical or sales	27	9	36	--	9	--	18	--	100	(11)
Services	6	--	44	6	25	--	12	6	100	(16)
Farm workers	--	100	--	--	--	--	--	--	100	(1)
Nonfarm laborers	--	14	23	--	--	--	18	46	100	(22)
Not working	--	13	13	13	7	--	7	47	100	(15)

phenomenon of hard-core unemployment should refer back to the fuller discussion of unemployment in Chapter 2, "Labor Force Participation," in which unemployed persons are distinguished from persons who moved out of the labor force.

There also appear to be important differences between migrants and long-termers. A broad spectrum of workers in both groups tended to be attracted to or retained in blue-collar positions (as craftsmen or foremen or as operatives). The white male migrants, however, appear to have a slight advantage in that the proportion moving to the higher-status jobs in the blue-collar world seems greater for white than for black males. For example, white males who had been working as craftsmen or foremen were most likely to be found in those occupations again at the time of their second interview. Black male migrants who had occupied positions of that sort were most likely to have moved into jobs as operatives. Among the small group of migrants who had been working in clerical or sales positions, white males were most likely to have moved into jobs as craftsmen or foremen while blacks were most likely to have shifted into operative jobs. Finally, among the laborers two-thirds of the white males had moved into operative jobs or had found work as craftsmen or foremen; almost half of the black male migrants who had been working as nonfarm laborers were without jobs at the time of their second interview.

Among the long-term residents, the retention of white males who had been working as craftsmen or foremen in positions of the same sort was particularly high (Table 3.16). Among long-termers who had been working as operatives when first interviewed, which was the only other group with a sufficient number of cases for reliable comparison, white and black males were likely to be found in the same kinds of jobs at their second interview.

The tabulations for type of work activity show the white male migrants more likely than the black males to be recruited to or retained in blue-collar positions (Table 3.17). Black male migrants were slightly more likely than white males from similar backgrounds to remain in white-collar occupations or to be without work at the time of the second interview when that had been their earlier position. When the occupational data for long-term residents are recombined to show type of work activities, the only group with a sufficient number of cases for comparison shows white and black male blue-collar workers equally likely to be retained in that kind of work (Table 3.18). The rate of movement into each of the other types of work activity by black and white male long-term residents who had been doing blue-collar work was also virtually identical.

TABLE 3.16

Changes in Occupation for Male Long-Term Residents: Occupation at First Interview to Occupation at Second Interview (percentages)

Occupation at First Interview	Occupation at Second Interview								Total	
	Professional, Technical, or Managerial	Craftsmen or Foremen	Operatives	Clerical or Sales	Services	Farm Workers	Nonfarm Laborers	Not Working	Percent	(N)
White										
Professional, technical, or managerial	33	50	--	--	--	--	--	17	100	(6)
Craftsmen or foremen	7	71	4	4	--	--	4	11	100	(28)
Operatives	2	9	52	4	4	--	4	23	100	(44)
Clerical or sales	--	10	10	50	--	--	--	30	100	(10)
Services	--	--	--	--	60	--	20	20	100	(5)
Farm workers	--	--	--	--	--	--	--	--	--	--
Nonfarm laborers	--	--	67	--	--	--	17	17	100	(6)
Not working	--	20	40	--	--	--	--	40	100	(5)
Black										
Professional, technical, or managerial	--	100	--	--	--	--	--	--	100	(1)
Craftsmen or foremen	--	25	50	--	--	--	--	25	100	(4)
Operatives	--	8	58	8	--	--	8	17	100	(36)
Clerical or sales	--	--	50	--	--	--	25	25	100	(4)
Services	20	20	--	--	40	--	--	20	100	(5)
Farm workers	--	--	--	--	--	--	--	--	--	--
Nonfarm laborers	--	29	14	14	14	--	14	14	100	(7)
Not working	50	--	50	--	--	--	--	--	100	(4)

TABLE 3.17

Changes in Type of Work Activity for Male Migrants: Occupation
at First Interview to Occupation at Second Interview
(percentages)

Occupation at First Interview	Occupation at Second Interview					
	White Collar	Blue Collar	Service	Not Working	Total Percent	(N)
White						
White collar	31	62	--	6	100	(16)
Blue collar	3	79	2	16	100	(207)
Service	--	75	17	8	100	(12)
Not working	5	50	5	40	100	(20)
Black						
White collar	43	43	5	10	100	(21)
Blue collar	5	71	4	20	100	(103)
Service	12	56	25	6	100	(16)
Not working	13	33	7	47	100	(15)

TABLE 3.18

Changes in Type of Work Activity for Male Long-Term Residents:
Occupation at First Interview to Occupation at Second Interview
(percentages)

Occupation at First Interview	Occupation at Second Interview					
	White Collar	Blue Collar	Service	Not Working	Total Percent	(N)
White						
White collar	44	31	--	25	100	(16)
Blue collar	8	72	3	18	100	(78)
Service	--	20	60	20	100	(5)
Not working	--	60	--	40	100	(5)
Black						
White collar	--	80	--	20	100	(5)
Blue collar	8	72	2	17	100	(47)
Service	20	20	40	20	100	(5)
Not working	50	50	--	--	100	(4)

     The data on skill level for male migrants (Table 3.19) show
the same general pattern of movement for whites and for blacks.
But again, blacks who had been working at middle-- or low-skill-level
jobs were less likely than whites to hold their position or move up.
By contrast, the between-interview movement of white and black
male long-term residents who had been working at middle-skill-level
jobs was not markedly different (Table 3.20).

Ideal Occupation

     When asked what kind of work they would be doing if they were
to achieve their ideal life state, most of the men saw themselves in
a different class of work from their current one; the migrants were
even more likely than the long-term residents to aspire to mobility
(see Table 3.21). The general direction of the choices also suggests that the long-term residents, who are older and hence further
along in their work careers, are more conservative than the migrants in their occupational aspirations (Table 3.22). Among the
black long-term residents, only those without occupations were more
likely to choose some category of work other than the one they were
in at the time of their second interview. White male long-termers
who were laborers or without work were also more likely than those
with other jobs to make an out-of-category choice. All other categories of male long-term residents were at least as likely to choose
work in the occupational area they were in at the time of their second
interview as to name an occupation in some other particular area.
(The relative size of the groups naming occupations in the general
area of the work they were doing may, of course, merely reflect a
lack of imagination or knowledge about occupational options.) Among
the migrants, the whites were also more conservative in their aspirations. In five of the seven occupational categories with any appre-
ciable membership, white male migrants were at least as likely to
choose to remain in the same occupational area as to move to some
other category.
     Blacks were very different in this respect. In four of the
seven occupational categories black male migrants were more likely
to name some other occupational area in connection with an ideal life
than the occupational area in which they were found. In three of those
four groups, the category most often mentioned was professional,
technical, or managerial occupations. Thus blacks were not only
more likely than the white males to be looking toward other occupational activities; they also had their sights set higher. Some of the
negative choices are also instructive. No black male migrant named
a service occupation in conjunction with his ideal life situation. Only
4 of the 90 males who were not working would choose to remain so.

TABLE 3.19

Changes in Skill Level for Male Migrants: Occupation at First
Interview to Occupation at Second Interview
(percentages)

Occupation at First Interview	Occupation at Second Interview					
				Not	Total	
	High	Medium	Low	Working	Percent	(N)
White						
High	51	23	6	20	100	(35)
Medium	25	53	9	13	100	(153)
Low	30	38	13	19	100	(47)
Not working	15	35	10	40	100	(20)
Black						
High	41	34	3	21	100	(29)
Medium	26	49	15	10	100	(73)
Low	10	34	26	29	100	(38)
Not working	13	27	13	47	100	(15)

TABLE 3.20

Changes in Skill Level for Male Long-Term Residents: Occupation
at First Interview to Occupation at Second Interview
(percentages)

Occupation at First Interview	Occupation at Second Interview					
				Not	Total	
	High	Medium	Low	Working	Percent	(N)
White						
High	79	6	3	12	100	(34)
Medium	11	57	7	24	100	(54)
Low	--	36	46	18	100	(11)
Not working	20	40	--	40	100	(5)
Black						
High	40	40	--	20	100	(5)
Medium	8	65	10	18	100	(40)
Low	33	17	33	17	100	(12)
Not working	50	50	--	--	100	(4)

TABLE 3.21

Changes in Occupation for Male Migrants: Occupation at Second Interview to Ideal Occupation (percentages)

Occupation at Second Interview	Ideal Occupation								Total	
	Professional, Technical, or Managerial	Craftsmen or Foremen	Operatives	Clerical or Sales	Services	Farm Workers	Nonfarm Laborers	Not Working	Percent	(N)
White										
Professional, technical, or managerial	75	--	--	--	--	--	--	25	100	(4)
Craftsmen or foremen	36	41	12	--	2	--	--	9	100	(64)
Operatives	27	14	41	1	1	6	2	7	100	(97)
Clerical or sales	--	12	12	62	--	12	--	--	100	(8)
Services	43	14	--	--	43	--	--	--	100	(7)
Farm workers	--	--	--	--	--	--	--	--	--	--
Nonfarm laborers	6	50	12	--	--	--	25	6	100	(16)
Not working	3	36	39	--	9	--	9	3	100	(33)
Black										
Professional, technical, or managerial	89	--	--	--	--	--	--	11	100	(9)
Craftsmen or foremen	25	50	17	--	4	--	--	4	100	(24)
Operatives	34	18	32	8	4	--	2	2	100	(50)
Clerical or sales	50	--	--	50	--	--	--	--	100	(8)
Services	25	--	50	25	--	--	--	--	100	(4)
Farm workers	--	--	--	--	--	--	--	--	--	--
Nonfarm laborers	67	--	8	--	--	--	25	--	100	(12)
Not working	34	21	31	3	3	--	7	--	100	(29)

TABLE 3.22

Changes in Occupation for Male Long–Term Residents: Occupation at Second Interview to Ideal Occupation
(percentages)

Occupation at Second Interview	Ideal Occupation								Total	
	Professional, Technical, or Managerial	Craftsmen or Foremen	Operatives	Clerical or Sales	Services	Farm Workers	Nonfarm Laborers	Not Working	Percent	(N)
White										
Professional, technical, or managerial	100	--	--	--	--	--	--	--	100	(5)
Craftsmen or foremen	18	64	4	--	--	--	--	14	100	(28)
Operatives	19	15	38	4	4	4	--	15	100	(26)
Clerical or sales	14	14	14	57	--	--	--	--	100	(7)
Services	20	20	20	--	20	--	--	20	100	(5)
Farm workers	--	--	--	--	--	--	--	--	--	--
Nonfarm laborers	--	--	50	--	--	25	25	--	100	(4)
Not working	32	16	32	--	5	5	--	10	100	(19)
Black										
Professional, technical, or managerial	67	33	--	--	--	--	--	--	100	(3)
Craftsmen or foremen	14	71	--	--	--	--	--	14	99	(7)
Operatives	19	12	38	8	--	--	4	19	100	(26)
Clerical or sales	--	33	--	67	--	--	--	--	100	(3)
Services	--	33	--	--	67	--	--	--	100	(3)
Farm workers	--	--	--	--	--	--	--	--	--	--
Nonfarm laborers	20	--	40	--	--	--	40	--	100	(5)
Not working	44	--	11	11	--	--	22	11	99	(9)

Examination of the ideal occupation data in terms of type of work activity shows the pattern of majority choice to be identical in three of the four comparison groups (the fourth, black male long-term residents, lacks sufficient cases in three of the strata to permit a judgment). Both white- and blue-collar workers tended to opt for occupations in the same work activity area they were in at the time of their interview. Those without work tended to name blue-collar occupations as the kind of work they would be doing if their lives ever worked out in the best way they saw possible (Tables 3.23 and 3.24).

The choices in terms of skill level were less consistent. In each group, the majority of persons in high-skill-level jobs named ideal occupations that were also classified as high-skill-level (Tables 3.25 and 3.26). Black male migrants from all other skill levels also named ideal occupations that were high on skill level. White male migrants with low-skill-level jobs agreed; but white males without work and those with middle-level jobs tended to split their votes between high- and middle-skill-level occupations.

TABLE 3.23

Changes in Type of Work Activity for Male Migrants:
Occupation at Second Interview to Ideal Occupation
(percentages)

Occupation at Second Interview	Ideal Occupation				Total	
	White Collar	Blue Collar	Service	Not Working	Percent	(N)
White						
White collar	67	25	--	8	100	(12)
Blue collar	29	62	1	8	100	(177)
Service	43	14	43	--	100	(7)
Not working	3	85	9	3	100	(33)
Black						
White collar	94	--	--	6	100	(17)
Blue collar	41	54	4	2	100	(86)
Service	50	50	--	--	100	(4)
Not working	38	59	3	--	100	(29)

TABLE 3.24

Changes in Type of Work Activity for Male Long-Term Residents:
Occupation at Time of Second Interview to Ideal Occupation
(percentages)

Occupation at Second Interview	Ideal Occupation					
	White Collar	Blue Collar	Service	Not Working	Total Percent	(N)
White						
White collar	83	17	--	--	100	(12)
Blue collar	19	66	2	14	100	(58)
Service	20	40	20	20	100	(5)
Not working	32	53	5	10	100	(19)
Black						
White collar	67	33	--	--	100	(6)
Blue collar	24	60	--	16	100	(38)
Service	--	33	67	--	100	(3)
Not working	56	33	--	11	100	(9)

TABLE 3.25

Changes in Skill Level for Male Migrants: Occupation
at Second Interview to Ideal Occupation
(percentages)

Occupation at Second Interview	Ideal Occupation					
	High	Medium	Low	Not Working	Total Percent	(N)
White						
High	76	12	2	10	100	(68)
Medium	43	45	6	7	100	(105)
Low	56	9	30	4	100	(23)
Not working	39	39	18	3	100	(33)
Black						
High	79	12	3	6	100	(33)
Medium	52	41	5	2	100	(58)
Low	56	25	19	--	100	(16)
Not working	55	34	10	--	100	(29)

TABLE 3.26

Changes in Skill Level for Male Long-Term Residents:
Occupation at Second Interview to Ideal Occupation
(percentages)

| Occupation at Second Interview | Ideal Occupation | | | | Total | |
	High	Medium	Low	Not Working	Percent	(N)
White						
High	85	3	--	12	100	(33)
Medium	36	48	3	12	100	(33)
Low	22	33	33	11	100	(9)
Not working	47	32	10	10	100	(19)
Black						
High	90	--	--	10	100	(10)
Medium	31	48	3	17	100	(29)
Low	25	25	50	--	100	(8)
Not working	44	22	22	11	100	(9)

The slightly lower aspiration levels of whites are consistent with our earlier observations. Compared to whites, blacks have been slightly more successful in bettering themselves since they arrived in Cleveland, and they appear eager to continue to do so. One might speculate that aspirations to break out of blue-collar occupations and into technical and managerial jobs that characterize quite a few of these migrants may point to a persistent source of potential discontent among black males even if the currently more acute unemployment issues are resolved.

Locations of Change

Earlier in this discussion we dealt with the process of movement among occupations by examining the change probabilities, which partially specify the effect on subsequent mobility of earlier work force position. In this section, further attention is given to the process of occupational mobility by examining the total amount of, or gross, movement around each of the occupational positions, types of work activity, and skill levels (Table 3.27). In a sense,

TABLE 3.27

Location of Occupational Mobility for Males: Amount of Mobility into and out of Major Occupational Categories (percentages)*

Occupational Category	Type of Respondent			
	White		Black	
	Migrants	Long-Termers	Migrants	Long-Termers
Time Period				
Premigration to First Cleveland Job (White) / Premigration to First Interview (Black)				
Professional, technical, or managerial	4		4	
Craftsmen or foremen	14		11	
Operatives	47		33	
Clerical or sales	9		14	
Services	14		30	
Farm workers	5		10	
Nonfarm laborers	28		24	
Not working	14		14	
(N)	(255)		(155)	
Premigration to First Interview				
Professional, technical, or managerial	3		6	
Craftsmen or foremen	16		12	
Operatives	45		40	
Clerical or sales	10		12	
Services	13		19	
Farm workers	4		11	
Nonfarm laborers	26		19	
Not working	19		17	
(N)	(252)		(155)	
First Interview to Second Interview				
Professional, technical, or managerial	2	7	6	6
Craftsmen or foremen	28	16	23	16
Operatives	41	28	39	36
Clerical or sales	5	8	12	13
Services	6	4	1	6
Farm workers	--	--	--	--
Nonfarm laborers	19	9	18	16
Not working	19	21	21	23
(N)	(255)	(104)	(155)	(61)
Second Interview to Ideal Occupation				
Professional, technical, or managerial	24	19	34	21
Craftsmen or foremen	32	20	20	14
Operatives	35	29	37	34
Clerical or sales	2	6	7	7
Services	4	6	6	2
Farm workers	3	3	--	--
Nonfarm laborers	7	3	9	11
Not working	21	28	24	25
(N)	(229)	(94)	(136)	(56)

*Percentage bases are total number of males in each race and duration-of-residence category excluding cases for which occupational information was lacking for either of the times being compared.

this discussion is the inverse of the static descriptions of the structure of occupations, type of work activities, and skill levels, which
showed the end results of movement among occupations. In looking
at the total, or gross, movement among occupations, attention is
shifted to the level of disruption in the work force that occurred in
reaching the static end states. A hypothetical example may help.
At the extremes, a net change of four percentage points in the composition of the work force might be achieved by having 4 percent of
the total population move into or out of an occupation while everyone
else in the category remained there. The same net change might
also be achieved through the movement of 48 percent of the population into an occupational category while the other 52 percent of the
population moved out of the same category (that is, by having everyone in the population move into or out of occupations in the category).
In the one case the gross change is minimal; in the second example
the entire population moved into or out of the occupation. In this
sense, gross change or turnover is a measure of the efficiency of
the system. Small amounts of gross change represent lesser investments in the acquisition of new skills and patterns of behavior and
smaller losses through setting aside previously acquired skills and
behavioral patterns.

As an indicator of efficiency, gross change measures cannot
be pushed to the level of the individual actors, simply because we
cannot tell from movement between categories at the various times
how many moves between what other categories occurred in the interim. At the systems level, however, this indeterminancy is less
troubling. Return moves back to the original occupational status re-
store the original structure, and occupations temporarily set aside
are resumed.

Across time, for all of the male comparison groups, the largest amount of mobility is centered on operative occupations (Table
3.27). Other major sources of movement were into or out of the
group without occupations, around nonfarm laboring positions, and,
among black but not white males, with regard to occupations in the
service category. The prominence of the operative occupations in
these change data is, of course, an indication of where the jobs are
for working-class men in Cleveland. The instability centered on the
nonworking group is indicative both of the vulnerability of the kinds
of employment the majority of these men were able to find and the
effectiveness of various forces impelling those without work to find
jobs.

Through all time periods the amounts of change shown are considerable, particularly when one realizes that to be registered as a
change the movement must be across the boundaries of broad occupational categories. But while the amounts of occupational shift were

considerable, those actually experienced tended to be centered on
jobs that ordinarily require little training and for which employers
apparently demand little by way of prior experience. Not so, however, with the kinds of change indicated by occupational aspirations.
Here the location of change shifts upwards in the occupational structure to involve larger proportions of each comparison group in movement centered on professional, technical, and managerial occupations.
Except for the movement around service occupations among the black
males, the general locations of change are rather striking in their
similarity for white and black males at each of the observation points.

   Changes in type of work activities carry few surprises not already apparent in the more detailed information for major occupational groups; the locations of change are similar across time for
white and black males, except for the amount of change centered on
service occupations among black males (Table 3.28). The absolute
levels of movement around each of the types of work activity do, however, merit further comment. The categories are broad and the
work subsumed under them implies both different skills and different working conditions. Even in the same plant, the environment and
the rewards of blue- and white-collar workers are not the same.
Across time the types of work activity tables generally show at least
one category around which about a third or more of each of the comparison groups is moving; this is usually the blue-collar category,
which for some is a destination and for others a takeoff point.

   The gross change measures for skill level, however, are also
instructive (Table 3.29). First, at entry into the Cleveland work
force and up through the time of the first interview, for both white
and black male migrants, the largest amounts of mobility are centered on low- and middle-skill-level occupations (with roughly two-
fifths in each group moving into or out of each of these lower-skill-
level categories). Between interviews, the movement around high-
skill-level occupations increased and that around low-skill-level jobs
decreased. While the earlier movements had been at levels representing relatively modest investments in training, the rise in the
center of movement for skill levels indicates progressively larger
amounts of wastage of prior experience and heavier investments in
training for new work roles. Looking toward occupational aspirations, the desire for upward movement along personal career lad-
ders is even more apparent. Throughout this series of observations, the locus of mobility moves steadily upward to center on
occupations requiring greater investments by workers and employers to acquire the skills necessary to perform more highly skilled
work roles.

TABLE 3.28

Location of Type of Work Activity Mobility for Males: Amount of Mobility into or out of Type of Work Activity (percentages)*

Type of Respondent

Time Period

Type of Work Activity	White Migrants	White Long-Termers	Black Migrants	Black Long-Termers
Premigration to First Cleveland Job				
White collar	11		17	
Blue collar	32		39	
Service	14		30	
Not working	14		14	
(N)	(255)		(155)	
First Interview to Second Interview				
White collar	7	14	14	20
Blue collar	29	30	34	33
Service	6	4	12	6
Not working	19	21	21	23
(N)	(255)	(104)	(155)	(61)
Premigration to First Interview				
White collar	11		17	
Blue collar	34		39	
Service	14		19	
Not working	20		17	
(N)	(252)		(155)	
Second Interview to Ideal Occupation				
White collar	26	21	36	29
Blue collar	43	36	43	38
Service	4	6	6	2
Not working	21	28	24	25
(N)	(229)	(94)	(136)	(56)

*Percentage bases are total number of males in each race and duration-of-residence category excluding cases for which occupational information was lacking for either of the times being compared.

TABLE 3.29

Location of Skill Level Mobility for Males: Amount of Mobility into or out of Skill Levels (percentages)*

Skill Level	Type of Respondent			
	White		Black	
	Migrants	Long-Termers	Migrants	Long-Termers
Time Period				
Premigration to First Cleveland Job				
High	17		13	
Medium	48		41	
Low	39		44	
Not working	14		14	
(N)	(255)		(155)	
First Interview to Second Interview				
High	28	13	27	20
Medium	41	30	41	33
Low	23	11	27	20
Not working	19	21	21	23
(N)	(255)	(104)	(155)	(61)
Premigration to First Interview				
High	18		19	
Medium	48		39	
Low	38		36	
Not working	19		17	
(N)	(252)		(155)	
Second Interview to Ideal Occupation				
High	38	30	46	29
Medium	35	29	38	34
Low	13	10	15	12
Not working	21	28	24	25
(N)	(229)	(94)	(136)	(56)

*Percentage bases are total number of males in each race and duration-of-residence category excluding cases for which occupational information was lacking for either of the times being compared.

Patterns of Change

The fine-grained data on exchanges between pairs of occupational categories reveal the net flows that result in changes in the occupational structures over time for the migrants and long-term residents. Generally speaking, the net flows show the black migrants to be closing the gap in occupational advantage early in their Cleveland work history but to be falling behind later. Higher occupational aspirations by black than by white males may also be seen as indicative of dissatisfaction with current occupational positions. A note on the difference between net and gross change may be appropriate. Gross change, which was just examined, is an indicator of the amount of disruption in occupations experienced by the workers and their employers. As we have noted, to register as a change the movement must be across the boundaries of a major occupational group. Net change is an indicator of the transformation of the occupational distribution or structure. Because the persons departing from an occupational category are subtracted from the recruits to that line of work, net change is almost invariably smaller in magnitude than the amount of gross change. Contrary to gross change, net change shows the transformations of the occupational distributions or structures. Presented in the form of net turnover matrices, these data show the pattern of flow among occupational categories. As we have already seen, a great deal of motion may occur yet generate little change in structure, even though the turnover of workers is considerable. When focused on a few destinations or sources, relatively small amounts of movement may produce a sizable structural modification.

First Cleveland Occupation

The data on net changes, represented by differences in usual premigration occupation and first Cleveland job, emphasize the different routes taken by white and black male migrants in entering the Cleveland work force. The convergence of white males on operative occupations is evident in the third column of Table 3.30, which shows gains in the proportion of white male migrants in operative occupations over all other occupational categories. The drawing power of operative occupations in the Cleveland work force is particularly apparent in the net movement downward from occupations as craftsmen or foremen. The net proportion of white men moving down from the more skilled jobs was as large as the net proportion moving up into these middle-skill-level positions from jobs as laborers and nearly as large as the gain from the pool of men without prior work experience. By contrast, for black males the largest net flow of any consequence was into service occupations, which gained

from all other varieties of prior experience except among former
clerical and sales workers. A comparison of the last column in the
portions of the table for white and for black males shows clearly the
advantage white males without prior work experience enjoyed over
blacks in entering the Cleveland work force. Among the whites, the
net movement to operative occupations was almost three times as
great as the number recruited to any other occupational category and
almost four times as great as the proportion of black male migrants
who were recruited to operative positions in the absence of any prior
work experience. Although similar proportions of black and white
male migrants came to Cleveland without prior work experience, for
the black males the location of first Cleveland jobs was spread more
widely among occupations than it was for whites. The pattern of
movement for black male migrants most similar to the funneling toward operative occupations among the whites occurred in service
jobs. But the levels of recruitment from other occupations to service occupations were lower for black male migrants than the funneling effect, and the strength of the recruitment from the other occupational statuses--the change in the occupational structure for white
male migrants over what it had been prior to migration--was considerably greater than the aggregate amount of change experienced by
the black males (despite the fact that more of the latter had been employed in farm occupations, from which change is virtually mandatory on entering urban employment).

Occupation at First Interview

        The total amount of change in occupational structures for black
and for white male migrants by the time of their first interview was
almost identical and, furthermore, the growth tended to be located
in the same general area (Table 3.31). The net change in each distribution was just over 20 percent and in each instance most of the
growth occurred in the proportion employed as operatives or in
higher-level blue-collar work or, for the black males, in the number employed in top-level white-collar work. For both, entering
the Cleveland work force meant a general movement into employment, for those who had never worked before the move, and up out
of jobs as nonfarm laborers and as farm and service workers. This
improvement in occupational position is undoubtedly a fundamental
ingredient in the generally favorable views migrants had of the move,
of their jobs, and of the prospects for staying in Cleveland.

Occupation at Second Interview

        The generally favorable changes in the occupational structures
for male migrants resulting from differences in the kinds of work

TABLE 3.30

Net Exchanges Between Occupational Categories for White and Black Male Migrants: Comparing Usual Premigration Occupation with First Cleveland Occupation (percentages)[a]

Usual Pre-migration Occupation	First Cleveland Occupation[b]							
	1	2	3	4	5	6	7	8
White male migrants								
1		0.4	1.2	0.0	0.0	0.0	-0.4	0.0
2	-0.4		5.1	0.4	0.0	-0.4	0.0	-1.6
3	-1.2	-5.1		-2.0	-2.0	-0.8	-5.5	-7.1
4	0.0	-0.4	2.0		-0.4	0.0	1.2	-0.8
5	0.0	0.0	2.0	0.4		-0.8	0.0	-2.0
6	0.0	0.4	0.8	0.0	0.8		2.0	0.0
7	0.4	0.0	5.5	-1.2	0.0	-2.0		-2.4
8	0.0	1.6	7.1	0.8	2.0	0.0	2.4	
Total	-1.2	-3.1	23.5	-1.6	0.4	-3.9	-0.4	-13.7
N = 255[c]								
Black male migrants								
1		1.3	-0.6	-0.6	0.0	-0.6	0.0	-0.6
2	-1.3		-1.3	0.6	1.3	0.0	1.3	-1.3
3	0.6	1.3		0.6	1.3	-3.9	1.3	-1.9
4	0.6	-0.6	-0.6		-1.3	-0.6	0.6	-1.9
5	0.0	-1.3	-1.3	1.3		-1.9	-0.6	-3.2
6	0.6	0.0	3.9	0.6	1.9		1.9	0.0
7	0.0	-1.3	-1.3	-0.6	0.6	-1.9		-1.9
8	0.6	1.3	1.9	1.9	3.2	0.0	1.9	
Total	1.3	0.6	0.6	3.9	7.1	-9.0	6.5	-11.0
N = 155[c]								

[a]Data in each column are signed changes from the categories shown at left margin of table.

[b]Occupational categories are:

1. Professional, technical, or managerial
2. Craftsmen or foremen
3. Operatives
4. Clerical or sales
5. Services
6. Farm workers
7. Nonfarm laborers
8. Not working

[c]Percentage base excludes cases for which occupational information is lacking for either of the times being compared.

A Note on the Matrices in Chapter 3

A note on reading these matrices may be helpful. All of the net turnover matrices in this section have a similar format. The data are the result of subtracting the percentage of persons in the group who left a given occupational status from the percentage of the total group who were recruited to the same occupational status. The signed result of this simple bit of arithmetic is a description, in percentages, of the net result of the exchange between the two occupational categories and describes the amount of change in the total occupational structure for the group that is due to the interchange. In the form in which the matrices are presented for this report, the last figure in each column represents the total change occurring to each category from the earlier time to the subsequent time, with minuses indicating a decrease in the percentage of the group in the relevant category and unsigned nonzero numerals indicating growth in the category. Whether seen from position a or from position b, the amount of the flow between categories must be identical and differ in sign. While one-half of the data displayed are therefore redundant, because they differ only in sign from the data displayed on the other side of the major diagonal, we have retained both the upper and lower portions of the matrices so that columns may be read to show signed gains and losses.

As an illustration, let us consider the upper panel in Table 3.30. The third column displays the net exchanges between operative occupations and all other occupational positions. None of the entries have negative signs and none are zeroes, indicating that the net movement from usual premigration occupational position to first Cleveland jobs was such that all other occupational positions lost more workers to operative occupations in Cleveland than were gained from the ranks of former operatives. Reading across the third row, we find identical entries for each paired comparison that are opposite in sign to those shown in the third column. These show the net losses from each of the categories shown in the column captions to the ranks of operatives. In other words, positive entries in a column answer the question, "Where were the sources of net growth in this occupational category located?" Negatively signed entries in a column answer the question, "To which categories did the net losses from this occupational group go?"

TABLE 3.31

Net Exchanges Between Occupational Categories for White and
Black Male Migrants: Comparing Usual Premigration
Occupation with Occupation at First Interview
(percentages)[a]

Usual Pre-migration Occupation	Occupation at First Interview[b]							
	1	2	3	4	5	6	7	8
White male migrants								
1		0.4	0.8	0.4	0.0	0.0	-0.4	0.0
2	-0.4		3.2	-0.8	-2.8	-0.8	1.2	-1.6
3	-0.8	-3.2		-1.6	0.0	-1.6	-7.1	-4.8
4	-0.4	0.8	1.6		-0.4	0.0	-0.4	-0.4
5	0.0	2.8	0.0	0.4		-0.4	0.4	0.8
6	0.0	0.8	1.6	0.0	0.4		1.2	0.4
7	0.4	-1.2	7.1	0.4	-0.4	-1.2		-0.8
8	0.0	1.6	4.8	0.4	-0.8	-0.4	0.8	
Total	-1.2	2.0	19.0	-0.8	-4.0	-4.4	-4.4	-6.3
N = 252[c]								
Black male migrants								
1		0.0	-0.6	0.6	-0.6	-1.3	0.0	-1.3
2	0.0		0.6	-1.3	-0.6	0.0	0.0	-1.9
3	0.6	-0.6		-1.3	-6.5	-4.5	0.0	-0.6
4	-0.6	1.3	1.3		-1.9	-0.6	0.0	0.0
5	0.6	0.6	6.5	1.9		-1.3	0.0	0.6
6	1.3	0.0	4.5	0.6	1.3		1.9	0.0
7	0.0	0.0	0.0	0.0	0.0	-1.9		0.0
8	1.3	1.9	0.6	0.0	-0.6	0.0	0.0	
Total	3.2	3.2	12.9	0.6	-9.0	-9.7	1.9	-3.2
N = 252[c]								

[a]Data in each column are signed changes from the categories
shown at left margin of table.

[b]Occupational categories are:

1. Professional, technical, or managerial
2. Craftsmen or foremen
3. Operatives
4. Clerical or sales
5. Services
6. Farm workers
7. Nonfarm laborers
8. Not working

[c]Percentage base excludes cases for which occupational information is lacking for either of the times being compared.

they were doing in Cleveland when first interviewed in 1968 as compared with their occupational position before the move were somewhat eroded by changes that occurred between the first and second
interviews (Table 3.32). Instead of a net movement into active employment, there was a sizable increase of about the same magnitude
in the number without work among both black and white migrant
males. At the upper end of the occupational structure, however,
the position of the black male migrants had worsened between the interviews. The comparison of premigration jobs showed the occupational structures for black and white male migrants to be growing at
about the same rate in the cluster of occupations represented by
middle- and top-level blue-collar jobs and by top-level white-collar
occupations. But in the interval between interviews this picture
changed. Both groups experienced a decrease in the number employed as operatives, with the major destinations being movement
upward in the blue-collar job hierarchy into more skilled positions
in the craftsmen or foreman category or out of the active work force
altogether into the group without jobs. But the movement upward was
more than twice as great among the white males as among the blacks
while the size of the group involved in the skid out of the work force
was more nearly equal.

Among the long-term residents, however, the relative position
of the two groups was reversed (Table 3.33). There were decreases
in the number of operatives in the structures for both black and white
male long-term residents and large increases in the number without
work. In both cases, the largest component in the change was among
the groups that had jobs as operatives when first interviewed. But
the net growth of the group without jobs was larger among the white
male long-termers than among the blacks, mainly because of a small
countermovement among black male long-termers who had been without work and who moved into white-collar jobs at the top skill level.
In addition, the size of the group in top-skill-level blue-collar jobs
showed a greater increase among black long-termers than among the
whites. Again the direction of movement was different for the blacks
than for the whites. Both groups suffered losses from the ranks of
craftsmen and foremen into the group without work, but top-level blue-
collar workers were recruited from the group with laboring jobs
among the blacks while the net movement for whites was out of the
top-level blue-collar jobs into positions as nonfarm laborers.

Thus the net changes in the occupational structures for white
and for black male migrants suggest a general initial improvement
with blacks tending to make greater gains than whites over their premigration occupational position. Between interviews the black migrants lost ground in comparison with the whites, not because they
moved out of employment in greater numbers but because of a smaller

TABLE 3.32

Net Exchanges Between Occupational Categories for White and
Black Male Migrants: Comparing Occupation at First
Interview with Occupation at Second Interview
(percentages)[a]

Occupation at First Interview	Occupation at Second Interview[b]							
	1	2	3	4	5	6	7	8
White male migrants								
1		0.8	-1.2	0.0	0.0	--	0.0	0.0
2	-0.8		-8.6	-2.0	-1.2	--	-3.5	1.6
3	1.2	8.6		0.0	-1.6	--	0.0	5.1
4	0.0	2.0	0.0		0.0	--	0.0	0.0
5	0.0	1.2	1.6	0.0		--	-0.8	0.0
6	--	--	--	--	--		--	--
7	0.0	3.5	0.0	0.0	0.8	--		2.7
8	0.0	-1.6	-5.1	0.0	0.0	--	-2.7	
Total	0.4	14.5	-13.3	-2.0	-2.0	--	-7.1	9.4
N = 255[c]								
Black male migrants								
1		0.6	-0.6	-1.3	-0.6	0.0	0.6	1.3
2	-0.6		-3.2	-0.6	0.0	-0.6	-1.9	1.3
3	0.6	3.2		0.0	-1.9	0.0	-0.6	3.2
4	1.3	0.6	0.0		0.0	0.0	1.3	-1.3
5	0.6	0.0	1.9	0.0		0.0	1.3	0.0
6	0.0	0.6	0.0	0.0	0.0		0.0	0.0
7	-0.6	1.9	0.6	-1.3	-1.3	0.0		5.8
8	-1.3	-1.3	-3.2	1.3	0.0	0.0	-5.8	
Total	0.0	5.8	-4.5	-1.9	-3.9	-0.6	-5.2	10.3
N = 155[c]								

[a]Data in each column are signed changes from the categories
shown at left margin of table.

[b]Occupational categories are:

1. Professional, technical, or managerial
2. Craftsmen or foremen
3. Operatives
4. Clerical or sales
5. Services
6. Farm workers
7. Nonfarm laborers
8. Not working

[c]Percentage base excludes cases for which occupational information is lacking for either of the times being compared. The symbol
"--" denotes absence of respondents in occupational category at both
time periods.

TABLE 3.33

Net Exchanges Between Occupational Categories for White and
Black Male Long-Term Residents: Comparing Occupation
at First Interview with Occupation at Second Interview
(percentages)[a]

Occupation at First Interview	Occupation at Second Interview[b]							
	1	2	3	4	5	6	7	8
White male long-termers								
1		1.0	-1.0	0.0	0.0	--	0.0	1.0
2	-1.0		-2.9	0.0	0.0	--	1.0	1.9
3	1.0	2.9		1.0	1.9	--	-1.9	7.7
4	0.0	0.0	-1.0		0.0	--	0.0	2.9
5	0.0	0.0	-1.9	0.0		--	1.0	1.0
6	--	--	--	--	--		--	--
7	0.0	-1.0	1.9	0.0	-1.0	--		1.0
8	-1.0	-1.9	-7.7	-2.9	-1.0	--	-1.0	
Total	-1.0	1.0	-12.5	-1.9	0.0	--	-1.0	15.4
N = 104[c]								
Black male long-termers								
1		1.6	0.0	0.0	-1.6	--	0.0	-3.3
2	-1.6		-1.6	0.0	-1.6	--	-3.3	1.6
3	0.0	1.6		1.6	0.0	--	3.3	6.6
4	0.0	0.0	-1.6		0.0	--	0.0	1.6
5	1.6	1.6	0.0	0.0		--	-1.6	1.6
6	--	--	--	--	--		--	--
7	0.0	3.3	-3.3	0.0	1.6	--		1.6
8	3.3	-1.6	-6.6	-1.6	-1.6	--	-1.6	
Total	3.3	6.6	-13.1	0.0	-3.3	--	-3.3	9.8
N = 61[c]								

[a]Data in each column are signed changes from the categories
shown at left margin of table.

[b]Occupational categories are:

1. Professional, technical, or managerial
2. Craftsmen or foremen
3. Operatives
4. Clerical or sales
5. Services
6. Farm workers
7. Nonfarm laborers
8. Not working

[c]Percentage base excludes cases for which occupational information is lacking for either of the times being compared. The symbol "--" denotes absence of respondents in occupational category at both time periods.

net increase in top-level blue- or white-collar employment. Among
the long-term residents, however, the relative position of the black
and white males was changing in favor of the black males because of
gains at the top and lesser net growth of the group without employment, partly because of the movement out of that group into top-level
white-collar employment.

The initial gains tend to confirm the basic motive for migration: there are better jobs in Cleveland than at home. But the movement between interviews suggests that the opportunities may be better for white male migrants than for blacks. On the other hand, the
change data for the long-term residents are congruent with our suggestion that residence in a poor neighborhood has different meaning
for whites than it does for blacks. The relative rate of movement
out of the actively employed work force was about the same for the
two groups of long-term residents but there was no white counter-
part to the selective improvement in the status of black males.

Ideal Occupations

Contrasting present occupational positions with the positions
the respondents saw themselves occupying in the future, if their
lives were to work out in the best possible manner, yields two important similarities among all the male comparison groups. The
net changes that would result from moving into ideal occupational
positions from those they held at the time of the second interview
would result in sizable displacements in the occupational structure
for each group (ranging from more than one-fifth to almost two-fifths).
And, in each case, the largest growth was located in top-level white-
collar occupations, indicating substantial aspirations for positions as
professionals, technicians, or managers; the largest net movement
would shift a third of the black male migrants into this category
(Tables 3.34 and 3.35).

The amount of net change implicit in these occupational aspirations was greater for migrants than for long-term residents and higher
for black males than for whites, suggesting that it is the black males
who are least satisfied with their present occupational positions and
white long-termers who are most satisfied. The locations of the
major sources of change tend to support this view. In three of the
four groups, the largest share of the growth implicit for these upper
white-collar positions was from the ranks of men employed as operatives at the time of their second interview. But there was also substantial movement there from among the men without employment
among all except the white male migrants. Associated with these
aspirations for positions near the top are tendencies for men located

TABLE 3.34

Net Exchanges Between Occupational Categories for White and Black Male Migrants: Comparing Occupation at Second Interview with Ideal Occupation (percentages)[a]

Occupation at Second Interview	Ideal Occupation[b]							
	1	2	3	4	5	6	7	8
White male migrants								
1		-10.0	-11.4	0.0	-1.3	0.0	-0.4	0.0
2	10.0		-2.6	-0.4	0.0	0.0	-3.5	-2.6
3	11.4	2.6		0.0	0.4	2.6	0.0	-2.6
4	0.0	0.4	0.0		0.0	0.4	0.0	0.0
5	1.3	0.0	-0.4	0.0		0.0	0.0	-1.3
6	0.0	0.0	-2.6	-0.4	0.0		0.0	0.0
7	0.4	3.5	0.0	0.0	0.0	0.0		-0.9
8	0.0	2.6	2.6	0.0	1.3	0.0	0.9	
Total	23.1	-0.9	-14.4	-0.9	0.4	3.1	-3.1	-7.4
N = 229[c]								
Black male migrants								
1		-4.4	-12.5	-2.9	-0.7	---	-5.9	-6.6
2	4.4		-3.7	0.0	0.7	---	0.0	-3.7
3	12.5	3.7		2.9	0.0	---	0.0	-5.9
4	2.9	0.0	-2.9		-0.7	---	0.0	-0.7
5	0.7	-0.7	0.0	0.7		---	0.0	-0.7
6	---	---	---	---	---	---	---	---
7	5.9	0.0	0.0	0.0	0.0	---		-1.5
8	6.6	3.7	5.9	0.7	0.7	---	1.5	
Total	33.1	2.2	-13.2	1.5	0.0	---	-4.4	-19.1
N = 136[c]								

[a]Data in each column are signed changes from the categories shown at left margin of table.

[b]Occupational categories are:
1. Professional, technical, or managerial
2. Craftsmen or foremen
3. Operatives
4. Clerical or sales
5. Services
6. Farm workers
7. Nonfarm laborers
8. Not working

[c]Percentage base excludes cases for which occupational information is lacking for either of the times being compared. The symbol "--" denotes absence of respondents in occupational category at both time periods.

TABLE 3.35

Net Exchanges Between Occupational Categories for White and
Black Male Long-Term Residents: Comparing Occupation
at Second Interview with Ideal Occupation
(percentages)[a]

Occupation at Second Interview	Ideal Occupation[b]							
	1	2	3	4	5	6	7	8
White male long-termers								
1		-5.3	-5.3	-1.1	-1.1	0.0	0.0	-6.4
2	5.3		-3.2	-1.1	-1.1	0.0	0.0	1.1
3	5.3	3.2		0.0	0.0	1.1	-2.1	-2.1
4	1.1	1.1	0.0		0.0	0.0	0.0	0.0
5	1.1	1.1	0.0	0.0		0.0	0.0	0.0
6	0.0	0.0	-1.1	0.0	0.0		-1.1	-1.1
7	0.0	0.0	2.1	0.0	0.0	1.1		0.0
8	6.4	-1.1	2.1	0.0	0.0	1.1	0.0	
Total	19.1	-1.1	-5.3	-2.1	-2.1	3.2	-3.2	-8.5
Black male long-termers								
1		0.0	-8.9	0.0	0.0	--	-1.8	-7.1
2	0.0		-5.4	-1.8	-1.8	--	0.0	1.8
3	8.9	5.4		3.6	0.0	--	-1.8	7.1
4	0.0	1.8	-3.6		0.0	--	0.0	-1.8
5	0.0	1.8	0.0	0.0		--	0.0	0.0
6	--	--	--	--	--	--	--	--
7	1.8	0.0	1.8	0.0	0.0	--		-3.6
8	7.1	-1.8	-7.1	1.8	0.0	--	3.6	
Total	17.9	7.1	-23.2	3.6	-1.8	--	0.0	-3.6

[a]Data in each column are signed changes from the categories shown at left margin of table. Percentage base excludes cases for which occupational information is lacking for either of the times being compared. The symbol "--" denotes absence of respondents in occupational category at both time periods.
[b]Occupational categories are:

1. Professional, technical, or managerial
2. Craftsmen or foremen
3. Operatives
4. Clerical or sales
5. Services
6. Farm workers
7. Nonfarm laborers
8. Not working

in the middle of the occupational structure (in operative positions)
and at the bottom (without jobs) to opt for a change.

Two other choices deserve comment, mainly because they are
not in line with expectations or trends in the data. First, the net
movement implied by these aspirations is mainly away from the
kinds of work found by most of the migrants on entering the Cleveland work force. Except among the group of men without work, the
general movement is away from operative occupations (among black
male long-term residents, in fact, there is a net movement toward
being outside the work force from the men employed in operative
positions, perhaps a comment on the kinds of jobs they held). Second-
ly, there is little evidence of a pastoral urge. No black male saw
farming as any part of his ideal life state and only 3 percent of the
males in each of the white comparison groups named farming as the
kind of work they would be doing in the future if their lives worked
out in the best imaginable manner. These men have become committed to urban living and working, but many of them (and especially
the blacks) want to experience it away from the assembly line and in
more skilled or technical positions than they have been able to secure
up to the time they participated in this study.

4

WOMEN AND THEIR
OCCUPATIONS

The interpretation of our findings pertaining to the occupational experience of women must take into account the ground rules for inclusion in the study, which differed for women and men. In addition to women who were working or looking for work when first contacted by the interviewers, the original study population also included female heads of house irrespective of labor force status. This special rule for defining the study population was adopted in light of the welfare potential migrant Southern women supposedly bring to Northern cities.* Thus, from the outset, women who were marginally, if at all, attached to the labor force were included in the study population. Their differential attachment to the labor force is reflected in the work expectations reported in the first-round interviews. Fewer of the female migrants than of the male migrants said they had expected to work in Cleveland at the time they made the move (the proportions expecting to work were as follows: white male migrants, 96 percent; black males, 92 percent; black females, 89 percent; and white female migrants, 73 percent). The great marginality of work in the lives of women in the study is also indicated by the relative proportions reporting no occupation at each of the subsequent measurement points. Out of 16 comparisons over time between the sexes (within race and duration-of-residence categories), in only one are the proportions of men and women reporting "no occupation" even reasonably similar.

---

*In retrospect, this turned out to be a useful decision, given the trend since the late 1960s to develop employment alternatives for this category of women after their children reach school age, in particular under the Work Incentive Program (WIN), administered jointly by the Departments of Labor and Health, Education, and Welfare.

At all other times men were considerably more likely than women to be actively engaged in an occupation. (It would obviously be more convenient to use labor force status as the indicator here. Unfortunately, the difficulty of fixing labor force status retrospectively for the periods of time surrounding the move to Cleveland led us to adopt this more general measure.)

TRENDS IN OCCUPATIONS

Because the goal of our study was to assess the part played by migratory status in the work adjustment of the population we studied, the findings need to be viewed against the background of the occupational structure of the female labor force in Cleveland.

On this point, the occupational data from the 1960 and 1970 censuses are instructive about the kinds of jobs available in the Cleveland area for women and provide some clues as to the changes that occurred in employment opportunities, especially for black women (Table 4.1).* Over the decennial period the number of employed women of both races had increased, by almost 40 percent for white women and by over 70 percent for black women, or at twice as high a rate as for white and black males respectively. Still, black women were a decided minority in the Cleveland work force (14 percent of the total in 1960, 17 percent in 1970). Despite the increase in the number of employed white women, their distribution among occupations differed little between the censuses. In both censuses, roughly half of the employed white females were found working in clerical and sales occupations with the remainder being relatively evenly distributed among professional, technical, and managerial occupations, operatives, or service workers. But between the two censuses the occupational distribution for employed black women changed markedly. In 1960 half of the employed black women in the Standard Metropolitan Statistical Area (SMSA) were working in service occupations, with operatives and clerical and sales being the next largest categories. By 1970 the proportion of employed black women working in clerical and sales occupations had almost doubled

---

*Once again, data on the distribution of employed persons are a rough proxy measure of employment opportunities. Such distributions only show where others have been successful in finding employment, not where unfilled vacancies are located. Under mandatory listing procedures such as those recently promulgated by the U.S. Employment Service, a comprehensive list of job vacancies would provide more exact information on the structure of opportunities.

TABLE 4.1

Occupational Structure Comparison of Census Data (1960 and 1970) and Survey Migrants (First Jobs and Occupation at Second Interview): Females
(percentages)

Category	White Females				Black Females			
	Census		Migrants		Census		Migrants	
	1960	1970	First Cleveland Job	Second Interview	1960	1970	First Cleveland Job	Second Interview
Professional, technical, and managerial	17	19	2	3	10	13	5	12
Craftsmen and foremen	1	2	4	6	1	1	1	2
Operatives	15	12	52	57	18	17	20	19
Clerical and sales	51	51	12	13	17	31	15	31
Service	15	15	29	21	53	36	58	36
Farm workers	--	--	--	--	--	1	--	--
Nonfarm workers	--	1	1	--	1	2	1	--
Total	100	100	100	100	100	100	100	100
(N)	184,190	256,717	112	67	30,821	53,004	173	100

Note: Data base for both years is number of employed females. The 1960 data for black females include other nonwhite females. The 1970 data for white females include other nonblack females. Persons without reported occupations are excluded from the 1960 data.

Sources: 1960 data from U.S. Bureau of the Census, U.S. Census of Population: 1960 General Social and Economic Characteristics, Ohio. Final Report PC(1)-37C, Table 74, p. 37-288 and Table 78, p. 37-335. 1970 data from U.S. Bureau of the Census, U.S. Census of Population: 1970 General Social and Economic Characteristics. Final Report PC(1)-C37, Ohio, Table 86, p. 37-433 and Table 93, p. 37-517.

(though it was still smaller than the corresponding figure for white women) and the proportion in service occupations had dropped by about one-third.

As one would expect in light of the selection criteria for the study subjects, one important difference between the data for the Cleveland SMSA and the experiences of our female study population in the Cleveland labor force (ranging from first Cleveland job, which was between 1962 and 1967, and job at time of second interview in 1971 or 1972) was the low proportion of women in professional, technical, and managerial jobs in the latter group; such women are unlikely to reside in low-income areas. As Table 4.1 shows, the difference was especially notable for white women: whereas close to 20 percent of women working in Cleveland were in this highest occupational category, this was true of only 2 percent of the migrants with respect to their first job, and 3 percent with respect to the job held at the time of the second interview. For black women, the findings are quite different; by the time of the second interview 12 percent of them--compared to 13 percent in the Cleveland black female population in 1970--held jobs in this category. Although one might conclude that a select group of black female migrants experienced noteworthy mobility and success, and we are inclined to accept this conclusion on the basis of other survey data, an alternative explanation must be considered; namely, the continued residence in ghetto areas of more successful blacks than whites because of lack of housing options.

There are other instructive differences between female migrants and all employed women in Cleveland. Among the white migrants, operative jobs accounted for over one-half of all jobs held at both times, clerical and sales jobs for less than 20 percent. For all employed white women in Cleveland, the proportions are almost exactly reversed, with the bulk of white female employment in clerical and sales occupations. As will be shown, white female migrants were also less likely to be placed in clerical and sales jobs than those inner-city residents who had lived in Cleveland for a longer period of time. For black women, the distribution of jobs held by migrants closely parallels the census data. One can thus conclude that the occupations of white female migrants were like those of their male counterparts, while black female migrants entered the more general realm of black women in Cleveland.

In the balance of this chapter, we are concerned with the occupational experiences of all women in our study, not only those who were employed at the times shown in Table 4.1. (See Chapter 2 for a detailed discussion of labor force participation by women in the study.) We will follow the same approach as used for the men by examining the occupation itself, the nature of the work performed (white-collar, blue-collar, or service), and the skill level involved.

The histograms for occupations, skill level, and functional activities (Figures 4.1, 4.2, and 4.3) for our entire female study population provide the first indication of why analysis of the place of work in the lives of these women is both more interesting and more challenging than study of the parallel data for men. There is, first of all, a clear and persistent racial difference over time on all three of these "kinds of work" indicators. There is also an indication of change, which was already apparent in Table 4.1. Finally, the proportions without occupations, who were not working at each of the various observation points, clearly establishes the position of these women on the periphery of the labor force. In terms of the development of human resources, "potential" would seem to be the term that best describes the extent of their participation in the labor force. Both quantitatively and qualitatively, it is difficult to see how, for the majority of these women, work in the occupations most of them found could be a source of major personal satisfaction, or income from their labors the basis for an adequate living or a secure future. Data on wages and income will be found in Chapter 5 of this study.

Summary of Occupation Data Categories

Usual Premigration Occupation

In comparison with those of the white female migrants, the credentials black female migrants had to offer prospective Cleveland employers were mixed. The black migrants were more likely than the white female migrants to have worked prior to the move to Cleveland and were, therefore, in a better position to claim prior employment experience. But they were also far more likely than the white female migrants to have been employed in one of the service occupations. In fact, examination of the detailed information on occupations shows that white women engaged in service occupations were more likely to have been employed in food service jobs than as private household workers, while the reverse was true of the black female migrants (6 percent of the whites, 28 percent of the black female migrants gave domestic employment as their customary premigration occupation).* The differences in premigration occupations

---

*As indicated early in Chapter 3, the use of the standard Bureau of the Census definition for the service category creates analytic difficulties since this category includes both traditionally low-paid and low-prestige jobs (in the case of black females often domestic service work) as well as many of the better paid and more

FIGURE 4.1

Occupational Distributions for Female Migrants and Long-Term Residents

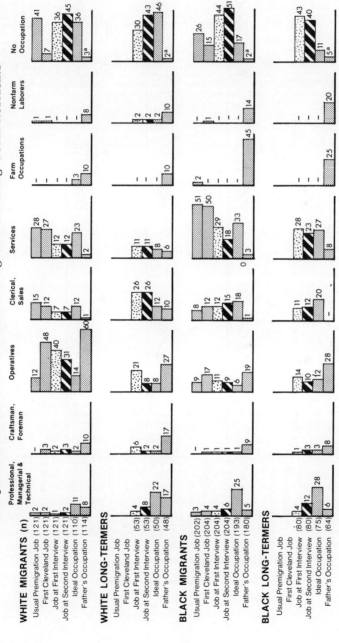

Figures in Percent

Note: "a" category includes respondents without a father or father surrogate as well as respondents whose father or father surrogate was unemployed when he was the respondent's age.

107

FIGURE 4.2

Skill Level Distributions for Female Migrants and Long-Term Residents

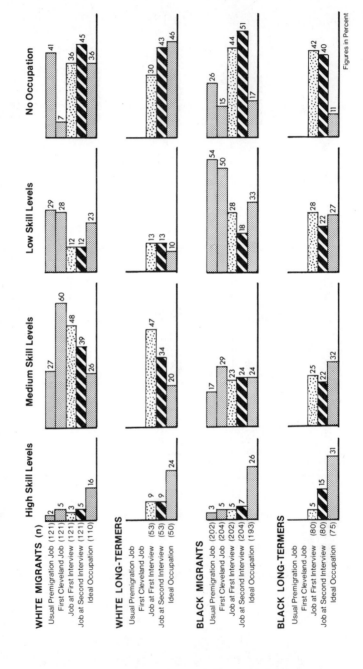

Figures in Percent

FIGURE 4.3

Distribution of Type of Work for Female Migrants and Long-Term Residents

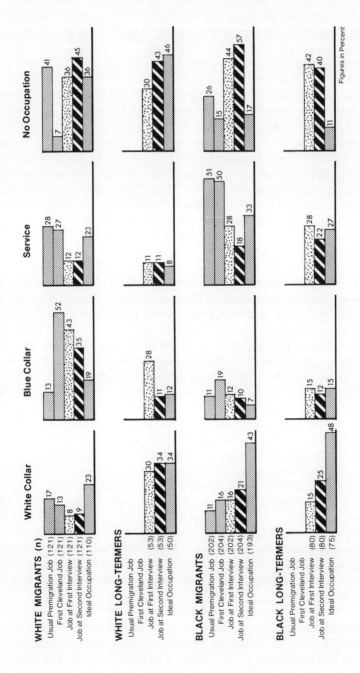

are, of course, reflected in the distribution of occupational skill
level and functional activities. Despite their lesser amount of work
experience, a larger proportion of white than black female migrants
had experience in white- or blue-collar work, the occupations most
prevalent among white women in the Cleveland work force (see Table
4.1). A larger proportion of white than black female migrants had
also accumulated work experience in high- or middle-skill-level
jobs. In confronting a work force in which service occupations predominated for black women, the black female migrants arrived in
Cleveland with the largest share of their experience in the same kind
of work or without prior work experience. In comparison with the
men, the employment credentials the female migrants brought with
them were meager; 70 percent of the white female migrants, 80 percent of the black female migrants either had no work experience or
had usually worked in a low-skill-level occupation.

First Cleveland Occupation

Relative to the kinds of work they had been doing before the
move, the major change in the occupational distribution for both
black and white female migrants was in the larger numbers working
as operatives and the corresponding decreases in the proportions
who reported no occupation. Part of the difference is due to differences in the span of the measurement intervals. Data on occupation
on first Cleveland job convey no information in terms of duration of
that employment. Usual premigration occupation data relate to the
customary occupation of those who had worked at any time prior to
the move. In both instances those without occupations are those who
had not worked at all during the time being considered (that is, before moving to Cleveland or since arrival in the city).

However, while the proportion of black and of white women in
operative jobs prior to the move was roughly similar, there was a
fourfold increase in the number of operatives among the white female
migrants while the number of black female operatives was about
twice as large as before coming to Cleveland. As was the case for
male migrants, the detailed occupational information shows that the
assembly lines of Cleveland's factories were more open to white than
to black female migrants. White females were about six times as

desirable service occupations, for example, practical nurses, cos-
metologists, or health or welfare service aides. Furthermore, the
low pay and prestige of domestic service reflects the status, rather
than skill level of this type of work; like the unpaid housewife, the
domestic worker is often highly skilled and a competent manager.

likely as blacks to have begun work in Cleveland as sorters, assemblers, or machine operators. Similarly, while the number of white migrant females reporting no occupation was only about a fifth as great as before the move, among the black female migrants the number without occupations dropped by about half.

Without further specification of the sort attempted in Chapter 2, "Labor Force Participation," being without work is an ambiguous indicator of social position, especially for women. Indeed, this situation probably has different origins and implications for white and black women. In the years after leaving school and before retirement, men who are not working, unless disabled, temporarily ill, or institutionalized, are most often found still in the labor force as unemployed persons or on the boundaries of it as discouraged workers. Among women, the category includes those who have withdrawn from the labor force to assume full-time maternal or domestic roles, both legitimated by the social system. But one might argue that women of the two races are subject to different risks and that the assumption of full-time maternal or domestic roles by white women in this study population is likely to signify an improvement in economic and social position, while for black women in these low-income neighborhoods movement into full-time maternal domestic roles often implies a deterioration of social relationships and economic position. In either case, however, the relatively large number of women without work reflects the options women have in social roles and at the same time constitutes what is probably the largest source of elasticity in the labor force (or, alternatively, wastage of human resources).

White female migrants were drawn into Cleveland's work force in greater numbers than the black female migrants; they were drawn into blue-collar occupations rather than service jobs and at middle rather than low-skill levels. Half of the white female migrants found their first Cleveland employment in a blue-collar job; half of the black female migrants had begun work in Cleveland in a service occupation.

Occupation at First Interview

With the data on current work situation at time of first interview, it becomes possible to make comparisons between the migrants and the long-term residents. Among each group of women the occupational distributions are dominated by the relatively large proportions of women who were not working (ranging between 30 and 44 percent). (Again, the marked increase in the number of persons without work is largely artifactual, stemming from the measurement interval. Whereas the occupational distributions on first Cleveland employment encompass everyone who had ever worked in Cleveland, these data are centered on the moment of the first interview and necessarily show higher proportions not working.) Occupational similarities within race are clearly greater than the differences across durations of Cleveland residence.

For the black females, the occupational distributions for migrants and long-term residents are virtually identical. Just over two-fifths were not working; just under a third were in service occupations. Between 10 and 15 percent in each group were in clerical or sales jobs or were working as operatives (the proportions in each grouping were reversed with migrants slightly more likely than long-termers to be in clerical and sales jobs). Service occupations continued to be a main source of employment for black women with more than twice as many working in service occupations as in any other occupational category. But the importance of employment in private households had dropped sharply. Fourteen percent of the black female migrants began work in Cleveland as domestic employees; at the time of their first interview only 9 percent of the black female migrants had this sort of job.

The distributions for migrants and long-term residents among the white females differ mainly in the proportions that were working in white-collar (largely clerical and sales) jobs as opposed to being operatives. Long-term residents had a clear edge over migrants in the clerical and professional, technical, or mangerial occupations.

More than twice as many of the white long-termers as any other of the female comparison groups were working in a clerical or sales capacity. White females from both groups were less than half as likely as black females to be working in service occupations; moreover, none of the white women were working in private households. Looking across the boundaries of race and sex, white women were about as likely as black men to have found employment as operatives.

Excluding those who were not working, it is apparent that modest changes were occurring in the aggregate structure of the migrant work force. Among both black and white female migrants, the proportion engaged in service occupations was shading off. Among the white female migrants the largest increase was in the number employed as operatives; for the black female migrants the largest gain was the number of clerical and sales workers.

Roughly twice as many black women were working in service occupations as in any other type of work. Among the white female migrants, the proportion of blue-collar workers overshadows other activities, while among the white long-termers there was a more even division between white- and blue-collar occupations. In terms of skill level, the white females had a clear advantage over the black women. The greatest proportion of white women were working in middle-skill-level occupations; among the black women there was a more even split between middle- and low-skill-level occupations.

Occupation at Second Interview

As at the time of the first interview, the occupational distributions for the black female migrants and long-term Cleveland residents at the time of the second interview were nearly identical while those for the white female migrants and long-termers differed from each other and from the distributions for the black women. All showed large proportions (ranging from two-fifths to one-half) of the women to be without jobs. Black women who were working were most likely to be employed in service occupations. Among the white female migrants with jobs the most likely employment was as an operative; for white female long-term residents who were working, employment in a clerical or sales capacity predominated. The relative advantage of the white women is clear. White migrant females were three times as likely as either group of black women to be employed as operatives; white female long-termers were found in clerical or sales positions about twice as often as the black females.

These general patterns are, of course, reflected in the type of work and skill level distributions. For the black women there was a rough balance between white-collar and service occupations. White female migrants were roughly three times as likely as any other group of the women to be found in blue-collar occupations. Middle-skill-level occupations tended to predominate among all groups of women; but black female long-termers were more likely than any other group to be in high- or low-skill-level occupations. In comparison with occupational positions held at the time of the first interview, the increase in the number of black long-termers in high-skill-level occupations (resulting from increases in the number of top-level white-collar and blue-collar workers) is the only noticeable improvement in the occupational distributions for the women. For black women, the earlier predominance of service occupations was also sharply reduced. (The detailed occupational information reveals that only one black female migrant was working in domestic service as compared to the 14 percent who began work in Cleveland in private households; private household workers were 5 percent of the black female long-term residents.) The data suggest that a minority of black women were able to make a breakthrough, and that these women tended to reach job levels seldom attained by their white counterparts. However, looking at the two female migrant populations as a whole, it is clear that white women had better opportunities to improve their situation primarily because blue-collar jobs were more open to them.

Ideal Occupations

It is clear that work was less central to the ideal life states of white women in the study population than it was for the black women. Even when asked the direct probe about what kind of work they would be doing in their ideal life situation, over two-fifths of the white women but fewer than half as many of the black women said they would not be working at all. The ideal occupation distributions for the black women also differ from those for the white women in the larger proportions naming professional, technical, or managerial occupations. Black women were also more likely than white women to name a service occupation (mainly health) or a clerical or sales job in describing their ideal life situation. This is a case where the service category should be viewed as encompassing relatively skilled, high-paying, high-prestige jobs.

These occupational choices describing ideal life states provide important contrasts between life aspirations and the situations the women were found in at the time of their second interview. The lower number of black, but not white, women who envisioned themselves as being without work has already been noted. There was also a general increase among all groups of women in the proportion opting for professional, technical, or managerial positions. Realization of occupational aspirations would result in more of the black than of the white women being in top skill-level positions and in white-collar jobs. The dominance of blue-collar occupations in the distributions is also noticeably lessened. What emerges from these data is a picture of lower-class women who are considerably more work- and career-oriented than their white counterparts, and who resemble the men in the black community in seeking to break out of low-skill and low-paid jobs.

Net Changes in the Composition
of the Groups

Prior to moving to Cleveland, fewer of the white than of the black female migrants had worked. As a result there was a larger pool of inexperienced white females available for employment in Cleveland. The data on net changes in the structure of occupational distributions for the two groups (Table 4.2) shows this strong effect of the difference in premigration experience. A third of the group of white female migrants moved out of the nonworking group, with operative occupations showing a parallel increase. Among the black female migrants, there were net losses in the group without an established occupation and lesser losses from the ranks of service and farm workers. As for the whites, but on a far lesser scale, the

TABLE 4.2

Net Changes in the Occupational Structure for Females
(percentages)*

	Type of Respondent							
	White		Black		White		Black	
Occupational Category	Migrants	Long-Termers	Migrants	Long-Termers	Migrants	Long-Termers	Migrants	Long-Termers
Time Period								
	Premigration to First Cleveland Job				Premigration to First Interview			
Professional, technical, or managerial	-1		1		-2		1	
Craftsmen or foremen	3		1		2		1	
Operatives	36		8		28		2	
Clerical or sales	-3		4		-7		4	
Services	-1		-2		-16		-23	
Farm workers	--		-2		-1		-2	
Nonfarm laborers	--		1		--		--	
Not working	-34		-11		-5		18	
(N)	(121)		(202)		(121)		(202)	
	First Interview to Second Interview				Second Interview to Ideal Occupation			
Professional, technical, or managerial	1	4	2	9	9	14	19	15
Craftsmen or foremen	1	-4	--	1	--	--	--	--
Operatives	-9	-13	-2	-4	-16	2	-2	3
Clerical or sales	--	--	3	1	4	-16	2	7
Services	-1	--	-11	-5	12	-4	15	5
Farm workers	--	--	--	--	--	--	--	--
Nonfarm laborers	--	--	--	--	3	--	--	--
Not working	8	13	7	-2	-11	4	-34	-29
(N)	(121)	(53)	(204)	(80)	(110)	(50)	(193)	(75)

*Percentage bases are total number of females in each race and duration-of-residence category excluding cases for which occupational information was lacking for either of the times being compared.

major increase was in the number of operatives. These changes are
reflected in the distribution of type of work activities and skill levels
by growth in the proportion with blue-collar and middle-skill-level
occupations (Tables 4.3 and 4.4).

Changes in the interval between the first Cleveland job and the
first interview substantially eroded these movements out of the pool
of nonworking women. Nonetheless, among white female migrants,
more were working in Cleveland at the time of their first interview
than had been employed prior to the move. Among the black female
migrants, who had considerably more employment experience than
the white female migrants, the number of nonworking women had increased almost 20 percentage points. For the white female migrants
the major changes were in the increase of operatives and the decrease
in the proportion of service workers. Among the black women, the
major increase over premigration activities was the noted rise in the
number without work and a parallel drop in the proportion employed
in service occupations. Again these are shown as rises in the proportion of blue-collar and middle-skill-level occupations among the
white female migrants and declines in the proportion of service and
low-skill-level workers among the black female migrants.

Comparison of the changes in occupational situation from the
time of the first to the time of the second interview shows the black
female long-term residents to be in a markedly different position
from that of the other groups of women. For the three other groups of
women the pattern of change is a decrease in the largest substantive
occupational category (operative occupations for white women, service occupations for black migrants) and a parallel increase in the
size of the group without jobs. Among the black female long-termers
there was a small but important increase in the number with top-level
white-collar positions and corresponding losses in the proportions
employed as service workers or operatives and in the group without
employment. This, of course, is reflected in losses in all types of
work activities other than white-collar work and from all except
high-skill-level occupations among the black female long-term Cleveland residents.

Comparison of occupations named in conjunction with ideal life
states and position at the time of the second interview shows that the
orientation of three of the four groups of women in the study implies
an aggregate movement out of the groups without jobs into a working
status. For both white and black female migrants the net shifts from
occupation at second interview to ideal occupation would enlarge both
the number of white-collar and service workers. Similar changes
among black female long-termers would mainly enlarge the number
of white-collar workers. Changes among white female long-termers
were of such small magnitude that little modification of the distribution

TABLE 4.3

Net Changes in Structure of Type of Work Activity for Females
(percentages)*

	Type of Respondent							
	White		Black		White		Black	
Occupational Category	Migrants	Long-Termers	Migrants	Long-Termers	Migrants	Long-Termers	Migrants	Long-Termers
	Premigration to First Cleveland Job				Premigration to First Interview			
White collar	-4		5		-9		4	
Blue collar	39		8		30		1	
Service	-1		-2		-16		-23	
Not working	-34		-11		-5		18	
(N)	(121)		(121)		(121)		(202)	
	First Interview to Second Interview				Second Interview to Ideal Occupation			
White collar	2	--	2	10	13	-2	21	21
Blue collar	-9	-13	2	-2	-14	2	-2	3
Service	-1	--	-11	-5	12	-4	15	5
Not working	8	13	7	-2	-11	4	-34	-29
(N)	(121)	(53)	(204)	(80)	(110)	(50)	(193)	(75)

*Percentage bases are total number of females in each race and duration-of-residence category excluding cases for which occupational information was lacking for either of the times being compared.

TABLE 4.4

Net Changes in Structure of Skill Levels for Females
(percentages)*

	Type of Respondent			
	White		Black	
Skill Level	Migrants	Long-Termers	Migrants	Long-Termers
Premigration to First Cleveland Job				
High	2		2	
Medium	32		12	
Low	-1		-4	
Not working	-34		-11	
(N)	(121)		(202)	
First Interview to Second Interview				
High	1	4	5	10
Medium	-8	-17	-2	-2
Low	-1	--	-11	-5
Not working	8	13	7	-2
(N)	(121)	(53)	(204)	(80)
Premigration to First Interview				
High	1		2	
Medium	21		5	
Low	-16		-25	
Not working	-5		18	
(N)	(121)		(202)	
Second Interview to Ideal Occupation				
High	12	14	19	15
Medium	-13	-14	--	9
Low	12	-4	15	5
Not working	-11	4	-34	-29
(N)	(110)	(50)	(193)	(75)

*Percentage bases are total number of females in each race and duration-of-residence category excluding cases for which occupational information was lacking for either of the times being compared.

among type of work activities would result. For all groups these
changes would also entail increases in the proportion in top-skill-
level jobs. But for both black and white migrants, movement into
low-skill jobs would be nearly as large.

The data presented so far in this chapter and other findings,
shown in Chapter 3, point in several clear directions. White female
migrants had better access than their black peers to factory jobs in
Cleveland, but their employment was more episodic than that of the
black female migrants and their duration of tenure on the same job
or with the same employer less. These data, and those that will
follow in the next section on the patterns of individual moves, suggest that, with greater frequency than is true for the black women,
the white female migrants move in and out of the labor force, alter-
nating between employment mainly as operatives and nonwork roles.
The mere fact of their greater movement suggests that for them
there exists a real alternative to work. The data on occupational aspirations support this view: white women more often than black
women indicated that in an ideal state they would not be working at
all. Black women, even those out of the labor force when interviewed, more often envisioned themselves actively at work. These
findings are, of course, in line with the main findings of the New
Jersey negative income tax experiment; with the additional security
of a guaranteed income white women were more likely than black
women to withdraw from the work force. [1]

In the remainder of this chapter, these main findings are refined and extended. At this point the analysis changes from consideration of the panel data in its aggregate, cross-sectional aspect to
consideration of patterns of individual change. For example, we will
examine individual mobility to assay the effect of earlier occupational
positions on subsequent ones and consider the pattern of exchanges
among occupations and the changes in occupational structure they
generate.

Several of our findings are greatly strengthened or clarified by
the analysis of individual mobility. Most important, the consideration of subsequent positions of the same individuals strengthens our
interpretation of the role of employment in the lives of these working-
class wives and their contribution, thereby, to elasticity of the labor
force, particularly in manufacturing occupations. Another area that
is considerably refined by the more detailed analyses is that of the
respective work behavior and aspirations of the black and white
women in the study. In brief, since they came to Cleveland, black
women seem to have shown stronger work orientations, expressed
higher aspirations, and actually experienced as much mobility as
the white women, or more; unfortunately, they also entered the work
force on a lower level.

We feel that the fine-grained data, and the analyses based on them, add materially to our conclusions and enrich our understanding of the dynamics of work force participation and adjustment among the migrant women. On the other hand, we recognize that some of the data displays are difficult to decipher and that the text is long and makes slow reading. Readers whose interest is limited to the general transformations created as the migrants settled into Cleveland may wish to pass over the detail by turning now to Chapter 5.

CHANGING OCCUPATIONS

Occupational Stability

With the shift of the analytic focus from the aggregate experience to the case-specific panel analysis, we encounter some special problems in the interpretation of the data on occupational stability for women that are not present to so large a degree in the data for men, because of the greater proportions of women than men not actively pursuing an occupation. For men, it was convenient to use occupational stability as a measure of the degree to which previously acquired skills and talents were utilized in subsequent employment. Without further information on the nonwork activities of the women, it is difficult to assert that retention of relatively large proportions of these women in statuses similar to those observed for them at earlier times is also indicative of a conservative use of human resources and skills. In fact, to a large degree, the total size of the group remaining in their earlier position in the occupational structure is strongly affected by the relative numbers in each comparison group who were not actively pursuing an occupation at the earlier time. For example, relative to their usual premigration occupation, white women were less likely than black female migrants to be found in the same general area in the Cleveland work force on their first Cleveland job. But that is largely because so many fewer white than black female migrants had established an occupation before their move to Cleveland. However, movement is a prerequisite of structural change. Therefore, the stability in the structures contributed by women without occupations, while not indicative of conservative use of resources, is a factor in reducing the motility of the structure. Pragmatically this is of considerable importance. We have measures both of actual movement (which is an outcome of the interaction of elements including aspiration, motivation, and opportunity) and also of occupational aspirations under rather ideal conditions (as indexed by occupational position associated with ideal life states). Thus we have measures both on the mobility the women have actually

achieved and on the kinds of positions the women aspire to under
the best of all perceivable personal life conditions. Broadly, the potential for movement exceeds that movement actually achieved and
is a particularly important feature of the occupational orientations
of the black women, both migrant and long-term residents.

The data on the two earliest time periods show almost identical
amounts of stability in the occupational positions of women in each of
the comparison groups, but because these data only reflect movement
from occupations in one broad category to occupations in another
category, the amount of actual change in occupations is considerably
understated. The major sources of the stability at the two times,
however, are different. For the earliest period, the major share
of the stability in the structure for both white and black women is
contributed by persons who had worked in service occupations before
the move (Table 4.5). By the time of the first interview, a sizable
proportion of the white female migrants without established premigration occupations had again moved back to nonwork status so that
the greatest share of the stability in the occupational structure for
white female migrants was due to the women who had not worked
prior to the move reverting to a nonwork status. For black female
migrants, continuity in service occupations contributed the main
share of the stability; but among these women, too, reversion to a
nonwork status was an important factor in the stability of the occupational structure for the group. Comparison of skill-level positions (Table 4.6) shows white female migrants to have a substantial
advantage over black female migrants at both times. At entry into
the Cleveland work force more of the white than black female migrants had retained middle-skill-level positions. This advantage
was still evident at the time of the first interview.

Comparisons between occupational position at the time of the
first and second interviews show the degree of stability of the occupational structures to have risen markedly, with roughly half or
more in each of the comparison groups being in the same position at
the latter time as when first interviewed. In each case roughly half
of the total stable population was found among the group of women
who had not been actively employed at the time of the first interview.
The data on type of work activities for the same time period show a
rising proportion of black women stable in white-collar activities,
though that share is still below the figure for white female long-
term residents (Table 4.7). The proportion of black women, both
migrants and long-termers, stable in (or locked into) low-skill-
level jobs was also higher than that of either group of white women.

In comparison with mobility between the 1968 and 1972 interviews, realization of occupational aspirations would result in greater
occupational movement. In fact, almost as much change would be

TABLE 4.5

Stability of Occupational Status: Females
(percentages)*

	Type of Respondent			
	White		Black	
Occupational Category	Migrants	Long-Termers	Migrants	Long-Termers
Time Period				
Premigration to First Cleveland Job				
Professional, technical, or managerial	--		1	
Craftsmen or foremen	--		--	
Operatives	7		3	
Clerical or sales	4		2	
Services	14		28	
Farm workers	--		--	
Nonfarm laborers	--		--	
Not working	2		4	
Total	27		37	
(N)	(121)		(202)	
Premigration to First Interview				
Professional, technical, or managerial	--		1	
Craftsmen or foremen	--		--	
Operatives	6		1	
Clerical or sales	2		3	
Services	7		18	
Farm workers	--		--	
Nonfarm laborers	--		--	
Not working	12		10	
Total	27		33	
(N)	(121)		(202)	
First Interview to Second Interview				
Professional, technical, or managerial	--	2	3	2
Craftsmen or foremen	--	--	1	1
Operatives	16	6	3	6
Clerical or sales	2	19	8	4
Services	6	8	13	12
Farm workers	--	--	--	--
Nonfarm laborers	--	--	--	--
Not working	20	23	29	30
Total	45	57	57	56
(N)	(121)	(53)	(204)	(80)
Second Interview to Ideal Occupation				
Professional, technical, or managerial	--	6	5	11
Craftsmen or foremen	1	--	--	--
Operatives	7	2	2	7
Clerical or sales	1	8	5	9
Services	4	4	8	16
Farm workers	--	--	--	--
Nonfarm laborers	--	--	--	--
Not working	18	16	6	7
Total	32	36	26	49
(N)	(110)	(50)	(193)	(75)

*Percentage bases are total number of females in each race and duration-of-residence category excluding cases for which occupational information was lacking for either of the times being compared.

TABLE 4.6

Stability of Skill Level Position: Females
(percentages)*

Type of Respondent

Time Period

Premigration to First Cleveland Job

Skill Level	White Migrants	White Long-Termers	Black Migrants	Black Long-Termers
High	1	2	1	4
Medium	18	24	7	10
Low	15	8	30	12
Not working	3	23	4	30
Total	36	57	41	56
(N)	(121)	(53)	(202)	(80)

First Interview to Second Interview

Skill Level	White Migrants	White Long-Termers	Black Migrants	Black Long-Termers
High	1	2	3	4
Medium	22	24	12	10
Low	6	8	13	12
Not working	20	23	29	30
Total	49	57	58	56
(N)	(121)	(53)	(204)	(80)

Premigration to First Interview

Skill Level	White Migrants	White Long-Termers	Black Migrants	Black Long-Termers
High	1	1	1	1
Medium	12	8	5	5
Low	7	10	18	18
Not working	12	4	10	10
Total	31	23	35	35
(N)	(121)	(50)	(202)	(80)

Second Interview to Ideal Occupation

Skill Level	White Migrants	White Long-Termers	Black Migrants	Black Long-Termers
High	1	8	5	11
Medium	11	10	9	16
Low	4	4	8	7
Not working	18	16	6	7
Total	34	38	28	49
(N)	(110)	(50)	(193)	(75)

*Percentage bases are total number of females in each race and duration-of-residence category excluding cases for which occupational information was lacking for either of the times being compared.

123

TABLE 4.7

Stability of Position in Type of Work Activity: Females
(percentages)*

Occupational Category	Type of Respondent							
	White		Black		White		Black	
	Migrants	Long-Termers	Migrants	Long-Termers	Migrants	Long-Termers	Migrants	Long-Termers
	Premigration to First Cleveland Job				Premigration to First Interview			
White collar	6		5		3		5	
Blue collar	7		3		6		1	
Service	14		28		7		18	
Not working	2		4		12		10	
Total	30		39		28		35	
(N)	(121)		(202)		(121)		(202)	
	First Interview to Second Interview				Second Interview to Ideal Occupation			
White collar	2	28	11	10	2	20	14	21
Blue collar	20	9	3	9	9	2	2	7
Service	6	8	13	12	4	4	8	16
Not working	20	23	29	30	18	16	6	7
Total	48	68	57	61	34	42	31	51
(N)	(121)	(53)	(204)	(80)	(110)	(50)	(193)	(75)

*Percentage bases are total number of females in each race and duration-of-residence category excluding cases for which occupational information was lacking for either of the times being compared.

generated by the realizations of occupational aspirations as was experienced between migration and early entry into the Cleveland work
force. Once again the white and black women differ markedly in the
sources of their groups' stability in occupational structure. Remaining outside the active work force in a nonwork status was a far
more important source of stability in occupational structure for
white than for black women.

The Differential Attractiveness of Occupations

Because of the size of the group and its importance for changing the composition of the labor force, as well as for the economic
and social salience of the issue of labor force participation by women
in low-income statuses, a critical issue is the rate of movement from
various occupational categories into the nonwork category and conversely the rate of movement out of the nonwork category into employment and the exercise of an occupation. Tables 4.8 through
4.25 show subsequent positions in the work force in terms of positions occupied at earlier times. As in other sections of this study,
these data are retabulated to reflect type of work and skill levels for
each pair of observations, but unlike the data in Tables 4.2 through
4.4, which showed aggregate movement, these tabulations reflect
the movement of smaller cohorts, respondents occupying similar
positions in the work force. In addition to describing the differential mobility of race and duration-of-residence groups, this section
investigates the differences in mobility arising out of having one
kind of employment at one point in time, say as an operative, as opposed to being located somewhere else in the work force. From
these data, we are able to discuss the holding power of various positions (represented by the percentages of women, found along the
major diagonal in the tables, who are found in the same occupational
group as the one they occupied earlier). The probability of moving
to any other position is represented by the complement (100 minus
the stable percentage) of the stable proportion. Finally, the probability of moving to each of the major categories from each origin is
found along the row following each originating category. Due to the
small number of cases in some categories, not all points of origin
can be given full discussion.

As is the case for most data, evaluation of the mobility outcomes depends a good deal on one's personal interests. In an earlier time, before the National Organization for Women enunciated
the principle that "the hand that rocks the cradle should rock the
boat," and when concern about the ability of men, and especially
black men, to provide for their families was seen as an important

indicator of social progress, one would be interested in indications that women were finding life's fulfillment in the home. High proportions stable in the nonworking category and movement to that category from other origins would be partial indication of that idyllic state. Today, the priorities are less clear-cut. In the case of the particular population that is the focus of this study, one might still be inclined to see the presence of women, and especially wives, in the labor force primarily as an indication of inadequate earnings on the part of men and a consequent threat to family stability. To some extent, the persistent finding that many women in this study frequently do not work and aspire to a nonworking status no doubt reflects the reality that many of these women work out of sheer economic necessity and not because it is their personal preference. Yet, and especially if these women could be helped to find more rewarding and better-paid jobs, those with an interest in the fuller participation and integration of women into the labor force would like to see the magnitude of these proportions reversed, with low proportions stable in the nonworking category and scant movement to that category from other origins. Those whose interest lies in promoting the best utilization of manpower resources are concerned with the impact of skill and experience on channeling job searches and career mobility and on deriving continued return on prior investments in worker training on the job; they would be interested in seeing high proportions in the stable cells along the major diagonal (except in the nonwork category). Those concerned about the channeling effect of local opportunity structures will be interested in seeing the extent to which these women flow toward the jobs that are most prevalent in the Cleveland area.

The changes that occurred between our three observation periods for Cleveland, as well as the aspiration data obtained at the second interviews, are examined in detail in the following sections and tables.

First Cleveland Occupation

It is quite apparent that white and black female migrants enter the Cleveland labor force on different tracks. First, consider female migrants without prior work experience. These newcomers to the Cleveland work force have no credentials to present to employers other than their prior socialization and their own personal appearance. Nearly three-fifths of the white female migrants without any prior work experience began work in Cleveland as operatives; for over half of the inexperienced black female migrants the first job was in a service occupation (Table 4.8). This is also broadly true of those workers with prior employment experience. Except for the white female migrants whose usual premigration employment was in service

TABLE 4.8

Changes in Occupation for Female Migrants: Usual Premigration Occupation to First Cleveland Occupation (percentages)

Usual Premigration Occupation	First Cleveland Occupation								Total	
	Professional, Technical, or Managerial	Craftsmen or Foremen	Operatives	Clerical or Sales	Services	Farm Workers	Nonfarm Laborers	Not Working	Percent	(N)
White										
Professional, technical, or managerial	--	33	33	33	--	--	--	--	100	(3)
Craftsmen or foremen	--	--	--	--	--	--	--	--	--	--
Operatives	--	7	53	7	20	--	--	13	100	(15)
Clerical or sales	6	6	44	28	11	--	--	6	100	(18)
Services	3	--	35	3	50	--	--	8	100	(34)
Farm workers	--	--	--	--	--	--	--	--	--	--
Nonfarm laborers	--	--	--	--	100	--	--	--	100	(1)
Not working	--	2	58	12	20	--	2	6	100	(50)
Black										
Professional, technical, or managerial	33	--	--	33	17	--	--	17	100	(6)
Craftsmen or foremen	--	--	--	--	--	--	--	--	--	--
Operatives	--	--	33	11	39	--	--	17	100	(18)
Clerical or sales	12	6	12	24	29	--	2	18	100	(17)
Services	2	--	18	9	54	--	--	15	100	(103)
Farm workers	--	--	--	20	40	--	--	40	100	(5)
Nonfarm laborers	--	--	--	--	--	--	--	--	--	--
Not working	4	2	15	13	53	--	--	13	100	(53)

occupations, white female workers tended to start work in Cleveland as operatives; blacks in similar proportions tended to begin work in Cleveland as service workers. (The proportions not actively employed are not discussed here. Other tabulations show a high correlation between time elapsed since arrival and the proportion having found employment.) In short, among the females in the study, experience did not seem to be a significant factor either in directing the search for work or as a hiring qualification.

The tabulations for type of work activity show one aspect that is less evident in the comparison of occupations before and after the move (Table 4.9): black white-collar workers deviated from the pattern of most other black female migrants. Those with premigration experience in white-collar work did not gravitate toward service occupations in Cleveland and were more likely than any other group of black female migrants to begin work in Cleveland in white-collar occupations. The skill level tabulations show a white advantage with higher proportions of white than black female migrants from all levels moving into middle- or high-skill-level jobs in Cleveland (Table 4.10).

Once again the availability of repeated measures on the same respondents provides strategic information beyond that available from the cross-sectional measures. From the cross-sectional data, one might infer that there is considerable occupational stability among the service workers, since the proportions of both white and black female migrants who began work in Cleveland are nearly identical with the proportions who had done that kind of work before the move. But, in the tabulations that show the mobility of individuals, we find that in both groups only about half of the service workers continued to work in that class of occupations (Table 4.8). The remainder of the group who began work in service occupations in Cleveland was composed of women entering these occupations for the first time. Thus, though the work force includes similar proportions from each group in service occupations at both times, these are not the same individuals. What appears in the aggregate distributions of occupations as stability is the result of complementary mobility among the individuals.

Occupation at Time of First Interview

With the exception of white female migrants who had not worked prior to migration, both black and white female migrants from all varieties of premigration work experience had moved into the non-work category at rates equal to or greater than their rate of movement into any other substantive occupational category (Table 4.11).

TABLE 4.9

Changes in Type of Work Activity for Female Migrants: Usual
Premigration Occupation to First Cleveland Occupation
(percentages)

Usual Premigration Occupation	First Cleveland Occupation				Total	
	White Collar	Blue Collar	Service	Not Working	Percent	(N)
White						
White collar	33	52	10	5	100	(21)
Blue collar	6	56	25	12	100	(16)
Service	6	35	50	9	100	(34)
Not working	12	62	20	6	100	(50)
Black						
White collar	44	13	26	17	100	(23)
Blue collar	13	26	39	22	100	(23)
Service	11	20	54	15	100	(103)
Not working	17	17	53	13	100	(53)

TABLE 4.10

Changes in Skill Level for Female Migrants: Usual Premigration
Occupation to First Cleveland Occupation
(percentages)

Usual Premigration Occupation	First Cleveland Occupation				Total	
	High	Medium	Low	Not Working	Percent	(N)
White						
High	33	67	--	--	100	(3)
Medium	9	67	15	9	100	(33)
Low	3	37	51	9	100	(35)
Not working	2	70	22	6	100	(50)
Black						
High	33	33	17	17	100	(6)
Medium	9	40	34	17	100	(35)
Low	2	27	56	16	100	(108)
Not working	6	28	53	13	100	(53)

TABLE 4.11

Changes in Occupation for Female Migrants: Usual Premigration Occupation to Occupation at First Interview*
(percentages)

Usual Premigration Occupation	Occupation at First Interview								Total	
	Professional, Technical, or Managerial	Craftsmen or Foremen	Operatives	Clerical or Sales	Services	Farm Workers	Nonfarm Laborers	Not Working	Percent	(N)
White										
Professional, technical, or managerial	--	33	33	33	--	--	--	--	100	(3)
Craftsmen or foremen	--	--	--	--	--	--	--	--	--	--
Operatives	--	--	47	--	7	--	--	47	100	(15)
Clerical or sales	--	6	22	17	17	--	--	39	100	(18)
Services	--	--	29	--	26	--	--	44	100	(34)
Farm workers	--	--	--	--	--	--	--	--	--	--
Nonfarm laborers	--	--	--	--	--	--	--	100	100	(1)
Not working	2	2	54	10	4	--	--	28	100	(50)
Black										
Professional, technical, or managerial	33	--	--	17	--	--	--	50	100	(6)
Craftsmen or foremen	--	--	--	--	--	--	--	--	--	--
Operatives	--	--	11	11	11	--	--	67	100	(18)
Clerical or sales	12	--	--	35	18	--	--	35	100	(17)
Services	2	1	12	8	35	--	--	43	100	(103)
Farm workers	--	--	--	20	20	--	--	60	100	(5)
Nonfarm laborers	--	--	--	--	--	--	--	--	--	--
Not working	4	2	15	11	28	--	--	40	100	(53)

*Occupation at time of first interview is compared with premigration occupation rather than first Cleveland job because many respondents were still on their first job at the time of the first interview.

(Occupation at time of first interview is compared with premigration occupation, rather than first Cleveland job, because many respondents were still on their first job at the time of the first interview.) Both the general trend, which was somewhat more marked for the black than the white female migrants, and the exception are instructive. The general trend indicates that the skills and experience of these female workers are not fully utilized in continuous employment in any of the occupational strata and that the mobility among occupations is often exceeded by the movement out of employment in this population. The strength of the movement by white female migrants from being without work into sporadic operative occupations is an early indication of the more general pattern of utilization of female workers in the group we studied, to which we have only alluded. The changes in the division of type of work activities again show black female migrants with experience in white-collar occupations to be remaining in those jobs at rates greater than for white female migrants with similar prior experience (Table 4.12). As in the comparison with first Cleveland jobs, from all levels of premigration work skills white female migrants moved into middle- or high-skill-level jobs at rates exceeding those for black female migrants (Table 4.13).

Occupation at Second Interview

Comparison of the positions held at the time of the second interview with those held at the time of the first round of fieldwork shows the continued importance of the nonwork status for the women in the study. The rate of retention in the nonwork status for both white and black female migrants exceeded rates for all other strata with significant numbers of cases (Table 4.14). In all except one stratum, rates of movement into or retention in the nonwork status for black female migrants were equal to or higher than the rates for white female migrants. As noted with respect to the two earlier observation points, the stability of black female migrants who had acquired experience in white-collar occupations equaled or exceeded most other mobility rates. Among those who had been working as operatives, one of the key occupations for this group, white female migrants were about a quarter more likely than the black females to be found in operative occupations at the time of the second interview. But the data also show the retention in service occupations to be virtually identical for black and white female migrants. Clearly the disadvantage occurs at the time of entry into this category of occupations, not through unequal mobility from the occupations once a precedent in service occupations is set.

TABLE 4.12

Changes in Type of Work Activity for Female Migrants: Usual
Premigration Occupation to Occupation at First Interview
(percentages)

Usual Premigration Occupation	Occupation at First Interview					
	White Collar	Blue Collar	Service	Not Working	Total Percent	(N)
White						
White collar	19	33	14	33	100	(21)
Blue collar	--	44	6	50	100	(16)
Service	--	29	26	44	100	(34)
Not working	12	56	4	28	100	(50)
Black						
White collar	48	--	13	39	100	(23)
Blue collar	13	9	13	65	100	(23)
Service	10	13	35	43	100	(103)
Not working	15	17	28	40	100	(53)

TABLE 4.13

Changes in Skill Level for Female Migrants: Usual
Premigration Occupation to Occupation at First Interview
(percentages)

Usual Premigration Occupation	Occupation at First Interview					
	High	Medium	Low	Not Working	Total Percent	(N)
White						
High	33	67	--	--	100	(3)
Medium	3	42	12	42	100	(33)
Low	--	29	26	46	100	(35)
Not working	4	64	4	28	100	(50)
Black						
High	33	17	--	50	100	(6)
Medium	6	29	14	51	100	(35)
Low	3	19	34	44	100	(108)
Not working	6	26	28	40	100	(53)

TABLE 4.14

Changes in Occupation for Female Migrants: Occupation at First Interview to Occupation at Second Interview (percentages)

Occupation at First Interview	Occupation at Second Interview								Total	
	Professional, Technical, or Managerial	Craftsmen or Foremen	Operatives	Clerical or Sales	Services	Farm Workers	Nonfarm Laborers	Not Working	Percent	(N)
White										
Professional, technical, or managerial	—	—	100	—	—	—	—	—	100	(1)
Craftsmen or foremen	33	—	67	—	—	—	—	—	100	(3)
Operatives	—	4	41	6	8	—	—	41	100	(49)
Clerical or sales	—	—	11	33	—	—	—	56	100	(9)
Services	—	7	7	7	47	—	—	33	100	(15)
Farm workers	—	—	—	—	—	—	—	—	—	—
Nonfarm laborers	—	—	—	—	—	—	—	—	—	—
Not working	2	2	30	4	7	—	—	54	100	(44)
Black										
Professional, technical, or managerial	75	—	—	12	—	—	—	12	100	(8)
Craftsmen or foremen	—	50	—	—	—	—	—	50	100	(2)
Operatives	4	—	27	9	14	—	—	46	100	(22)
Clerical or sales	—	—	4	67	—	—	—	29	100	(24)
Services	2	—	7	3	46	—	—	42	100	(59)
Farm workers	—	—	—	—	—	—	—	—	—	—
Nonfarm laborers	—	—	—	—	—	—	—	—	—	—
Not working	4	1	9	11	7	—	—	67	100	(89)

The small size of the groups providing percentage bases for long-term residents seriously hampers comparative analyses involving this population (Table 4.15). The data have, however, been displayed to provide as much parallel information as possible. Two broad features of Table 4.15 are worthy of comment. First, white female long-term residents moved into the nonwork category at greater rates than the black female long-term residents. Second, the mobile black long-termers tended to make greater improvements than the whites in their position (that is, a somewhat higher proportion of cases for the blacks than for the whites is located below the major diagonal).

Looking at the data from the perspective of type of work activities (Tables 4.16 and 4.17), some of the differences between the races emerge in bolder relief. Among the migrants, a lower proportion of white than black white-collar workers held on to their positions in the work force. But white blue-collar workers were more likely than blacks to remain in their positions and white service workers who were mobile were more likely than mobile blacks in the same stratum to improve their position. Among the long-termers two of these outcomes were reversed. Among the white-collar workers, whites were more likely than blacks to hold on to their positions. Among the blue-collar workers, blacks were more likely than whites to remain in similar occupations. Finally, though the number of white females employed in service occupations is too small for accurate comparisons, black service workers were more likely than whites to make a change and the direction of the change tended to be more toward an improved position in the work force.

Skill level comparisons show little difference among the migrants except that at the lowest skill level white female migrants were somewhat more likely than blacks to move to a higher skill level occupation (Tables 4.18 and 4.19). Among the long-termers at the lowest skill level, black females were more likely than whites to improve their position.

For women, the modal pattern of participation in the Cleveland work force is one of instability, dominated by movement into and out of the nonworking group but also including smaller amounts of movement between major occupational groupings, type of work divisions, and skill levels.

Ideal Occupation

The data on movement from occupational position at the time of the second interview to ideal occupation are consistent with our suggestion that being in the nonwork category has different social and economic meanings for white and for black women. Except for the

TABLE 4.15

Changes in Occupation for Female Long-Term Residents: Occupation at First Interview to Occupation at Second Interview (percentages)

Occupation at First Interview	Occupation at Second Interview								Total	
	Professional, Technical, or Managerial	Craftsmen or Foremen	Operatives	Clerical or Sales	Services	Farm Workers	Nonfarm Laborers	Not Working	Percent	(N)
White										
Professional, technical, or managerial	50	--	--	50	--	--	--	--	100	(2)
Craftsmen or foremen	--	--	--	33	--	--	--	67	100	(3)
Operatives	--	--	27	--	9	--	9	54	100	(11)
Clerical or sales	21	--	--	71	--	--	--	7	100	(14)
Services	--	--	--	--	67	--	--	33	100	(6)
Farm workers	--	--	--	--	--	--	--	--	--	--
Nonfarm laborers	--	100	--	--	--	--	--	--	100	(1)
Not working	--	--	6	12	6	--	--	75	100	(16)
Black										
Professional, technical, or managerial	67	--	--	--	33	--	--	--	100	(3)
Craftsmen or foremen	--	100	--	--	--	--	--	--	100	(1)
Operatives	--	9	46	--	9	--	--	36	100	(11)
Clerical or sales	33	--	--	33	11	--	--	22	100	(9)
Services	18	--	9	18	46	--	--	9	100	(22)
Farm workers	--	--	--	--	--	--	--	--	--	--
Nonfarm laborers	--	--	--	--	--	--	--	--	--	--
Not working	3	--	3	9	15	--	--	71	100	(34)

TABLE 4.16

Changes in Type of Work Activity for Female Migrants: Occupation
at First Interview to Occupation at Second Interview
(percentages)

Occupation at First Interview	Occupation at Second Interview					
	White Collar	Blue Collar	Service	Not Working	Total Percent	(N)
White						
White collar	30	20	--	50	100	(10)
Blue collar	8	46	8	38	100	(52)
Service	7	13	47	33	100	(15)
Not working	7	32	7	54	100	(44)
Black						
White collar	72	3	--	25	100	(32)
Blue collar	12	29	12	46	100	(24)
Service	5	7	46	42	100	(59)
Not working	16	10	7	67	100	(89)

TABLE 4.17

Changes in Type of Work Activity for Female Long-Term Residents:
Occupation at First Interview to Occupation at Second Interview
(percentages)

Occupation at First Interview	Occupation at Second Interview					
	White Collar	Blue Collar	Service	Not Working	Total Percent	(N)
White						
White collar	94	--	--	6	100	(16)
Blue collar	7	33	7	53	100	(15)
Service	--	--	67	33	100	(6)
Not working	12	6	6	75	100	(16)
Black						
White collar	67	--	17	17	100	(12)
Blue collar	--	58	8	33	100	(12)
Service	36	9	46	9	100	(22)
Not working	12	3	15	71	100	(34)

TABLE 4.18

Changes in Skill Level for Female Migrants: Occupation
at First Interview to Occupation at Second Interview
(percentages)

| Occupation at First Interview | Occupation at Second Interview | | | | Total | |
	High	Medium	Low	Not Working	Percent	(N)
White						
High	25	75	--	--	100	(4)
Medium	3	47	7	43	100	(58)
Low	7	13	47	33	100	(15)
Not working	4	34	7	54	100	(44)
Black						
High	70	10	--	20	100	(10)
Medium	2	54	6	37	100	(46)
Low	2	10	46	42	100	(59)
Not working	6	20	7	67	100	(89)

TABLE 4.19

Changes in Skill Level for Female Long-Term Residents:
Occupation at First Interview to Occupation at Second Interview
(percentages)

| Occupation at First Interview | Occupation at Second Interview | | | | Total | |
	High	Medium	Low	Not Working	Percent	(N)
White						
High	20	40	--	40	100	(5)
Medium	12	52	8	28	100	(25)
Low	14	--	57	27	100	(7)
Not working	--	19	6	75	100	(16)
Black						
High	75	--	25	--	100	(4)
Medium	20	40	10	30	100	(20)
Low	18	27	46	9	100	(22)
Not working	3	12	15	71	100	(34)

black migrants who were working in service occupations, white female migrants in every stratum were more likely than black females
to indicate that if their life were to work out in the best possible manner, they would not be working (Table 4.20). Three times as many
white as black women who were not working when interviewed the
second time said that under ideal conditions they would be similarly
situated in respect to the labor force. The story is similar for the
long-term residents (Table 4.21). Wherever there are sufficient
cases for analysis, the white women were more likely than the black
women to say that under ideal conditions they would not be working.
These data clearly suggest that, at least in 1972, lower-class white
women did not seek liberation through work; obviously, burdened by
low-paying and unrewarding jobs as well as household responsibilities, they saw an improvement in their life situation through freedom
from employment. We can only question why the same attitudes do
not prevail among black women; certainly their job market experience
was, if anything, less favorable on the whole. Very high levels of
aspiration, greater drive, higher educational levels, a longer tradi-
tion of female wage-earning roles, and less stable marital structures
are possible explanations.

While there was a strong movement toward the nonwork status
for each of the white female groups, there was also a sizable counter-
trend. In three of the four comparison groups (migrants of both
races and black female long-term residents), the number of women
who opted to move out of the nonwork status into employment exceeded the number who indicated that they would prefer to be outside
the labor force. Hence, the size of the net shift in the distributions
is largely due to differences between the races in the proportions of
women who were not working at the time of the second interview.
Among both migrants and long-term residents, whites who were not
working were twice or more as likely as similarly situated black
women to prefer to be outside the labor force, if their lives were to
go as well as they could conceive possible.

The data on type of work activities follow this same general
outline. In each area of the work force, black female migrants were
more likely than the white females to indicate that under ideal conditions they would move into white-collar occupations (Table 4.22).
Where desires of long-term residents can be compared on this point,
the same is true for them (Table 4.23). Except for the black service
workers noted above, from each work activity area black women in
the study were less likely than white women to indicate that, if their
aspirations were realized, they would not be working at all. With
respect to skill level, black female migrants, but not long-term residents, tended to be more likely than whites to aspire to a high-skill-
level occupation (Tables 4.24 and 4.25).

TABLE 4.20

Changes in Occupation for Female Migrants: Occupation at Second Interview to Ideal Occupation (percentages)

Occupation at Second Interview	Ideal Occupation								Total	
	Professional, Technical, or Managerial	Craftsmen or Foremen	Operatives	Clerical or Sales	Services	Farm Workers	Nonfarm Laborers	Not Working	Percent	(N)
White										
Professional, technical, or managerial	—	—	50	—	50	—	—	—	100	(2)
Craftsmen or foremen	—	50	—	—	—	—	—	50	100	(2)
Operatives	15	—	24	9	15	3	—	35	100	(34)
Clerical or sales	11	—	—	11	11	11	—	56	100	(9)
Services	17	—	17	8	42	8	—	8	100	(12)
Farm workers	—	—	—	—	—	—	—	—	—	—
Nonfarm laborers	—	—	—	—	—	—	—	—	—	—
Not working	8	2	10	16	26	—	—	39	100	(51)
Black										
Professional, technical, or managerial	75	—	—	—	—	—	—	25	100	(12)
Craftsmen or foremen	50	—	—	50	—	—	—	—	100	(2)
Operatives	19	—	25	12	31	—	—	12	100	(16)
Clerical or sales	30	3	3	33	7	—	—	27	100	(30)
Services	23	—	—	11	43	—	—	20	100	(35)
Farm workers	—	—	—	—	—	—	—	—	—	—
Nonfarm laborers	—	—	—	—	—	—	—	—	—	—
Not working	19	1	7	17	43	—	—	12	100	(98)

TABLE 4.21

Changes in Occupation for Female Long-Term Residents: Occupation at Second Interview to Ideal Occupation (percentages)

Occupation at Second Interview	Ideal Occupation								Total Percent	(N)
	Professional, Technical, or Managerial	Craftsmen or Foremen	Operatives	Clerical or Sales	Services	Farm Workers	Nonfarm Laborers	Not Working		
White										
Professional, technical, or managerial	75	—	—	—	—	—	—	25	100	(4)
Craftsmen or foremen	100	—	—	—	—	—	—	—	100	(1)
Operatives	—	—	33	—	—	—	—	67	100	(3)
Clerical or sales	21	—	—	29	—	—	—	50	100	(14)
Services	—	—	—	—	33	—	—	67	100	(6)
Farm workers	—	—	—	—	—	—	—	—	—	—
Nonfarm laborers	—	—	—	—	—	—	—	100	100	(1)
Not working	19	5	14	10	10	—	5	38	100	(21)
Black										
Professional, technical, or managerial	80	—	—	—	20	—	—	—	100	(10)
Craftsmen or foremen	—	—	—	—	50	—	—	50	100	(2)
Operatives	14	—	71	—	14	—	—	—	100	(7)
Clerical or sales	10	—	—	70	10	—	—	10	100	(10)
Services	6	—	6	6	75	—	—	6	100	(16)
Farm workers	—	—	—	—	—	—	—	—	—	—
Nonfarm laborers	—	—	—	—	—	—	—	—	—	—
Not working	33	7	10	23	10	—	—	17	100	(30)

TABLE 4.22

Changes in Type of Work Activity for Female Migrants:
Occupation at Second Interview to Ideal Occupation
(percentages)

| Occupation at Second Interview | Ideal Occupation | | | | Total | |
	White Collar	Blue Collar	Service	Not Working	Percent	(N)
White						
White collar	18	18	18	46	100	(11)
Blue collar	22	28	14	36	100	(36)
Service	25	25	42	8	100	(12)
Not working	24	12	26	39	100	(51)
Black						
White collar	67	2	5	26	100	(42)
Blue collar	39	22	28	11	100	(18)
Service	34	3	43	20	100	(35)
Not working	37	8	43	12	100	(98)

TABLE 4.23

Changes in Type of Work Activity for Female Long-Term Residents:
Occupation at Second Interview to Ideal Occupation
(percentages)

| Occupation at Second Interview | Ideal Occupation | | | | Total | |
	White Collar	Blue Collar	Service	Not Working	Percent	(N)
White						
White collar	56	--	--	44	100	(18)
Blue collar	20	20	--	60	100	(5)
Service	--	--	33	67	100	(6)
Not working	29	24	10	38	100	(21)
Black						
White collar	80	--	15	5	100	(20)
Blue collar	11	56	22	11	100	(9)
Service	12	6	75	6	100	(16)
Not working	57	17	10	17	100	(30)

TABLE 4.24

Changes in Skill Level for Female Migrants: Occupation at Second Interview to Ideal Occupation
(percentages)

Occupation at Second Interview	Ideal Occupation				Total	
	High	Medium	Low	Not Working	Percent	(N)
White						
High	25	25	25	25	100	(4)
Medium	19	28	14	40	100	(43)
Low	25	25	42	8	100	(12)
Not working	10	26	26	39	100	(51)
Black						
High	71	7	--	21	100	(14)
Medium	26	37	15	22	100	(46)
Low	26	11	43	20	100	(35)
Not working	20	24	43	12	100	(98)

TABLE 4.25

Changes in Skill Level for Female Long-Term Residents: Occupation at Second Interview to Ideal Occupation
(percentages)

Occupation at Second Interview	Ideal Occupation				Total	
	High	Medium	Low	Not Working	Percent	(N)
White						
High	80	--	--	20	100	(5)
Medium	18	29	--	53	100	(17)
Low	--	--	29	71	100	(7)
Not working	24	24	14	38	100	(21)
Black						
High	67	--	25	8	100	(12)
Medium	12	71	12	6	100	(17)
Low	6	12	75	6	100	(16)
Not working	40	33	10	17	100	(30)

At the opening of this section of the study, we noted that the availability of data on actual movement as well as occupational aspirations was an important advantage to the analysis. Quite simply, in their movement the black women seem to be making considerable strides toward overcoming the initial disadvantage they had relative to white women in the position they occupy in the labor force. These data on aspirations indicate that the hope for future movement is in the same direction. When asked where they would be if their lives worked out as best they might, a larger proportion of white than black women indicated that they would not be working. In general, the answers the black women gave were consistent with their own previous behavior and the statements of women in the civil rights movement. Ideally, they would like to push on toward better jobs, in the direction in which they have actually been heading.

Locations of Change

As in the preceding chapter dealing with the men, we took gross turnover* as an indication of the amount of instability in the system or structure of occupations. In that sense, examination of the gross turnover data complements the data and discussion in the section entitled "Occupational Stability." Though the amounts and location of turnover in occupations, skill level, and type of work activity could be anticipated from the data and discussion already presented, the data on gross turnover (shown in Tables 4.26, 4.27, and 4.28) emphasize the level of change in ways that the other tables do not. It is no surprise to note that movement centered on the nonworking category tends to predominate from the time prior to migration through the two interview periods and into ideal occupations. This is merely to repeat what has been said before on the probabilities of moving to or from that category. Here, however, those probabilities are applied to the occupational distributions existing at the time of each of the observations to show the magnitude of the movement. The lowest level of movement into or out of the nonwork category is between the first and second interviews. Between those two interviews, more than one in every five of the black female migrants and nearly three in ten of the white female migrants moved into or out of the group without jobs. Rates for migrants, who were younger and presumably less well settled into the life patterns

---

*Gross turnover for each category is the sum of the proportion moving into the category and of those moving out of the same category.

TABLE 4.26

Location of Occupational Mobility for Females: Amount of Mobility into and out of Major Occupational Categories (percentages)*

Type of Respondent

Upper category band — Time Period:

Occupational Category	Premigration to First Cleveland Job				Premigration to First Interview			
	White Migrants	White Long-Termers	Black Migrants	Black Long-Termers	White Migrants	White Long-Termers	Black Migrants	Black Long-Termers
Professional, technical, or managerial	4	7	5	11	3	18	5	20
Craftsmen or foremen	3	7	1	1	2	4	1	5
Operatives	47	17	20	11	41	10	18	8
Clerical or sales	18	15	17	16	17	24	14	15
Services	27	8	45	25	26	12	44	16
Farm workers	--	--	2	--	--	--	2	--
Nonfarm laborers	2	4	1	--	1	4	--	--
Not working	44	28	35	22	55	56	50	37
(N)	(121)	(53)	(202)	(80)	(121)	(50)	(202)	(75)

Lower category band — Time Period:

Occupational Category	First Interview to Second Interview				Second Interview to Ideal Occupation			
	White Migrants	White Long-Termers	Black Migrants	Black Long-Termers	White Migrants	White Long-Termers	Black Migrants	Black Long-Termers
Professional, technical, or managerial	2		4		13	18	22	20
Craftsmen or foremen	6		1		2	4	2	5
Operatives	39		14		31	10	10	8
Clerical or sales	10		11		18	24	23	15
Services	12		20		25	12	36	16
Farm workers	--		--		--	--	--	--
Nonfarm laborers	--		--		3	4	--	--
Not working	41		36		46	56	55	37
(N)	(121)	(53)	(204)	(80)	(110)	(50)	(193)	(75)

*Percentage bases are total number of females in each race and duration-of-residence category excluding cases for which occupational information was lacking for either of the times being compared.

TABLE 4.27

Location of Skill Level Mobility for Females: Amount of Mobility into or out of Skill Levels (percentages)*

Skill Level	Type of Respondent			
	White		**Black**	
	Migrants	Long-Termers	Migrants	Long-Termers
Time Period				
Premigration to First Cleveland Job				
High	6		6	
Medium	50		33	
Low	27		44	
Not working	44		35	
(N)	(121)		(202)	
First Interview to Second Interview				
High	7	15	5	12
Medium	42	32	23	28
Low	12	11	20	25
Not working	41	28	36	22
(N)	(121)	(53)	(204)	(80)
Premigration to First Interview				
High	4		6	
Medium	52		30	
Low	26		45	
Not working	55		50	
(N)	(121)		(202)	
Second Interview to Ideal Occupation				
High	17	18	23	25
Medium	44	34	30	23
Low	25	16	36	16
Not working	46	56	55	37
(N)	(110)	(50)	(193)	(75)

*Percentage bases are total number of females in each race and duration-of-residence category excluding cases for which occupational information was lacking for either of the times being compared.

TABLE 4.28

Location of Type of Work Activity Mobility for Females: Amount of Mobility into or out of Functional Divisions (percentages)*

Occupational Category	Type of Respondent			
	White		**Black**	
	Migrants	Long-Termers	Migrants	Long-Termers
Time Period				
Premigration to First Cleveland Job				
White collar	19		18	
Blue collar	50		25	
Service	27		45	
Not working	44		35	
(N)	(121)		(202)	
Premigration to First Interview				
White collar	19		16	
Blue collar	45		21	
Service	26		44	
Not working	55		50	
(N)	(121)		(202)	
First Interview to Second Interview				
White collar	12	8	14	20
Blue collar	38	21	15	10
Service	12	8	20	25
Not working	41	28	36	22
(N)	(121)	(53)	(204)	(80)
Second Interview to Ideal Occupation				
White collar	29	30	36	32
Blue collar	34	18	12	13
Service	25	12	36	16
Not working	46	56	55	37
(N)	(110)	(50)	(193)	(75)

*Percentage bases are total number of females in each race and duration-of-residence category excluding cases for which occupational information was lacking for either of the times being compared.

associated with middle years, were somewhat higher than those of
the long-term residents. Change in work status from the time before migration to that observed during the first interview was of
greater magnitude with half or more of the migrants moving into or
out of the group without employment. Movement around the substantive occupational categories follows the pattern already described.
The centrality of operative occupations for the white women in the
study and service occupations for the black women has already been
emphasized. We see that the magnitude of change around these occupations affected more than two-fifths of the migrant women in the
early phases of their settling-in period and continued at nearly the
same level for white migrant females over the interval between the
two interviews. These levels of change are, of course, reflected in
changes in skill level and in type of work activities. Since the changes
in the nonworking category are carried forward from the occupational
tables, no further discussion is needed concerning the weight of the
movement centered there. Up to the point of comparison with ideal
future occupation, most of the change occurs where the majority of
the women were located, at the middle and lowest skill levels. At
that point, the increase in the movement in the highest skill level reflects the aspirations these women held. These aspirations also pro-
duced the increase in movement centered on white-collar occupations
shown in the tabulations for type of work activities. As with the men,
what is important to notice throughout is the absolute size of the populations affected by mobility; almost everywhere at least a fifth, and
generally much more, of the population is changing occupational positions, type of work activities, or skill levels.

 While the gross turnover data reveal considerable movement,
the data on net changes and on exchanges between pairs of occupational statuses (Tables 4.29 through 4.34) tend to show substantially
less change in the structure of occupations for the women in the study.
Behind this apparent anomaly lies a relatively simple pattern of movement. In most of the comparisons, the main share of the movement
is between the largest categories (generally the nonwork category and
operatives for white women and service workers for black women)
and it is largely compensatory. When the movement to a category is
nearly balanced by movement from the same category little change
in structure results.

 The data show two important exceptions to this generalization.
The move to Cleveland is associated with a strong change in occupational statuses, particularly for the white female migrants, and
the potential for change represented in the comparison of occupational aspirations with occupational position at the time of the
second interview is also sizable.

TABLE 4.29

Net Exchanges Between Occupational Categories for White and
Black Female Migrants: Comparing Usual Premigration
Occupation with First Cleveland Occupation
(percentages)[a]

Usual Premigration Occupation	First Cleveland Occupation[b]							
	1	2	3	4	5	6	7	8
White female migrants								
1		0.8	0.8	0.0	-0.8	--	0.0	0.0
2	-0.8		-0.8	-0.8	0.0	--	0.0	-0.8
3	-0.8	0.8		-5.8	-7.4	--	0.0	-22.3
4	0.0	0.8	5.8		0.8	--	0.0	-4.1
5	0.8	0.0	7.4	-0.8		--	-0.8	-5.8
6	--	--	--	--	--		--	--
7	0.0	0.0	0.0	0.0	0.8	--		-0.8
8	0.0	0.8	22.3	4.1	5.8	--	0.8	
Total	-0.8	3.3	35.5	-3.3	-0.8	--	0.0	-33.9
N = 121[c]								
Black female migrants								
1		0.0	0.0	0.0	-0.5	0.0	0.0	-0.5
2	0.0		0.0	-0.5	0.0	0.0	0.0	-0.5
3	0.0	0.0		0.0	-5.9	0.0	0.0	-2.5
4	0.0	0.5	0.0		-2.0	-0.5	0.0	-2.0
5	0.5	0.0	5.9	2.0		-1.0	1.0	-6.4
6	0.0	0.0	0.0	0.5	1.0		0.0	1.0
7	0.0	0.0	0.0	0.0	-1.0	0.0		0.0
8	0.5	0.5	2.5	2.0	6.4	-1.0	0.0	
Total	1.0	1.0	8.4	4.0	-2.0	-2.5	1.0	-10.9
N = 202[c]								

[a]Data in each column are signed changes from the categories shown at left margin of table.

[b]Occupational categories are:
1. Professional, technical, or managerial
2. Craftsmen or foremen
3. Operatives
4. Clerical or sales
5. Services
6. Farm workers
7. Nonfarm workers
8. Not working

[c]Percentage base excludes cases for which occupational information is lacking for either of the times being compared. The symbol "--" denotes absence of respondents in occupational category at both time periods.

A Note on the Matrices in Chapter 4

A note on reading these matrices may be helpful. All of the net turnover matrices in this section have a similar format. The data are the result of subtracting the percentage of persons in the group who left a given occupational status from the percentage of the total group who were recruited to the same occupational status. The signed result of this simple bit of arithmetic is a description, in percentages, of the net result of the exchange between the two occupational categories and describes the amount of change in the total occupational structure for the group that is due to the interchange. In the form in which matrices are presented for this report, the last figure in each column represents the total change occurring to each category from the earlier time to the subsequent time, with minuses indicating a decrease in the percentage of the group in the relevant category and unsigned nonzero numerals indicating growth in the category. Whether seen from position a or from position b, the amount of the flow between categories must be identical but opposite in sign. While one-half of the data displayed are therefore redundant, because they differ only in sign from the data displayed on the other side of the major diagonal, we have retained both the upper and lower portions of the matrices so that columns may be read to show signed gains and losses.

An example, drawn from the upper panel of Table 4.29, may be enlightening. The third column shows the change in the percentage of white migrant females employed as operatives on their first Cleveland job in comparison with their usual premigration occupation. The total growth (35.5 percent) is seen to come mainly from the net movement into operative occupations by women who had never worked prior to coming to Cleveland (22.3 percent). Secondary sources of growth are the net flow toward operative occupations on the part of women who have worked in service occupations (7.4 percent) and on the part of those who had clerical and sales experience (5.8 percent). Across the diagonal, the entry in row 3 column 4 (-5.8 percent) describes the loss from clerical and sales occupations to operative occupations. Returning to column 3, the negatively signed entry in the second row describes the small net movement (-0.8 percent) from persons in operative occupations into positions as craftsmen and foremen. Thus, reading down the columns as displayed here, positive entries answer the question, "Where did the net growth in this category come from?" Negative entries answer the question, "To which categories did the net losses from this category go?"

Patterns of Mobility

Generally speaking, the fine-grained data on net exchanges between pairs of occupational categories (Tables 4.29 through 4.34)
tend to show greater changes in actual occupational structures for
the white women than for the black women and greater potential for
change in the occupational aspirations of the black women in comparison with the white women.

First Cleveland Occupation

Because of the criteria used to select the subjects for the study,
the greater net change in occupational structure for white female migrants than for black female migrants on entry into the Cleveland
work force is inherent in the difference in premigration occupational
distributions. Fewer of the white than the black female migrants had
worked prior to the move, and study subjects were required to be
members of the labor force, discouraged workers, or female heads
of house. Because there was a very small difference in the proportion of female heads of house, the labor force attachment criterion
built in higher probabilities for change in occupational status for
white than for black female migrants. Differences in the distributions of the jobs members of each group moved into was not a consequence of the selection process, however, and it is this difference
that runs so consistently through the data. A third of the white female migrants entered the labor force for the first time in Cleveland
prior to their first interview. Of that number, two-thirds went into
operative occupations (Table 4.29). Among the black female migrants
the direction of flow was also out of the nonworking category into employment, but the volume was smaller and directed more to service
occupations than to operative positions. The second largest net shift
for the black female migrants was in the increase in the number of
operatives (8 percent) but, unlike the white migrants, most of this
group had been working in service occupations. Thus, the first
Cleveland jobs of the white female migrants tended to move them
directly from the pool of inexperienced job applicants into Cleveland's factories and assembly lines. First jobs for black female
migrants tended to be service jobs. Comparing those with prior
work experience, black female migrants were far less likely than
whites to move into operative occupations.

Occupation at First Interview

In comparison with usual premigration occupations, by the
time of the first interview the main changes in the occupational

TABLE 4.30

Net Exchanges Between Occupational Categories for White and Black
Female Migrants: Comparing Usual Premigration Occupation
with Occupation at First Interview
(percentages)[a]

Usual Premigration Occupation	Occupation at First Interview[b]							
	1	2	3	4	5	6	7	8
White female migrants								
1		0.8	0.8	0.8	0.0	--	0.0	-0.8
2	-0.8		0.0	-0.8	0.0	--	0.0	-0.8
3	-0.8	0.0		-3.3	-7.4	--	0.0	-16.5
4	-0.8	0.8	3.3		2.5	--	0.0	1.7
5	0.0	0.0	7.4	-2.5		--	0.0	10.7
6	--	--	--	--	--		--	--
7	0.0	0.0	0.0	0.0	0.0	--		0.8
8	0.8	0.8	16.5	-1.7	-10.7	--	-0.8	
Total	-1.7	2.5	28.1	-7.4	-15.7	--	-0.8	-5.0
N = 121[c]								
Black female migrants								
1		0.0	0.0	-0.5	-1.0	0.0	--	0.5
2	0.0		0.0	0.0	-0.5	0.0	--	-0.5
3	0.0	0.0		1.0	-5.0	0.0	--	2.0
4	0.5	0.0	-1.0		-2.5	-0.5	--	0.0
5	1.0	0.5	5.0	2.5		-0.5	--	14.4
6	0.0	0.0	0.0	0.5	0.5		--	1.5
7	--	--	--	--	--	--		--
8	-0.5	0.5	-2.0	0.0	-14.4	-1.5	--	
Total	1.0	1.0	2.0	3.5	-22.8	-2.5	--	17.8
N = 202[c]								

[a]Data in each column are signed changes from the categories shown at left margin of table.

[b]Occupational categories are:

1. Professional, technical, or managerial
2. Craftsmen or foremen
3. Operatives
4. Clerical or sales
5. Services
6. Farm workers
7. Nonfarm workers
8. Not working

[c]Percentage base excludes cases for which occupational information is lacking for either of the times being compared. The symbol "--" denotes absence of respondents in occupational category at both time periods.

151

structures for white and black female migrants were among service
workers, those in the nonwork category, and, for white migrants,
among the operatives. The two racial groups are alike in that they
showed a strong net movement out of service occupations (Table
4.30). But again the pathways of the two groups are different.
Among the white migrant females, the net flow of those leaving service occupations was almost evenly divided between women moving
into operative occupations and into the group without occupations.
Among the black female migrants, most of the net flow out of service occupations was into the ranks of those without employment.
Despite the larger net proportion moving out of service occupations
among black female migrants, the net shift from this group into operative occupations was slightly smaller than among the whites.
The groups are further differentiated by the difference in volume
and direction of the net shifts between operative occupations and being in the nonworking group. For white female migrants the largest
net movement in this time comparison is from the ranks of previously inexperienced workers into operative occupations. Black female
migrants, on the other hand, showed a minute net increase in the
nonworking proportion. For the white female migrants the size of
the group without work was declining, and for the black female migrants it was increasing relative to premigration activities. The
white migrants were moving into operative occupations; the black
migrants were moving out of service occupations. The size of the
group without work was greatly increased by the movement of black
female migrants out of service work. Among the former service
workers who remained in the active work force, there was a modest
upward movement into more skilled work.

Occupation at Second Interview

        The categories most prominent in the histograms for the dis-
tribution of occupations at the time of the first and second interviews
also dominate the net change matrices. For both the white and the
black female migrants the largest growth category (a net increase of
roughly 8 percent in each case) was in the size of the nonworking
group (Table 4.31). Again, the major source of that increase in
each case was from the occupational category with the largest share
of the group's workers. For the white female migrants the net flow
was from operative occupations; for the black female migrants it was
from service occupations. But while the net flow to the nonworking
group from the dominant category was larger for the black than for
the white female migrants, the net change was countered by slight
shifts into employment. The size of the group without work was increasing in both groups but at a rate marginally smaller for the black,
where so many were already out, than for the white female migrants.

TABLE 4.31

Net Exchanges Between Occupational Categories for White and Black
Female Migrants: Comparing Occupation at First
Interview with Occupation at Second Interview
(percentages)[a]

Occupation at First Interview	Occupation at Second Interview[b]							
	1	2	3	4	5	6	7	8
White female migrants								
1		-0.8	0.8	0.0	0.0	--	--	-0.8
2	0.8		0.0	0.0	-0.8	--	--	-0.8
3	-0.8	0.0		1.7	2.5	--	--	5.8
4	0.0	0.0	-1.7		-0.8	--	--	2.5
5	0.0	0.8	-2.5	0.8		--	--	1.7
6	--	--	--	--	--		--	--
7	--	--	--	--	--	--		--
8	0.8	0.8	-5.8	-2.5	-1.7	--	--	
Total	0.8	0.8	-9.1	-0.0	-0.8	--	--	8.3
N = 121[c]								
Black female migrants								
1		0.0	-0.5	0.5	-0.5	--	--	-1.5
2	0.0		0.0	0.0	0.0	--	--	0.0
3	0.5	0.0		0.5	-0.5	--	--	1.0
4	-0.5	0.0	-0.5		-1.0	--	--	-1.5
5	0.5	0.0	0.5	1.0		--	--	9.3
6	--	--	--	--	--		--	--
7	--	--	--	--	--	--		--
8	1.5	0.0	-1.0	1.5	-9.3	--	--	
Total	2.0	0.0	-1.5	3.4	-11.3	--	--	7.4
N = 204[c]								

[a]Data in each column are signed changes from the categories
shown at left margin of table.

[b]Occupational categories are:

1. Professional, technical, or managerial
2. Craftsmen or foremen
3. Operatives
4. Clerical or sales
5. Services
6. Farm workers
7. Nonfarm laborers
8. Not working

[c]Percentage base excludes cases for which occupational information is lacking for either of the times being compared. The symbol "--" denotes absence of respondents in occupational category at
both time periods.

Among the long-term residents there was a net flow from operatives into the nonworking group, but the rate was almost three times as great for the white females as for the blacks (Table 4.32). For the whites, in fact, the net change matrix is dominated by the decline in the number in operative occupations and an equally large increase in the number without employment. For the black female long-termers, the predominant feature of the matrix is the increase in the proportion with top-level white-collar jobs (possibly because so few held these jobs before and the reserve in lower-ranked occupations was so large). The black long-termers were moving in opposite directions from the white female long-termers and in nearly equal volume. Whereas the size of the nonworking group was increasing among the whites, among the blacks the size of the group of top-level white-collar workers was increasing. The aggregate structure for the black long-termers also manifests a "promotional" aspect. Though the changes are smaller, there is a net upward ripple in the structure. Women from the group without jobs moved into service occupations, service workers moved into clerical and sales jobs and into top-level white-collar positions, and there was a minute upward movement from the ranks of operatives into supervisory and crafts occupations in blue-collar activities.

Ideal Occupation

The aspirations for top-level white-collar positions, largely technical occupations, show clearly in the net change matrices. Each group shows a relative strong increase in these occupations and in all four comparison groups a substantial share of the increase is from women who were not working when interviewed the second time. Aspirations also indicate the potential for a second strong movement, evident in the matrices for both black and white female migrants, out of the nonworking group and into presumably higher-level service occupations (Table 4.33). This polarity of movement from the nonworking category into service occupations and top-level white-collar occupations is more apparent than real. What is represented here is the attraction of occupations in the health services field for women who were not working when interviewed. The differentiation springs from the proportions opting for technical positions as opposed to personal health care. Among both black and white female migrants, the net shift toward service occupations from the nonworking group was about twice as large as the net increase indicated in the choice of professional, managerial, or technical occupations in conjunction with their image of their ideal life state.

TABLE 4.32

Net Exchanges Between Occupational Categories for White and Black Female Long-Term Residents: Comparing Occupation at First Interview with Occupation at Second Interview (percentages)[a]

Occupation at First Interview	Occupation at Second Interview[b]							
	1	2	3	4	5	6	7	8
White female long-termers								
1		0.0	0.0	-3.8	0.0	--	0.0	0.0
2	0.0		0.0	1.9	0.0	--	-1.9	3.8
3	0.0	0.0		0.0	1.9	--	1.9	9.4
4	3.8	-1.9	0.0		0.0	--	0.0	-1.9
5	0.0	0.0	-1.9	0.0		--	0.0	1.9
6	--	--	--	--	--		--	--
7	0.0	1.9	-1.9	0.0	0.0	--		0.0
8	0.0	-3.8	-9.4	1.9	-1.9	--	0.0	
Total	3.8	-3.8	-13.2	0.0	0.0	--	0.0	13.2
N = 53[c]								
Black female long-termers								
1		0.0	0.0	-3.7	-3.7	--	--	-1.2
2	0.0		-1.2	0.0	0.0	--	--	0.0
3	0.0	1.2		0.0	-1.2	--	--	3.7
4	3.7	0.0	0.0		-3.7	--	--	-1.2
5	3.7	0.0	1.2	3.7		--	--	-3.7
6	--	--	--	--	--		--	--
7	--	--	--	--	--	--		--
8	1.2	0.0	-3.7	1.2	3.7	--	--	
Total	8.7	1.2	-3.7	1.2	-5.0	--	--	-2.5
N = 80[c]								

[a]Data in each column are signed changes from the categories shown at left margin of table.

[b]Occupational categories are:

1. Professional, technical, or managerial
2. Craftsmen or foremen
3. Operatives
4. Clerical or sales
5. Services
6. Farm workers
7. Nonfarm laborers
8. Not working

[c]Percentage base excludes cases for which occupational information is lacking for either of the times being compared. The symbol "--" denotes absence of respondents in occupational category at both time periods.

TABLE 4.33

Net Exchanges Between Occupational Categories for White and Black
Female Migrants: Comparing Occupation at Second
Interview with Ideal Occupation
(percentages)[a]

Occupation at Second Interview	Ideal Occupation[b]							
	1	2	3	4	5	6	7	8
White female migrants								
1		0.0	-3.6	-0.9	-0.9	0.0	--	-3.6
2	0.0		0.0	0.0	0.0	0.0	--	0.0
3	3.6	0.0		2.7	2.7	0.9	--	6.4
4	0.9	0.0	-2.7		0.0	0.9	--	-2.7
5	0.9	0.0	-2.7	0.0		0.9	--	-10.9
6	0.0	0.0	-0.9	-0.9	-0.9		--	0.0
7	--	--	--	--	--	--		--
8	3.6	0.0	-6.4	2.7	10.9	0.0	--	
Total	9.1	0.0	-16.4	3.6	11.8	2.7	--	-10.9
N = 110[c]								
Black female migrants								
1		-0.5	-1.6	-4.7	-4.1	--	--	-8.3
2	0.5		0.0	0.5	-0.5	--	--	-0.5
3	1.6	0.0		0.5	2.6	--	--	-2.6
4	4.7	-0.5	-0.5		-1.0	--	--	-4.7
5	4.1	0.5	-2.6	1.0		--	--	-18.1
6	--	--	--	--	--		--	--
7	--	--	--	--	--	--		--
8	8.3	0.5	2.6	4.7	18.1	--	--	
Total	19.2	0.0	-2.1	2.1	15.0	--	--	-34.2
N = 193[c]								

[a]Data in each column are signed changes from the categories
shown at left margin of table.

[b]Occupational categories are:

1. Professional, technical, or managerial
2. Craftsmen or foremen
3. Operatives
4. Clerical or sales
5. Services
6. Farm workers
7. Nonfarm laborers
8. Not working

[c]Percentage base excludes cases for which occupational information is lacking for either of the times being compared. The symbol "--" denotes absence of respondents in occupational category at both time periods.

Difference in the movement around the nonwork category also distinguishes both black female comparison groups from those of the white women. Among both groups of black women, in every instance the net exchange with the nonwork category is away from that status into a substantive occupation. More simply, both groups of black women in the study population were considerably more likely to say that, in conjunction with their image of an ideal life state for themselves, they would rather be working than not working. Among both groups of white women there is some net flow from a substantive occupation (operative for the migrants, clerical and sales for the long-termers) toward being out of the work force. Part of the movement out of the work force is from the general departure from operative occupations white female migrants envisioned for themselves. They are reasonably well agreed that, ideally, they would be in something other than an operative position. They are less well agreed on what that occupation would be. The white female migrants expressed ideal work choices that would shift their occupational structure toward top-level white-collar jobs, clerical and sales occupations, and certain types of service occupations. White female long-term residents were predisposed to make changes that would decrease their participation in clerical and sales jobs (Table 4.34). While the flow from these occupations is of the same magnitude as the departures from operative occupations for the white female migrants, the destinations were less diverse. The aspirations expressed by the white female long-term residents resulted in an either/or flow-out of clerical and sales occupations. In the balance, most preferred to leave the work force; about half as many would aim for higher-level white-collar positions. The pattern revealed by the turnover data, which show the positions of the same individuals at different points in time, suggests that Cleveland employers of operatives may find the elasticity in work force needed to adjust to changing economic conditions mainly among working-class white women. On the other hand, the alternation between being without an occupation and being employed as an operative may also indicate that the women find short-term employment as operatives a prime opportunity to adjust to short-range economic needs. Since these routine, highly repetitive jobs generally demand little in the way of prior training, and the necessary skills are rapidly learned by casual instruction on the job, prior employment of any sort may establish the reliability of the worker. If the women are not looking for long-term employment, usual sources of worker dissatisfaction such as task boredom and uncertainty of employment may count for less than the immediate economic reward.

Though we are constrained here by the number of cases available for analysis and the number of timed observations, it is tempting to speculate on what information on an adequate number of prior

TABLE 4.34

Net Exchanges Between Occupational Categories for White and Black
Female Long-Term Residents: Comparing Occupation at
Second Interview with Ideal Occupation
(percentages)[a]

Occupation at Second Interview	Ideal Occupation[b]							
	1	2	3	4	5	6	7	8
White female long-termers								
1		-2.0	0.0	-6.0	0.0	--	0.0	-6.0
2	2.0		0.0	0.0	0.0	--	0.0	-2.0
3	0.0	0.0		0.0	0.0	--	0.0	-2.0
4	6.0	0.0	0.0		0.0	--	0.0	10.0
5	0.0	0.0	0.0	0.0		--	0.0	4.0
6	--	--	--	--	--		--	--
7	0.0	0.0	0.0	0.0	0.0	--		0.0
8	6.0	2.0	2.0	-10.0	-4.0	--	0.0	
Total	14.0	0.0	2.0	-16.0	-4.0	--	0.0	4.0
N = 50[c]								
Black female long-termers								
1		0.0	-1.3	-1.3	1.3	--	--	-13.3
2	0.0		0.0	0.0	1.3	--	--	-1.3
3	1.3	0.0		0.0	0.0	--	--	-4.0
4	1.3	0.0	0.0		0.0	--	--	-8.0
5	-1.3	-1.3	0.0	0.0		--	--	-2.7
6	--	--	--	--	--		--	--
7	--	--	--	--	--	--		--
8	13.3	1.3	4.0	8.0	2.7	--	--	
Total	14.7	0.0	2.7	6.7	5.3	--	--	-29.3
N = 75[c]								

[a]Data in each column are signed changes from the categories shown at left margin of table.

[b]Occupational categories are:

1. Professional, technical, or managerial
2. Craftsmen or foremen
3. Operatives
4. Clerical or sales
5. Services
6. Farm workers
7. Nonfarm laborers
8. Not working

[c]Percentage base excludes cases for which occupational information is lacking for either time being compared. The symbol "--" denotes absence of respondents in occupational category at both time periods.

occupations would reveal for those who were employed when first
interviewed, or what a subsequent measure would reveal regarding
the later occupations of women who were not working when last seen.
Our best hunch at this time is that the mobility patterns for these
two groups of women are similar because they represent different
initial employment opportunities (with different vulnerabilities to
sources of work dissatisfaction). It would appear that white women
found it far easier than black women to find employment as operatives in Cleveland in the late 1960s, with black women seeking employment being relegated to less attractive jobs in service industries.
Later, moving out of the nonwork category back into employment,
the diversity of destinations for both groups suggests a departure
from traditional occupations for each of the groups into new and perhaps more attractive occupational fields. If this inference is correct, the mixed mobility model is, in fact, quite similar to the pattern of mobility for earlier generations of immigrants to America
from European countries.

                                   NOTE

    1. Harold W. Watts and Albert Rees, eds., Central Labor
Supply Response, Part A; Part B, Chapters 1-4, Final Report of
the New Jersey Graduated Work Incentive Experiment (Madison:
Institute on Research on Poverty, University of Wisconsin).

5

ECONOMIC POSITION AND DEPENDENCY

In Chapters 1 through 4 we have examined the integration of the Southern newcomers into the Cleveland work force and the kinds of work they did before and after arriving in Cleveland. In this chapter we turn toward indicators of economic position. First we examine the progress of the individual wage earners by comparing, as we did with occupation, premigration positions with wages earned subsequently in Cleveland. This is followed by a discussion of household structures and the contributions made by working spouses. We then turn to the problem of money management and emergency assistance by asking the respondents whether they needed help with money, how they would cope if no one in the household were working, and what their actual contact with public service agencies had been. Finally, we consider changes in receipt of welfare, location of the respondents in terms of the Department of Labor's definition of disadvantaged households, and the subjects' own evaluations of their real income position in Cleveland as compared to that in their home towns.

WAGES

The data on wages for these migrants are the least equivocal assertion of our generalization that, when advantage can be attributed from the measures used in this study, men fare better than women, and whites are generally in a more favorable position than blacks. In the comparisons over time, with only one exception, the rankings on median hourly wage were as follows: white men, black men, white women, black women (Figures 5.1 and 5.2). The rank ordering, however, does not reveal the marked and continued

FIGURE 5.1

Hourly Wage Distributions for Males

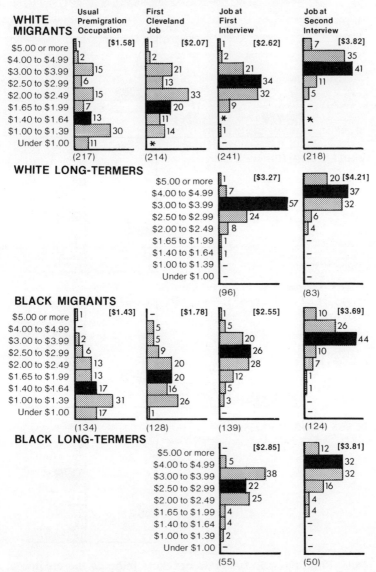

*0.5 percent or less.

Note: Solid bar and figure in brackets indicate the median or midpoint in the distribution. Distributions exclude cases for which wages were not convertible into an hourly rate and those from whom wage information was not obtained.

161

FIGURE 5.2

Hourly Wage Distributions for Females

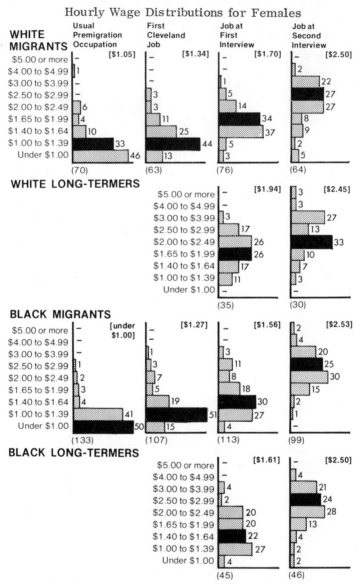

Note: Solid bar and figure in brackets indicate the median or midpoint in the distribution. Distributions exclude cases for which wages were not convertible into an hourly rate and those from whom wage information was not obtained.

difference in the wage rates for men and women. Before the move
to Cleveland the median income of the white male migrants was about
50 percent higher than that of the black female migrants. At the
time of the second interview in Cleveland it was still about 50 percent
higher. Though whites in each instance had higher median wages,
the main difference in wage rates was between the sexes, not between
race groups.

In response to questions on their reasons for moving to Cleveland, most of the migrants replied simply that they had come seeking work or better-paying jobs. The wage data show how fundamental
that motivation was. More than four-fifths of the women had never
earned as much as the then current federal minimum wage in their
usual premigration occupation; half of the black women had never
earned more than a dollar an hour. Men had fared only slightly better; the median for black male migrants shaded just over the current
federal minimum wage while the median for white male migrants was
less than 20 cents an hour higher than the minimum wage. The impact of federal wage standards seems evident in the Cleveland data,
particularly for men (who were more likely than women to find jobs
in industries to which federal controls applied). Even so, more than
a quarter of the black male migrants and more than half of the female migrants of both races began employment in Cleveland in jobs
paying less than the standard minimum wage. As would be expected
from the differences in entry occupations, median wages for first
Cleveland jobs were lower among black than white males. But among
the women there was little difference in median wages on first jobs,
merely because so large a share of these new entrants to Cleveland's
work force found initial employment in low-paying occupations.

At the time of the first interview, when comparison with the
long-term residents can first be made, long-termers (who were
better established in the local work force) had higher wage medians
than the migrants. Among the males, the white migrants ranked
below the black long-term residents. Among the women, the white
migrants ranked higher on wages than the black female long-termers;
this is another sign of the advantage of finding employment in the
operative occupations over those in the service categories. At that
time, medians for males straddled the average hourly earnings for
all workers in the private sector, while the medians for all groups
of females were considerably lower than the national averages.
Generally, of course, medians would tend to be slightly lower than
means for the same range of wage data. The medians reported here
are also lower than average hourly earnings in 1969 for women
workers in the private sector.[1]

Medians for all groups in the study had risen markedly by the
time of the second interview, to the extent that the median hourly

wages for all groups of employed men were above the national norms. Among the women the median hourly wages were approximately a dollar an hour below the national level for all workers but at about the same level as the average wage for women in the private sector computed by Fuchs.

It is obvious that sizable increases in hourly wages occurred between the first and second interviews. However, since the amount of the increases was decidedly uneven across groups (Table 5.1), the rise in medians cannot be attributed solely to the general upward trend in wages. Increases in median hourly wages over the time between the first and second interviews for white long-term residents (those in the study most firmly established in the city) were virtually identical to the change in median wages for workers in private industry in the nation as a whole for the same period (27 percent). (The national increase is estimated from the hourly return to workers in private industry for the years 1967-68 and 1971-72.)[2] Migrants, whose wages had initially been lower, made greater advances; this is merely to say that their median incomes had converged on the national median. Insofar as we can tell, behind this convergence is increasing employment in occupations similar to those held by long-term residents of the city's working-class neighborhoods. While the wages returned to the migrants were initially considerably lower than those paid to long-term residents, by the time of the second interview the gap in median wages had narrowed considerably among the males and disappeared among the females. The amount of the increases relative to initial earnings and the convergence on the wages of neighbors who are old-timers in the city are probably important components of the belief that the move to Cleveland was a good thing and that future advantage lies more in the city than back home.

TABLE 5.1

Percentage Increase in Median Hourly Wages
from First to Second Interview

	Migrants	Long-Term Residents
White		
Males	46	29
Females	47	26
Black		
Males	45	34
Females	62	55

The patterns of net change in wage position show clearly the general rise in earnings (Table 5.2). Relative to their premigration wage level, male migrants tended as a group to enter the Cleveland work force at a higher level, with larger proportions of white than black male migrants improving their position. However, as will be shown later in this chapter, these group data conceal some important individual variations to the general trend. For example, many migrants actually experienced an earnings decline in their first Cleveland job compared with their premigration wages. Jobs held at the first interview advanced the black males further, relative to premigration wage positions, than the white males; but this is partly due to the larger number of black males whose highest premigration wages had been at the lowest end of the earnings scale. In the aggregate, a larger number of black than white male migrants moved up, but not far enough to overcome the initial wage disadvantage experienced by the black male migrants.

In the last interval, between the first and second interviews, both groups of male migrants moved sharply upward. Long-term residents of both races showed little net change, with most of the increases being in the number earning wages between $2.00 and $4.00 an hour but also with some growth in the proportion earning very low wages. Thus, for the male migrants, we see the steady growth in wage position while the long-term residents as a group were doing considerably less well in advancing their position.

Among the female migrants, there were also initial gains but they tended to occur lower down on the wage scale, representing very modest gains over the extremely low premigration wage levels. Like the men, the female migrants continued to gain over time, but the centers of growth were consistently at a lower level for the women than for the men. Black female long-termers who were employed at the time of both interviews were, however, making considerable shifts upward, much more so than was the case among any of the other long-term residents (but, again, they were catching up with other workers rather than surpassing them in earnings).

The data on premigration wages and wages on earlier Cleveland jobs provide important additional evidence toward unraveling the myth about the ways in which Southern newcomers fit into the metropolitan work force. They are reputedly willing to do kinds of work that other people won't, but are also considered unreliable as employees. As we have seen in the chapters on occupations, a good many newcomers from the South did start out in Cleveland on jobs well down on the occupational ladder; at the same time, however, we also found that when age is taken into account, the black migrants tend to have worked longer for their employers than had black workers in a national sample and that job tenure of white newcomers did

TABLE 5.2

Net Changes in Hourly Wage Rates
(percentages)

	Time Period							
	Highest Premigration Wage to Wage on First Cleveland Job		Highest Premigration Wage to Wage on Job at First Interview		Wage on Job at First Interview to Wage on Job at Second Interview			
				Type of Respondent				
	White	Black	White	Black	White		Black	
	Migrants	Migrants	Migrants	Migrants	Migrants	Long-Term Residents	Migrants	Long-Term Residents
Hourly Wage								
Males								
Under $1.00	-10	-16	-11	-19	-2	-1	-4	-2
$1.00 to $1.39	-15	-5	-26	-23	-2	1	-4	2
$1.40 to $1.64	-2	-2	-11	-12	-10	-3	-11	2
$1.65 to $1.99	13	9	3	--	-29	8	-26	-9
$2.00 to $2.49	17	6	17	15	-22	-18	-14	9
$2.50 to $2.99	6	2	25	18	22	14	24	-11
$3.00 to $3.99	-7	2	6	16	36	-13	25	9
$4.00 to $4.99	-1	5	-2	5	7	--	11	--
$5.00 or more	--a	-1	--	1	--	--	--	--
(N)b	(214)	(128)	(201)	(120)	(205)	(78)	(112)	(45)
Females								
Under $1.00	-30	-36	-38	-45	4	4	-3	-3
$1.00 to $1.39	10	12	-12	-7	-18	-8	-21	-3
$1.40 to $1.64	16	15	20	27	-20	-8	-31	-22
$1.65 to $1.99	6	1	25	8	-23	4	-3	-17
$2.00 to $2.49	-3	5	2	7	14	-12	16	14
$2.50 to $2.99	3	2	5	8	16	16	16	6
$3.00 to $3.99	--	1	--	1	25	--	20	22
$4.00 to $4.99	-2	--	-2	--	2	4	4	-3
$5.00 or more	--	--	--	--	--	--	3	--
(N)b	(63)	(107)	(40)	(71)	(44)	(25)	(70)	(36)

a0.5 percent or less.

bPersons from whom wage data at either of comparison points was not obtained and whose wages were not convertible to an hourly rate are excluded.

not differ markedly from that of white workers of similar age in the
national sample. The wage data here show that a number of the male
migrants initially accept jobs that pay less than they had earned in
their usual premigration occupation, but that they subsequently shift
to jobs paying more than they had earned before (Table 5.3). This
evidence of initial instability and the loyalties disclosed in the data
on job tenure is entirely consistent with patterns of search behavior
that put priority on immediately finding some kind of work (remem-
ber the proportion of newcomers who arrived with less than $50.00
at their disposal) and with subsequent exploration of avenues leading
toward better paying jobs. In a sense, the charges of unreliability
and lack of tenacity on the part of the migrants may merely be drawing attention to the kinds of jobs initially offered to them and the
relative attractiveness of the rewards they bring. The need for immediate income is great, but taking a stopgap job assures initial
dissatisfaction and the likelihood of an early quit.

The same logic does not hold for the analysis of the data on the
female migrants, simply because so many had been paid so little in
the work they had done before the move. Among the women who had
worked both at home and in Cleveland prior to the first interview,
more than four-fifths had never earned as much back home as the
then current federal minimum wage. From so low a floor, their
initial upward wage mobility in the economy of an urban industrial
milieu was almost assured. We have seen that, like the men, the
women generally were initially hired into low-level jobs. But, low
as they were, they almost invariably paid at least as well as or
better than the women had ever been paid prior to migration.

Compared to the long-term residents, the migrants were still
rising (but this may merely reflect the fact that persons who have
lived considerably longer in a place also tend to be somewhat older,
and thereby further onto earnings plateaus, than persons who have
recently arrived). The chapters on labor force participation and
occupations have both stressed the observations on the intermittent
labor force participation of the women. These data would seem to
suggest that, in addition to need (which is not here controlled), improved earnings positions also lead to continued labor force participation. While there is considerable evidence from other research
that lower earnings are associated with intermittent labor force
participation among women,[3] the nature of the causal connection is
not clear. Low earnings may precipitate withdrawal from the labor
force, but entry-level positions also tend to receive less pay.
Roughly the same share of women as of men who were employed at
the time of both interviews had improved their earnings position
over what it had been at the earlier time. Among the comparable
long-term residents, on the other hand, there was considerable

TABLE 5.3

Changes in Wages Received
(percentages)

Comparison Points and Relative Position	Type of Respondent							
	Male				Female			
	White		Black		White		Black	
	Migrant	Long-Term Resident	Migrant	Long-Term Resident	Migrant	Long-Term Resident	Migrant	Long-Term Resident
Highest premigration wage/ wage on first Cleveland job								
Higher	54		59		49		55	
Same	19		18		38		36	
Lower	27		23		13		8	
Total	100		100		100		100	
(N)	(214)		(128)		(63)		(107)	
Highest premigration wage/ wage on job at first interview								
Higher	67		82		70		75	
Same	17		9		22		20	
Lower	15		9		8		6	
Total	100		100		100		100	
(N)	(201)		(120)		(40)		(71)	
Wage on job at first interview/ wage on job at second interview								
Higher	91	30	88	40	84	52	94	64
Same	8	51	9	33	4	24	3	22
Lower	2	19	3	27	11	24	3	14
Total	100	100	100	100	100	100	100	100
(N)	(205)	(78)	(112)	(45)	(44)	(25)	(70)	(36)

stagnation in earnings position and even a sizable amount of decline to less favorable positions.

Closer examination of the wage levels of those whose position was unchanged between the several observation times provides additional information about the immediate employment prospects of the female migrants (Table 5.4). We have already noted that women were far more likely than men to be hired into jobs that provided no substantial improvement in earnings position. They were also less likely than men to land jobs paying less than they had been earning prior to the move in earnings position, a fact that we attributed to the low level of their wages back home. But, as is evident from Table 5.4, the failure of women to make an improvement in earnings in their first job in Cleveland is also due to relatively large proportions being locked into low-paying jobs. More than a third of the female migrants began work in Cleveland on jobs that paid about what they had been earning at home. Most of that stagnation in earnings, for both black and white female migrants, was among workers who were earning less than the federal minimum wage both as a highest premigration earning and in their first Cleveland job. The female migrants were also somewhat less likely than the males to move quickly out of the bottom-of-the-barrel positions they found on entering the Cleveland work force; at the time of the first interview more of the female migrants than of the males were still on about the same level, near the bottom of the wage scale, as they had been at the peak of their earnings before moving.

CHANGES IN RATES OF PAY

As with occupations, the individual data on wage mobility add an extra dimension and insight not available from the aggregate data. The individual wage mobility data, like the occupational data, suggest that the prevalent factor in fixing entry wage levels is the kind of jobs available in Cleveland rather than the kind of work the migrants had been accustomed to doing. In reviewing changes in occupation relative to premigration experiences, we came to the conclusion that the opportunity structure in Cleveland, the kind of jobs readily available there, tends to override the specific occupational experience the migrants brought with them. As far as first jobs go, an image of foremen and personnel directors shopping to fill vacancies in their plants and offices prevails over the alternative image of entrepreneurial workers using migration as a means to transfer their crafts and trades to more hospitable milieus.

We have noted the strong convergence of white male migrants on operative jobs as the locus of first Cleveland employment. That

TABLE 5.4

Stability of Earnings Position
(percentages)

Time Period and Hourly Wage	Type of Respondent							
	Male				Female			
	White		Black		White		Black	
	Migrant	Long-Term Resident	Migrant	Long-Term Resident	Migrant	Long-Term Resident	Migrant	Long-Term Resident
Highest premigration wage to wage on first Cleveland job								
Under $1.00	--		1		8		11	
$1.00 to $1.39	6		8		21		22	
$1.40 to $1.64	2		3		8		1	
$1.65 to $1.99	1		2		--		1	
$2.00 to $2.49	5		5		2		--	
$2.50 to $2.99	2		--		--		1	
$3.00 to $3.99	3		--		--		--	
$4.00 to $4.99	--		--		--		--	
$5.00 or more	--		--		--		--	
Total	19		18		38		36	
(N)	(214)		(128)		(63)		(107)	

170

Highest premigration wage to wage at first interview

Under $1.00	—	—	—	—	2	—
$1.00 to $1.39	2	—	1	—	8	17
$1.40 to $1.64	*	—	1	—	5	—
$1.65 to $1.99	1	—	2	2	2	1
$2.00 to $2.49	6	—	4	—	5	—
$2.50 to $2.99	2	—	2	4	—	1
$3.00 to $3.99	6	10	—	11	—	—
$4.00 to $4.99	—	1	—	—	—	—
$5.00 or more	—	1	—	—	—	—
Total	17	12	9	17	22	20
(N)	(201)	(78)	(120)	(45)	(40)	(71)

Wage at first interview to wage at second interview

Under $1.00	—	—	—	—	—	—	—	3
$1.00 to $1.39	—	—	—	—	—	—	—	—
$1.40 to $1.64	—	—	—	—	2	—	—	3
$1.65 to $1.99	—	—	2	2	—	4	1	—
$2.00 to $2.49	2	—	1	—	—	4	1	6
$2.50 to $2.99	2	—	4	4	2	4	—	—
$3.00 to $3.99	3	10	1	11	—	4	—	3
$4.00 to $4.99	*	1	1	—	—	—	—	—
$5.00 or more	*	1	—	—	—	—	—	—
Total	8	12	9	17	4	12	3	15
(N)	(205)	(78)	(112)	(45)	(44)	(25)	(70)	(36)

*0.5 percent or less.

171

occupational concentration is clearly reflected in the wage structure. When wages on first Cleveland job are compared with highest wages in usual premigration occupation, a rather pronounced centering tendency is apparent (Table 5.5).*

Though the numbers at the upper end of the wage scale are not large, there is an apparent movement toward the middle wage groups (from $2.00 to $2.99 per hour) by persons with higher as well as lower premigration wages. In effect, this is further evidence that experience and earnings are not fully portable; that the demand structure at the destination strongly influences the extent to which more experienced and higher paid migrants may expect to retain their relatively advantageous prior position. (Selection of the premigration measure probably adds some unknown amount of error. In particular, we have no knowledge of whether the highest premigration wage occurred during some exceptional period or whether it was being received in the last employment before the move. Even so, it provides a conservative standard against which to measure successive levels of earnings.)

Female migrants were considerably more likely than males to have found initial jobs in Cleveland within the same general hourly ranges as their highest premigration wage (Table 5.6). Because the women had been paid so little as their highest premigration wage, they were less likely than the men to have landed initial employment that paid them less than they had earned before.

Whatever their premigration earning position had been, the most likely situation for an employed male migrant at the time of his first interview was a job paying somewhere between $2.00 and $2.99 (Table 5.7). This, of course, is primarily a reflection of the overwhelming importance of operative occupations for these workers. Exceptions to this general tendency for both white and black male migrants to move into these middle wage groups occurred at the upper ranges of premigration earnings for both white and

---

*The changing location of the empty rows and columns of these wage matrices is graphic evidence of the wage mobility of the study population and the relative advantage and disadvantage of the subgroups. For men, the comparison of first Cleveland wages with highest premigration wages shows the relative lack of earners in the upper wage categories at both times as well as the general tendency for workers from most prior earnings levels to find initial jobs in Cleveland in the middle hourly rate ranges. In contrast, the tight clustering of the data for women shows both concentration in low level premigration jobs and the relatively modest gains made in finding work in Cleveland.

TABLE 5.5

Hourly Wage on First Cleveland Job by Highest Hourly Wage
Before Moving to Cleveland: Male Migrants
(percentages)

Highest Hourly Wage Before Cleveland	Hourly Wage on First Cleveland Job									Total	(N)*
	Under $1.00	$1.00 to $1.39	$1.40 to $1.64	$1.65 to $1.99	$2.00 to $2.49	$2.50 to $2.99	$3.00 to $3.99	$4.00 to $4.99	$5.00 or More		
Whites											
Under $1.00	--	35	4	22	30	9	--	--	--	100	(23)
$1.00 to $1.39	--	20	12	23	30	9	5	--	--	100	(64)
$1.40 to $1.64	--	7	18	7	39	21	7	--	--	100	(28)
$1.65 to $1.99	--	--	7	20	60	7	7	--	--	100	(15)
$2.00 to $2.49	3	12	12	24	30	12	6	--	--	100	(33)
$2.50 to $2.99	--	21	14	7	21	29	7	--	--	100	(14)
$3.00 to $3.99	--	3	6	19	31	16	19	3	3	100	(32)
$4.00 to $4.99	--	--	--	--	33	--	67	--	--	100	(3)
$5.00 or more	--	--	--	100	--	--	--	--	--	100	(2)
Blacks											
Under $1.00	4	36	18	18	14	--	4	4	--	100	(22)
$1.00 to $1.39	--	26	23	31	15	--	5	--	--	100	(39)
$1.40 to $1.64	--	32	18	9	18	23	--	--	--	100	(22)
$1.65 to $1.99	--	33	7	13	20	13	7	7	--	100	(15)
$2.00 to $2.49	--	--	11	17	33	11	6	22	--	100	(18)
$2.50 to $2.99	--	12	--	38	38	--	12	--	--	100	(8)
$3.00 to $3.99	--	67	--	--	--	33	--	--	--	100	(3)
$4.00 to $4.99	--	--	--	--	--	--	--	--	--	--	--
$5.00 or more	--	--	--	--	--	100	--	--	--	100	(1)

*Persons without employment before migration or in Cleveland and those whose wages were not convertible to hourly rates are excluded from the tabulation.

TABLE 5.6

Hourly Wage on First Cleveland Job by Highest Hourly Wage
Before Moving to Cleveland: Female Migrants
(percentages)

Highest Hourly Wage Before Cleveland	Hourly Wage on First Cleveland Job									Total	(N)*
	Under $1.00	$1.00 to $1.39	$1.40 to $1.64	$1.65 to $1.99	$2.00 to $2.49	$2.50 to $2.99	$3.00 to $3.99	$4.00 to $4.99	$5.00 or More		
Whites											
Under $1.00	18	48	18	15	--	--	--	--	--	100	(27)
$1.00 to $1.39	4	59	18	14	--	4	--	--	--	100	(22)
$1.40 to $1.64	17	--	83	--	--	--	--	--	--	100	(6)
$1.65 to $1.99	--	67	33	--	--	--	--	--	--	100	(3)
$2.00 to $2.49	25	--	25	--	25	25	--	--	--	100	(4)
$2.50 to $2.99	--	--	--	--	--	--	--	--	--	--	--
$3.00 to $3.99	--	--	--	--	--	--	--	--	--	--	--
$4.00 to $4.99	--	--	--	--	100	--	--	--	--	100	(1)
$5.00 or more	--	--	--	--	--	--	--	--	--	--	--
Blacks											
Under $1.00	22	52	15	4	7	--	--	--	--	100	(54)
$1.00 to $1.39	10	57	21	5	5	2	--	--	--	100	(42)
$1.40 to $1.64	--	75	25	--	--	--	--	--	--	100	(4)
$1.65 to $1.99	--	--	25	25	--	--	50	--	--	100	(4)
$2.00 to $2.49	--	--	50	50	--	--	--	--	--	100	(2)
$2.50 to $2.99	--	--	--	--	100	--	--	--	--	100	(1)
$3.00 to $3.99	--	--	--	--	--	--	--	--	--	--	--
$4.00 to $4.99	--	--	--	--	--	--	--	--	--	--	--
$5.00 or more	--	--	--	--	--	--	--	--	--	--	--

*Persons without employment before migration or in Cleveland and those whose wages were not convertible to hourly rates are excluded from the tabulation.

TABLE 5.7

Hourly Wage at First Interview by Highest Hourly Wage
Before Moving to Cleveland: Male Migrants
(percentages)

Highest Hourly Wage Before Cleveland	Hourly Wage at First Interview									Total	(N)*
	Under $1.00	$1.00 to $1.39	$1.40 to $1.64	$1.65 to $1.99	$2.00 to $2.49	$2.50 to $2.99	$3.00 to $3.99	$4.00 to $4.99	$5.00 or More		
Whites											
Under $1.00	--	9	--	9	26	30	26	--	--	100	(23)
$1.00 to $1.39	--	5	3	16	28	36	12	--	--	100	(58)
$1.40 to $1.64	--	--	4	--	57	25	14	--	--	100	(28)
$1.65 to $1.99	--	--	--	14	14	57	14	--	--	100	(14)
$2.00 to $2.49	--	--	3	10	39	26	23	--	--	100	(31)
$2.50 to $2.99	--	--	--	15	38	38	8	--	--	100	(13)
$3.00 to $3.99	--	--	3	7	28	14	41	--	7	100	(29)
$4.00 to $4.99	--	--	--	--	33	33	33	--	--	100	(3)
$5.00 or more	--	--	--	--	--	100	--	--	--	100	(2)
Blacks											
Under $1.00	--	9	9	13	26	30	9	4	--	100	(23)
$1.00 to $1.39	--	3	6	15	29	21	26	--	--	100	(34)
$1.40 to $1.64	--	--	5	5	50	25	15	--	--	100	(20)
$1.65 to $1.99	--	7	7	14	21	21	21	--	7	100	(14)
$2.00 to $2.49	--	--	--	6	28	11	28	22	6	100	(12)
$2.50 to $2.99	--	14	--	14	29	29	--	14	--	100	(7)
$3.00 to $3.99	--	33	--	33	--	33	--	--	--	100	(3)
$4.00 to $4.99	--	--	--	--	--	--	--	--	--	--	--
$5.00 or more	--	--	--	--	--	100	--	--	--	100	(1)

*Persons without employment before Cleveland or at time of first interview and those whose wages were not convertible to hourly rates are excluded from the tabulation.

black males. Half of the white male migrants who had earned wages
of between $3.00 and $3.99 were able to move into work paying at
least as much in Cleveland; more than half of the black male migrants with highest premigration wages in the $2.00 to $2.49 range
managed to move into jobs in Cleveland paying over $3.00 an hour.

At the time of their first interview the majority of working
female migrants who had also worked prior to migration were found
in jobs in the $1.00 to $1.99 an hour range, or at rates about a dollar an hour lower than for the migrant male workers (Table 5.8).
Even so, since most of the women had been in even lower-paying
jobs before the move, these pay levels represented a modest improvement in their earnings position. Female migrants were less
likely than the males to have experienced changes in their earnings
position as a result of moving to Cleveland, and the changes that did
occur suggest a movement, for most, from bottom-level jobs in one
economy to similar jobs in another.

For the males, the change in wage rates between the two
Cleveland interviews has a distinct pattern, one suggestive of structural changes such as would be associated with a secular rise in
wages rather than a pattern of differential increments such as would
be associated with individual mobility (Tables 5.9, 5.10). Male
workers who had been paid up to $2.99 an hour ($2.50 for black
male migrants) tended to be receiving wages between $3.00 and
$3.99 an hour. Those who had been earning more initially were
found in jobs paying $4.00 or more an hour. With starting position
held constant, there appears to be little difference among the comparison groups in their progression to better paying jobs. This is
important because it suggests that once into roughly equivalent jobs,
the black males were about as able as whites to rise to better earnings. On the other hand, the crux of the matter is that it was initially harder for blacks than whites to get a start in even a middle-
level job in Cleveland in the early 1960s.

Similar comparisons for the women are hampered by the number of cases for which wage data were available for both points of
time (due, of course, to the number of women who shifted from
employment to being outside the labor force and from outside into
employment). But for the women there also seems to be a movement toward middle-level wage ranges ($2.00 to $2.99 an hour) with
a slight tendency for those who had been in this range earlier to
move up into positions paying above $3.00 an hour (Tables 5.11,
5.12).

TABLE 5.8

Hourly Wage at First Interview by Highest Hourly Wage
Before Moving to Cleveland: Female Migrants
(percentages)

Highest Hourly Wage Before Cleveland	Hourly Wage at First Interview									Total	(N)*
	Under $1.00	$1.00 to $1.39	$1.40 to $1.64	$1.65 to $1.99	$2.00 to $2.49	$2.50 to $2.99	$3.00 to $3.99	$4.00 to $4.99	$5.00 or More		
Whites											
Under $1.00	6	25	25	38	6	--	--	--	--	100	(16)
$1.00 to $1.39	--	23	46	15	8	8	--	--	--	100	(13)
$1.40 to $1.64	--	--	50	50	--	--	--	--	--	100	(4)
$1.65 to $1.99	--	50	--	50	--	--	--	--	--	100	(2)
$2.00 to $2.49	--	--	--	25	50	25	--	--	--	100	(4)
$2.50 to $2.99	--	--	--	--	--	--	--	--	--	--	--
$3.00 to $3.99	--	--	--	--	--	--	--	--	--	--	--
$4.00 to $4.99	--	--	--	--	100	--	--	--	--	100	(1)
$5.00 or more	--	--	--	--	--	--	--	--	--	--	--
Blacks											
Under $1.00	--	36	39	12	12	--	--	--	--	100	(33)
$1.00 to $1.39	3	40	20	13	10	13	--	--	--	100	(30)
$1.40 to $1.64	--	50	--	--	--	50	--	--	--	100	(2)
$1.65 to $1.99	--	--	33	33	--	33	--	--	--	100	(3)
$2.00 to $2.49	--	--	50	--	--	--	50	--	--	100	(2)
$2.50 to $2.99	--	--	--	--	--	100	--	--	--	100	(1)
$3.00 to $3.99	--	--	--	--	--	--	--	--	--	--	--
$4.00 to $4.99	--	--	--	--	--	--	--	--	--	--	--
$5.00 or more	--	--	--	--	--	--	--	--	--	--	--

*Persons without employment before Cleveland or at time of first interview and those whose wages were not convertible to hourly rates are excluded from the tabulation.

TABLE 5.9

Hourly Wage at Second Interview by Hourly Wage at First Interview: Male Migrants
(percentages)

Hourly Wage at First Interview	Hourly Wage at Second Interview										
	Under $1.00	$1.00 to $1.39	$1.40 to $1.64	$1.65 to $1.99	$2.00 to $2.49	$2.50 to $2.99	$3.00 to $3.99	$4.00 to $4.99	$5.00 or More	Total	(N)*
White male migrants											
Under $1.00	--	--	--	--	--	--	--	--	--	--	--
$1.00 to $1.39	--	--	--	--	20	--	60	20	--	100	(5)
$1.40 to $1.64	--	--	--	--	--	50	50	--	--	100	(4)
$1.65 to $1.99	--	--	--	--	5	35	40	15	5	100	(20)
$2.00 to $2.49	--	--	--	--	4	13	61	21	--	100	(67)
$2.50 to $2.99	--	--	--	--	2	7	34	48	9	100	(68)
$3.00 to $3.99	--	--	--	--	3	--	16	62	19	100	(37)
$4.00 to $4.99	--	--	--	--	--	--	--	50	50	100	(2)
$5.00 or more	--	--	--	--	50	--	--	--	50	100	(2)
Black male migrants											
Under $1.00	--	--	--	--	--	--	--	--	--	--	--
$1.00 to $1.39	--	--	--	--	20	--	40	20	20	100	(5)
$1.40 to $1.64	--	--	--	--	17	50	33	--	--	100	(6)
$1.65 to $1.99	--	--	--	--	8	31	46	8	8	100	(13)
$2.00 to $2.49	--	--	--	--	6	9	51	26	9	100	(35)
$2.50 to $2.99	--	--	--	4	4	4	56	30	4	100	(27)
$3.00 to $3.99	--	--	5	--	--	--	24	57	14	100	(21)
$4.00 to $4.99	--	--	--	--	--	--	--	25	75	100	(4)
$5.00 or more	--	--	--	--	--	--	--	--	100	100	(1)

*Persons without wages at either time and those whose wages were not convertible to an hourly rate are excluded from the tabulation.

TABLE 5.10

Hourly Wage at Second Interview by Hourly Wage at First Interview:
Male Long-Term Residents
(percentages)

Hourly Wage at First Interview	Hourly Wage at Second Interview										
	Under $1.00	$1.00 to $1.39	$1.40 to $1.64	$1.65 to $1.99	$2.00 to $2.49	$2.50 to $2.99	$3.00 to $3.99	$4.00 to $4.99	$5.00 or More	Total	(N)*
White male long-termers											
Under $1.00	—	—	—	—	—	—	—	—	—	—	—
$1.00 to $1.39	—	—	—	—	—	—	—	—	—	—	—
$1.40 to $1.64	—	—	—	—	—	100	—	—	—	100	(1)
$1.65 to $1.99	—	—	—	—	—	—	100	—	—	100	(1)
$2.00 to $2.49	—	—	—	—	—	—	83	—	17	100	(6)
$2.50 to $2.99	—	—	—	—	5	—	58	26	10	100	(19)
$3.00 to $3.99	—	—	—	—	2	7	18	54	18	100	(44)
$4.00 to $4.99	—	—	—	—	—	—	—	17	83	100	(6)
$5.00 or more	—	—	—	—	—	—	—	—	100	100	(1)
Black male long-termers											
Under $1.00	—	—	—	—	—	—	—	—	—	—	—
$1.00 to $1.39	—	—	—	—	—	—	100	—	—	100	(1)
$1.40 to $1.64	—	—	—	—	100	—	—	—	—	100	(1)
$1.65 to $1.99	—	—	—	100	—	—	—	—	—	100	(1)
$2.00 to $2.49	—	—	—	—	—	27	46	27	—	100	(11)
$2.50 to $2.99	—	—	—	10	—	20	30	40	—	100	(10)
$3.00 to $3.99	—	—	—	—	5	10	25	40	20	100	(20)
$4.00 to $4.99	—	—	—	—	—	—	—	—	100	100	(1)
$5.00 or more	—	—	—	—	—	—	—	—	—	—	—

*Persons without wages at either time and those whose wages were not convertible to an hourly rate are excluded from the tabulation.

TABLE 5.11

Hourly Wage at Second Interview by Hourly Wage at First Interview: Female Migrants

(percentages)

Hourly Wage at First Interview	Hourly Wage at Second Interview										
	Under $1.00	$1.00 to $1.39	$1.40 to $1.64	$1.65 to $1.99	$2.00 to $2.49	$2.50 to $2.99	$3.00 to $3.99	$4.00 to $4.99	$5.00 or More	Total	(N)*
White female migrants											
Under $1.00	—	—	—	—	—	—	—	—	—	—	—
$1.00 to $1.39	—	—	11	22	33	11	22	—	—	100	(9)
$1.40 to $1.64	17	8	8	—	25	33	8	—	—	100	(12)
$1.65 to $1.99	—	—	—	—	42	33	25	—	—	100	(12)
$2.00 to $2.49	—	—	17	—	—	17	67	—	—	100	(6)
$2.50 to $2.99	—	—	—	—	—	25	50	25	—	100	(4)
$3.00 to $3.99	—	—	—	—	100	—	—	—	—	100	(1)
$4.00 to $4.99	—	—	—	—	—	—	—	—	—	—	—
$5.00 or more	—	—	—	—	—	—	—	—	—	—	—
Black female migrants											
Under $1.00	—	—	—	—	50	50	—	—	—	100	(2)
$1.00 to $1.39	—	6	—	25	44	19	6	—	—	100	(16)
$1.40 to $1.64	—	—	—	17	26	35	22	—	—	100	(23)
$1.65 to $1.99	—	9	—	9	27	36	18	—	—	100	(11)
$2.00 to $2.49	—	—	—	—	12	38	38	—	12	100	(8)
$2.50 to $2.99	—	—	—	—	12	—	62	12	12	100	(8)
$3.00 to $3.99	—	—	—	—	—	—	—	100	—	100	(2)
$4.00 to $4.99	—	—	—	—	—	—	—	—	—	—	—
$5.00 or more	—	—	—	—	—	—	—	—	—	—	—

*Persons without wages at either time and those whose wages were not convertible to an hourly rate are excluded from the tabulation.

TABLE 5.12

Hourly Wage at Second Interview by Hourly Wage at First Interview:
Female Long-Term Residents
(percentages)

Hourly Wage at First Interview	Hourly Wage at Second Interview									Total	(N)*
	Under $1.00	$1.00 to $1.39	$1.40 to $1.64	$1.65 to $1.99	$2.00 to $2.49	$2.50 to $2.99	$3.00 to $3.99	$4.00 to $4.99	$5.00 or More		
White female long-termers											
Under $1.00	—	—	—	—	—	—	—	—	—	—	—
$1.00 to $1.39	—	—	—	—	67	33	—	—	—	100	(3)
$1.40 to $1.64	—	25	—	25	50	—	—	—	—	100	(4)
$1.65 to $1.99	—	—	—	14	43	14	14	—	14	100	(7)
$2.00 to $2.49	—	—	14	—	14	14	57	—	—	100	(7)
$2.50 to $2.99	—	—	—	—	—	33	33	33	—	100	(3)
$3.00 to $3.99	—	—	—	—	—	—	100	—	—	100	(1)
$4.00 to $4.99	—	—	—	—	—	—	—	—	—	—	—
$5.00 or more	—	—	—	—	—	—	—	—	—	—	—
Black female long-termers											
Under $1.00	100	—	—	—	—	—	—	—	—	100	(1)
$1.00 to $1.39	—	—	—	22	33	11	33	—	—	100	(9)
$1.40 to $1.64	—	—	10	20	40	20	10	—	—	100	(10)
$1.65 to $1.99	—	—	—	—	43	57	—	—	—	100	(7)
$2.00 to $2.49	—	—	—	—	29	29	43	—	—	100	(7)
$2.50 to $2.99	—	—	—	—	—	—	—	—	—	—	—
$3.00 to $3.99	—	—	—	—	—	—	50	50	—	100	(2)
$4.00 to $4.99	—	—	—	—	—	—	—	—	—	—	—
$5.00 or more	—	—	—	—	—	—	—	—	—	—	—

*Persons without wages at either time and those whose wages were not convertible to an hourly rate are excluded from the tabulation.

HOUSEHOLDS

Fuller understanding of the adaptation of the migrants to the city requires a brief examination of their households and the economic activities of other household members since, as in the general population, the household consisting almost solely of persons related by marriage and descent was the primary residential, economic, and social unit. We have already touched briefly on the importance of kinship ties. Making the move to Cleveland to be with or near family members was the second most frequently given reason for migration (after the search for employment or a better job). The move itself was far more often accomplished with family members than by the migrant alone or in the company of friends. Kin almost invariably provided shelter and hospitality for the first nights and days in Cleveland and, more often than any other single source, information about employment opportunities. While we expected family and kin to be potent centers in the lives of the migrants, we were not prepared for the predominance of family ties that we encountered. For example, at the time of the first interview so few respondents were found living alone or in households containing any unrelated persons such as roommates or boarders, that the relatedness of household members was not probed in the follow-up interviews.

For the men, migrants and long-termers, whites and blacks, the predominant living arrangement was with spouse. Generally, between the first and second interviews, there were modest increases in the proportion of men who were married and living with their wives, probably due in part to the low average age of the migrant population when they were first interviewed. As members of the study population, they were found at a time when many were in the initial stages of family formation. In the second round of interviews in 1972, we found about 75 percent of the black males and 85 percent of the white males living in conjugal units. Among the women the proportion married and living with spouse had also tended upward, generally to a lower level than for the men, with white women more likely than black women to be living with their spouses.* At the time of the most recent interview, migrants in each race-sex group were at least as likely as long-term residents

---

*In part, this is another manifestation of the selection procedures used. More black than white female heads of house were included in the original study population, thus making it more likely that more whites than blacks would be found in conjugal units the second time around.

to be married and living with their spouses. If other living arrangements are taken as indicators of personal or moral instability, then the migrants are generally in better shape than those who have lived in the city for longer periods of time. They are also more likely than the long-term residents to be in a position in which the economic contribution of a coearner to family finances is possible.

The households were also relatively small when first visited (except among black females, upwards of 70 percent were living in households containing five or fewer members). By the time of the second interview even more were living in small households and the households of black females had come to resemble those of other respondents.

WORKING MATES

The presence of a working spouse in a household has several benefits. On the social level, the presence of a spouse is generally held to be a preferable state to the absence of a spouse, or, among adults, to not being married at all. Economically, a working spouse means a measure of security somewhat advanced over having a nonworking spouse or no spouse at all. Among the men, except for the white migrants, the proportions living in households with a working spouse shaded upward from the first to the second interview, to the point that about a third of the black males, the group with the largest share of working wives, were living in a household in which there was a female wage earner. The women present a more mixed picture, partly because of the way they were originally selected for inclusion in the study.

Women were included in the study if they were female heads of house or if they were working, looking for work, or had stopped looking for work because they believed none existed for them in the community or in their usual line of work. Thus a fair share of the women, the female heads of house, were initially included precisely because they did not live in a household with a working spouse. Elsewhere we have shown that this was somewhat more likely to be true for the black than for the white women in the study. Among the women, the two racial groups moved in opposite directions regarding the presence of a working husband. Among the black women in the study, the proportion living in households with an employed husband remained constant among the migrants and fell off among the long-term residents (suggesting that, over time, inner-city black women's marital positions may gradually be eroded even before the ages at which dissolution of unions by death becomes an important factor).

Among white female migrants and long-term residents, the proportions living in households with husbands who were employed moved
upwards between the two interviews. Thus, at the time of the second
interview, the white females were considerably more likely than the
black females with equivalent amounts of residence in Cleveland to
be living in households with working husbands.

For a closer look at the economic activity of the spouses, we
retabulated the data eliminating all those without spouses living with
them while, at the same time, controlling for labor force position of
the respondents. Not much news comes from the data on the husbands of female respondents; wherever the data bases are adequate,
upwards of four-fifths of the husbands were found to be working.
(We lack the data necessary to partition those without jobs into the
unemployed and out-of-labor-force segments.) We take this merely
to be the working out of the general norm that prescribes gainful
employment or work as the central role for adult males living in
households. Among all groups of males except the white migrants,
there were substantial increases in the proportions of working wives,
with the wives of black migrants being almost half again as likely as
the wives of white males to be employed. Again, this is a basic difference in the structure of the household and the composition of the
earning unit. With working wives in black households contributing
between 30 and 40 percent of the total family money income, the importance to these black families of living in an intact conjugal unit
with two working spouses can hardly be overstated. The disadvantage
seems to stem not so much from having a wife who works as from
not having a wife or having one who does not work.*

OCCUPATIONS AND EARNINGS OF SPOUSES

Working mates tended to be found in the same general sectors
of the Cleveland work force as the primary study participants of the

---

*With respondents' labor force position controlled, the data
base becomes far too thin for interpretation in many categories. We
do wish to point out, however, the indication that wives are less likely
to be working when husbands are unemployed than when they are out
of the labor force altogether. At the root of this is probably the expectation that persons without work who are seeking work (that is,
are unemployed by the BLS definition) will, in fact, soon find work.
Put another way, this is another consequence of the definition of the
terms in the labor force concept. The "unemployed" state is, by
definition, likely to be of briefer duration than the employed or out-
of-labor-force state.

same sex (Figure 5.3). Their patterns of mobility were also similar to those of the primary participants. Husbands of white long-
termers and wives of black respondents showed the most distinctive
patterns of mobility. Among the husbands of white long-termers,
the proportion in operative occupations declined between the first
and second interviews while the number in lower-level white- and
blue-collar occupations and in service occupations increased.
Working wives of black respondents improved their position by
moving into technical, professional, and managerial occupations
from a variety of origins. All other groups showed gains in the
proportions working in supervisory and skilled blue-collar positions
and declines in the relative number of operatives. These changes
are particularly important in black households, where we found increments in the number of working wives as well as advancement in
occupational position for them and for their spouses.

Incomes also showed the same upward trend as among the
primary subjects, with the largest gains tending to occur among the
husbands of black respondents and among the wives of the white
males. These differences in increments in median wages resulted
in the median wages for husbands of black females being about on a
par with those of the husbands of the white female respondents.
Increments in median wages between the first and second interviews
were smaller for the wives of respondents and did not offset the initial disadvantage in earning observed for the wives of black respondents (Table 5.13).

FAMILY INCOME

The importance of the additional contribution to family income
made by the working spouses is evident from the distributions of
family income amounts for the 12 months preceding the first and
second interviews (Figure 5.4). Among the males, blacks and whites
have virtually identical medians at the time of the first interview
(except among the long-term residents, where the family income of
blacks was less). Blacks had achieved that parity through the additional contribution of the working wives. Among the women, which
at both times includes welfare mothers and working female heads of
house (statuses more likely to be occupied by black than by white
women), the black participants in the study at no time have parity
with the whites on median family income. Among both men and
women in the study, the rise in median family incomes had generally placed the most recent arrivals in the city alongside or near
the migrants that had come before them and the long-term residents.

FIGURE 5.3

Occupational Distributions for Spouses of Respondents at Time of First and Second Interviews

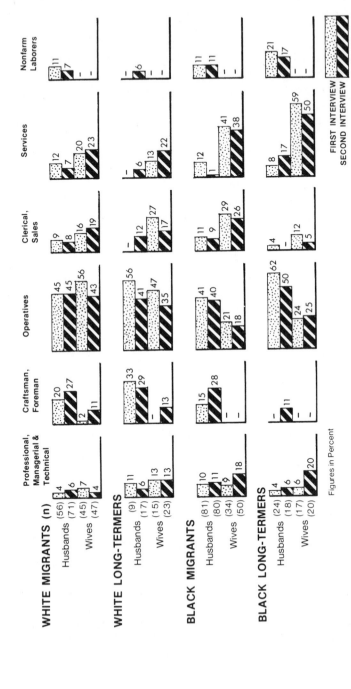

Figures in Percent

186

TABLE 5.13

Median Wage per Hour for Spouses Working (Excludes
Persons Without Working Spouse)
(dollars)

Type of Respondent	First Interview (T_1)	Reinterview (T_2)	Ns	
			(T_1)	(T_2)
Husbands of white women				
Latecomers	2.31	3.95	(15)	(23)
Early arrivals	2.78	3.73	(41)	(48)
Long-termers	2.94	3.92	(9)	(17)
Husbands of black women				
Latecomers	2.38	3.79	(37)	(31)
Early arrivals	2.67	3.86	(43)	(53)
Long-termers	2.96	4.38	(21)	(17)
Wives of white men				
Latecomers	1.57	2.75	(13)	(21)
Early arrivals	1.70	2.45	(32)	(27)
Long-termers	1.88	3.00	(14)	(24)
Wives of black men				
Latecomers	1.75	2.32	(14)	(27)
Early arrivals	1.65	2.70	(18)	(24)
Long-termers	1.63	2.41	(15)	(19)

FINANCIAL PROBLEMS

As has become painfully evident to more and more Americans
in recent years, how much one makes is less important than
whether one's income is adequate to meet one's needs and reason-
able desires. Median incomes for the Cleveland respondents were
not far off the national medians for 1970. About half were earning
less than the national median family income and about half were
earning more (though, from the income distributions, clearly not as
much more as the families above the median nationally). About
half or more of the respondents, generally many more than half,
reported that they had experienced periods of financial need at some

FIGURE 5.4

Family Income for Preceding 12 Months: First and Second Interviews

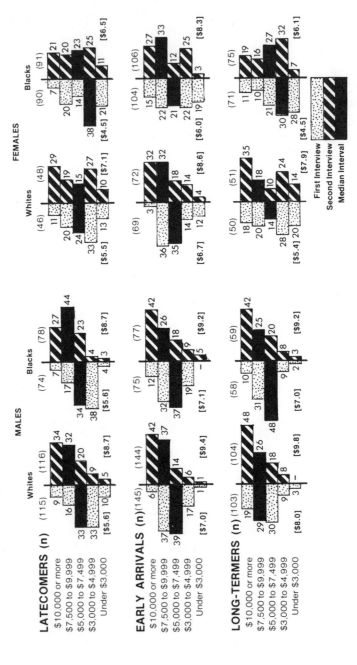

Note: Solid bar and figure in brackets indicate median family incomes for the preceding 12 months, in thousands of dollars.

time in Cleveland (Table 5.14).* Smaller, but still substantial,
proportions (ranging from about one-third to nearly half) reported
having needed financial assistance within the preceding 12 months.
Both the prevalence of need and its recency are consistent with the
reports we received on levels of income and experience with episodic unemployment. While the proportions reporting a recent need
for financial assistance are higher among the black women, they were
not much higher than in other groups. This may merely be an indication that the black women, whose number included a larger share
of female heads of house, are no less successful than others in cut-
ting their capes to fit the cloth. It is also important to note that,
despite rises in median income, there were no corresponding decreases between the first and the second interviews in the proportion
reporting a need for financial assistance within the preceding 12
months. Obviously, like most lower- and middle-income Americans,
our respondents had considerable difficulty keeping up with their ex-
penses and obligations.

SOURCES OF ASSISTANCE OR ADVICE

Students of the urban scene characteristically are somewhat
ambivalent in their approach to the use of public and private sources
of assistance and advice. For example, welfare agencies exist to
provide support for persons who have fallen on hard times, yet if
some segment of the population expresses a willingness to avail itself of these services, the individuals are said to be "welfare prone."
Or if, instead of letting nature run its course, some citizens ask the
police for assistance in restoring tranquillity to a household in the
midst of a domestic argument, they are faulted for burdening the
police force. Perhaps, as a middle ground, one might maintain that
these sources of emergency social and financial support are not unlike firehouses: everyone should know where they are and how to
gain access to their services. On the other hand, one would hope
that the need does not arise too often.

At the time of the first interview, the general level of awareness of sources of assistance and advice was low. However, in each
race-sex group, it was higher for the groups with longer periods of
residence in the city, suggesting that as people settle into the community they gain greater knowledge of its resources. To an extent,
this seems to be confirmed by the reports from the second round of

---

*Inconsistencies in the proportions reporting that they had
"ever" needed help with money in Cleveland may be due to redefini-
tion of level of need as well as errors in recall.

TABLE 5.14

Prevalence and Recency of Financial Problems
(percentages)

| | Needed Help with Money | | | | | |
| | Ever in Cleveland | | In the Preceding 12 Months | | Ns | |
Type of Respondent	First Interview (T_1)	Second Interview (T_2)	First Interview (T_1)	Second Interview (T_2)	(T_1)	(T_2)
White males						
Latecomers	70	61	47	35	(117)	(116)
Early arrivals	64	67	36	42	(145)	(144)
Long–termers	70	63	38	34	(104)	(105)
Black males						
Latecomers	56	46	32	35	(80)	(80)
Early arrivals	51	53	37	36	(78)	(77)
Long–termers	67	64	36	38	(61)	(61)
White females						
Latecomers	55	69	39	43	(49)	(49)
Early arrivals	57	68	35	35	(72)	(72)
Long–termers	72	58	42	45	(53)	(53)
Black females						
Latecomers	55	55	45	46	(95)	(93)
Early arrivals	65	60	47	39	(109)	(109)
Long–termers	71	58	52	43	(80)	(80)

interviews. At least, in all but one group of men, the proportion
reporting that they knew of somewhere one could go in the city for
help or advice was larger than in the preceding interview, and
groups with longer durations of residence in the city tended to be
more aware than those who had arrived more recently. But this
pattern did not appear in the responses of the women. Among the
women, awareness of sources of assistance or advice increased
only among the migrants who had most recently arrived in Cleveland.
In the other female comparison groups, the proportions who said
they knew of any place to go for help or advice had dropped sharply.

While other evidence is needed to confirm these interpretations, it may be that with greater experience the respondents tend
to change their perception of the environment and that what formerly
were perceived as sources of help are later perceived to be less than
helpful. It is also possible that the level of need shifts dramatically,
causing the appraisal to shift. If so, situations that formerly ap-
peared to call for outside intervention may later be dealt with without
such help. For the problems that remain and that now loom large,
few perceive sources of assistance sufficiently potent to be of any
benefit. While it is only a guess, our hunch is that the data are
consistent with both interpretations and that underlying the difference
in the pattern of change among the men in comparison with the women
is a change in the level of need. In any case, in the eyes of the respondents, the environment was far from teeming with sources of
help. There was only one group at the time of either interview in
which more than one-third thought they knew of somewhere to turn
in times of trouble.

PUBLIC ASSISTANCE FOR EMERGENCY SUPPORT

The potentiality for using welfare and other public assistance
agencies was probed in both interviews by asking respondents how
they managed or would manage when no one in the house was working.
Several dimensions are involved in the mention of welfare and other
assistance agencies as a means of support in such situations. The
question itself is variously real to the respondents; some have been
in the situation, while to others the situation is not only hypothetical
but also farfetched. To be mentioned as a potential source of support, agencies must also be known to the respondent and perceived
as an efficacious and personally acceptable means that is preferable
in some degree to a range of other options (for example, receiving
assistance from relatives or friends, hustling, or illegal activities).

The data suggest that the respondents acquire more favorable
perceptions of welfare and other agencies as their life situation

changes. In their first interviews, roughly half or more of the respondents in each group named welfare or other agencies as potential sources of emergency support. Within each comparison group,
mention of assistance agencies was more common among migrants
who had been in the city longer than among the more recent arrivals
or the long-term residents (except for black long-term residents,
who mentioned welfare sources more often than any other group of
respondents). Four years later, with more experience in the city
and with a general slump in economic activity, every group of respondents mentioned welfare or other assistance agencies more
often than they had in their first interviews. The frequency of these
mentions was at least 20 percentage points higher than in the first
interviews in all but three groups. In the first interviews welfare
agencies were mentioned by three-quarters or more of the respondents in only one group (black female long-termers). In the second
interviews these agencies were mentioned by at least three-quarters
of the respondents in all but one group (black male long-term residents). Aside from this general increase in the acceptability of welfare assistance, no other pattern is apparent. For example, among
the men, whites were more likely than black respondents to mention
welfare in two of the three comparison groups; but in two of the
three comparisons among the women, mention of welfare was more
prevalent among black than white women.

CONTACT WITH SOCIAL AGENCIES

Reports of prior contact with personnel from social assistance
agencies ranged widely in the first interview, from 4 percent for
white male recent migrants to 47 percent for black female long-
termers (Table 5.15). Contact with agency personnel was also clearly
patterned, with more women than men reporting such contacts, with
the level of contact being higher for blacks than whites, and (with
one exception) with persons with longer durations of Cleveland residence more likely than more recent arrivals to have been in contact
with someone from a social agency in Cleveland. Still, if agency
personnel were to be the mediators of services for migrants to speed
their integration into the community, the level of their activity
would need to be increased, for only in one group (black female
early arrivals) had more than one-fifth of the migrants had any contact with an agency worker in Cleveland. Cleveland social workers
barely existed in the lives of the male recent migrants; only 4 percent of the whites or blacks in the group reported any contact with
agency personnel.

TABLE 5.15

Contact with Social Agencies: Percentage Who Talked
with Anyone from Any Service Group or Agency
Prior to Their First Interview or Within
12 Months of Their Second Interview

Type of Respondent	First Interview (T_1)	Reinterview (T_2)
White males		
Latecomers	4	12
	(117)	(117)
Early arrivals	9	16
	(145)	(145)
Long-termers	23	18
	(105)	(105)
Black males		
Latecomers	4	13
	(80)	(79)
Early arrivals	15	9
	(78)	(78)
Long-termers	31	8
	(61)	(60)
White females		
Latecomers	18	12
	(49)	(49)
Early arrivals	18	21
	(72)	(72)
Long-termers	36	19
	(53)	(53)
Black females		
Latecomers	19	18
	(95)	(94)
Early arrivals	38	17
	(109)	(106)
Long-termers	47	26
	(78)	(80)

In the second interview, the time span for contact with social
agency personnel was reduced from "ever" to the preceding 12
months in order to better gauge the use of the services of assistance
groups by the respondents. With the time frame for contact short-
ened (for some of the recent arrivals, 12 months would be a longer
period of time than the duration of their residence in Cleveland prior
to the first interview), one would expect the level of contact to decrease among all but the most recent arrivals. Generally, the
respondents were somewhat less likely to report contacts with
agency personnel than they had been in their first interview. Two
of the four groups reporting greater contact with agencies were
those who had lived in Cleveland the least amount of time. The
level of contact was also less clearly patterned than in the first
interview. Within race-sex groups, levels of contact with agencies
were greater in four of the longer duration-of-residence groups,
unchanged in three, and lower in one. Reports of contacts with
agencies tended to be more numerous among white males than
blacks, but the reverse was true for the women. The lowest level
of agency contact within the preceding year was reported by black
male long-term residents and early arrivals (8 percent and 9 percent respectively), while black female long-term residents had had
the greatest contact with agencies (26 percent).

PUBLIC DEPENDENCY

In the eyes of others and, to some extent, in the migrants'
own, to be a newcomer from the South implies a high likelihood of
ending up on welfare roles. (See, for example, the quotation from
the Appalachian Regional Council's journal, Appalachia, on
page xxv of the Introduction.)   Indeed, the notion that people
leave the South because of the lure of high welfare payments in
Northern states has been popular. 4 Yet only one group of migrants
(black females who had been in Cleveland less than two years when
first interviewed) was more likely to have received welfare at any
time in Cleveland than to have been entirely without dependence on
public assistance since arriving in the city (Table 5.16). In all
groups except black women, the odds for never having been on welfare in Cleveland ran two to one or better. * Just over two-fifths of

----

*In a sense, this finding is even more compelling evidence
against the "migration for welfare" argument than the census data.
The latter are based on a national sample which, of course, includes
the better-off migrants who do not take up residence in inner-city

TABLE 5.16

Dependence on Public Assistance in Cleveland by Sex, Race, and Duration
of Cleveland Residence
(percentages)

	Type of Respondent					
	White			Black		
Dependency Status	Latecomers	Early Arrivals	Long-Termers	Latecomers	Early Arrivals	Long-Termers
Males						
Never on welfare	76	70	73	71	71	72
Last welfare was more than 12 months earlier	4	11	12	9	10	18
Welfare within 12 months, not at present	10	9	10	11	8	5
Currently receiving welfare payments	9	10	5	9	10	5
Total	100	100	100	100	100	100
(N)	(117)	(145)	(105)	(79)	(77)	(61)
Females						
Never on welfare	67	72	70	44	57	48
Last welfare was more than 12 months earlier	8	7	8	5	9	12
Welfare within 12 months, not at present	4	7	2	6	6	--
Currently receiving welfare payments	21	14	21	45	28	40
Total	100	100	100	100	100	100
(N)	(48)	(72)	(53)	(94)	(108)	(80)

the most recent arrivals among the black female migrants and just
under three-fifths of the black female migrants with longer durations
of residence in the city escaped being on welfare in Cleveland altogether.

Among the women, blacks were twice as likely as whites to be
living in welfare households. Within each of these race groups,
long-termers (contrary to conventional wisdom) were as likely as
the migrants to be living in welfare households (Table 5.17).

Due to the trends between the two interview periods, these
earlier patterns of involvement with welfare persist at the later
time, but with several differences. Involvement with welfare, as
indicated by living in a welfare household, is still more prevalent
among the women, and this male-female difference is accentuated in
all groups except among the white early arrivals. By the same
criterion, black women are still more likely to be involved with welfare than white women and this difference is also greater at the time
of the second interview, except among the early arrivals.

Stability, rather than change of status with respect to receipt
of welfare payments, was characteristic of the study population
(Table 5.18). But when change occurred, in the interval between
the two rounds of fieldwork during which the economy began to slip
downward and unemployment rates rose, the direction of change was
far more toward becoming a welfare client or living in a household
in which someone else was receiving welfare than it was toward
freeing oneself of dependency on public assistance. In both the first
and second rounds of interviewing, roughly nine in ten of the male
migrants were found to be living in households in which no one was
receiving welfare. Among the females (a group that, again, included all migrant female heads of house), the proportions living in
welfare households were higher, but, even so, half or more were
found outside welfare households in both interviews. While no particular disadvantage with respect to welfare was found among the
households in which the black males were living, continuance in a
welfare status or becoming a member of a welfare household was
far more common among the black than among the white women.

The unfavorable ratios between new welfare households and
households that had ceased receiving welfare are, of course, due to
the disparity of the size of the two groups at the time of the first

---

poor neighborhoods. Participants in this study were originally found
in Cleveland's lowest-income neighborhoods and included all female
heads of house, irrespective of labor force status, thus loading the
study population with a subgroup with high probability of becoming
welfare clients.

TABLE 5.17

Percentage of Households in Which Anyone Was Currently
Receiving Welfare Payments

Type of Respondent	First Interview (T_1)	Reinterview (T_2)
White males		
Latecomers	--	13
	(117)	(117)
Early arrivals	1	14
	(145)	(145)
Long-termers	4	7
	(105)	(105)
Black males		
Latecomers	1	10
	(80)	(79)
Early arrivals	6	12
	(78)	(77)
Long-termers	5	8
	(61)	(61)
White females		
Latecomers	6	25
	(49)	(48)
Early arrivals	4	15
	(72)	(72)
Long-termers	19	25
	(53)	(52)
Black females		
Latecomers	15	46
	(95)	(94)
Early arrivals	22	30
	(109)	(107)
Long-termers	34	44
	(79)	(80)

TABLE 5.18

Welfare Status at Time of Second Interview Compared to Status When First Interviewed
(percentages)

Welfare Status	White			Black		
	Latecomers	Early Arrivals	Long-Termers	Latecomers	Early Arrivals	Long-Termers
Males						
In same status at both times						
Not living in welfare household*	87	85	90	89	83	88
Living in welfare household	--	--	1	--	1	2
In different position at the two times						
Household began receiving welfare	13	14	6	10	10	7
Household ceased receiving welfare	--	1	3	1	5	3
Total Percent	100	100	100	100	100	100
(N)	(117)	(145)	(105)	(79)	(77)	(61)
Females						
In same status at both times						
Not living in welfare household	71	82	71	53	65	52
Living in welfare household	2	1	15	14	17	30
In different position at the two times						
Household began receiving welfare	23	14	10	32	13	14
Household ceased receiving welfare	4	3	4	1	5	4
Total Percent	100	100	100	100	100	100
(N)	(48)	(72)	(52)	(94)	(107)	(79)

*As used here, the term "welfare household" denotes one in which any person was receiving welfare.

interview. A larger number of cases were found in new welfare households than were found in households that had ceased receiving welfare assistance simply because there were so many more non-welfare than welfare households originally. Because there were so few welfare households in the first round of interviews, we cannot control original status in order to examine the relative probabilities of having the household move into or out of welfare recipiency. However, it is possible to examine the comparison groups in terms of their differential risk of having the household begin receiving welfare (Table 5.19). Among the men originally found in welfare-free households, no particular disadvantage for whites or blacks is apparent, though migrants were slightly more likely than the long-termers to be found in welfare households at the time of the second round of interviews. A black woman clearly stood a stronger chance than a white woman of having her household become one in which welfare was being received, and those more recently arrived in the city appear more likely than those who had come earlier of being found in welfare households at the time of the second interview.

TABLE 5.19

Vulnerability to Welfare: Percentage of Respondents
Originally in Nonwelfare Households Who Were
Found in Welfare Households at the Time
of the Second Interview

	White Males	Black Males
Latecomers	13	10
	(117)	(78)
Early arrivals	15	11
	(144)	(72)
Long-termers	6	7
	(101)	(58)
	White Females	Black Females
Latecomers	24	38
	(45)	(80)
Early arrivals	14	17
	(69)	(84)
Long-termers	12	21
	(42)	(52)

Note: Numbers in parentheses are percentage bases, cases found outside welfare households at the time of the first interview.

Here the stratification of the study population by duration of residence gets in the way of the evidence. To properly appraise the apparent greater vulnerability to welfare dependency of the more recently arrived migrants, it would be necessary to follow the groups over time. This is because the ranks of the early arrivals in this comparison are excluded male-headed households that were receiving welfare at the time of the first interview. The group most like the recent arrivals who subsequently became members of welfare households were excluded from the tabulation at the outset.

ECONOMICALLY DISADVANTAGED HOUSEHOLDS

Comparison of the study groups in terms of the concept of disadvantaged households developed by the Manpower Administration is complicated by the criteria used to select subjects for the study initially and by the terms of the definition itself. Under the definition, a household is classified as disadvantaged if any member of the household is receiving welfare payments.* But at the same time, because our concern for the progress of female heads of house led us to include them initially irrespective of labor force or welfare status, the female comparison groups contained excess numbers, over the male groups, of study participants whose future was already in jeopardy. These fine points should not obscure the main image. We have seen all along that the men tend to be better off than the women, that they have better jobs, are less likely to be out of work, get paid more, and so forth. Yet somewhere between 14 and 26 percent of the men were either living in a household that was clearly disadvantaged or in one that was in the boundary area (Table 5.20). Every group of white women in the study was better situated than the opposite black comparison group; yet in two of the white female groups roughly a third were living in households that were clearly or marginally disadvantaged. Among the black females, between one-third and one-half were living in households that were clearly

---

*The Bureau of Labor Statistics (BLS) definition of "disadvantaged" is presented in the note to Table 5.20. In use here, the BLS definition was modified to include a marginal group, not clearly below nor clearly above the disadvantaged line in income, to compensate for the fact that the source data used in the study were interval coded. These data, unlike those prepared for national estimates, are also based on the respondents' estimate of the approximate cash income for the 12 months preceding the interview.

disadvantaged. Fewer black than white females were in the marginal group because that group was established to accommodate the ranges in income intervals. The larger proportion of black than white females in households receiving welfare more clearly establishes them in the definitely disadvantaged group.

TABLE 5.20

Poverty Status of Respondent's Household at Time
of Second Interview by Sex, Race, and Duration
of Cleveland Residence*
(percentages)

Poverty Status	Males		Females	
	White	Black	White	Black
Latecomers				
Disadvantaged	15	11	24	49
Marginal	5	4	6	7
Not disadvantaged	80	85	69	44
Total	100	100	100	100
(N)	(117)	(79)	(49)	(94)
Early arrivals				
Disadvantaged	15	14	18	33
Marginal	1	12	1	6
Not disadvantaged	84	74	81	62
Total	100	100	100	100
(N)	(145)	(77)	(72)	(107)
Long-termers				
Disadvantaged	8	10	28	48
Marginal	6	10	6	7
Not disadvantaged	86	80	67	45
Total	100	100	100	100
(N)	(104)	(59)	(51)	(75)

*This variable differs from the 1973 Manpower Administration definition by the inclusion of the near-poor category "marginal," necessitated by the form of the family income data (which were interval coded) and by use of unadjusted cash income for families. Otherwise, as in the Manpower Administration definition, persons were deemed to be poor or disadvantaged if their family income did not exceed the following levels for each size household: one person, $2,200; two persons, $2,900; three persons, $3,600; four persons, $4,300; five persons, $5,000; six persons, $5,700; seven persons, $6,400, or if anyone in the household was receiving welfare payments.

SELF-EVALUATIONS OF ECONOMIC POSITION

In each interview the migrants were asked to evaluate their current situation in terms of real income relative to their home community. In an attempt to control for cost-of-living and earnings differentials, as well as changes over the time between the two interviews, the migrants were asked:

> Lots of people have told us that they make more money here than they did back home, but that it also costs more to live here. Taking into account differences in what it costs to live back home and what it costs to live here in Cleveland and what you are able to make in the two places, how do you feel? Would you say that you are much better off here, only a bit better off here, that there isn't much difference between the two, or that you were better off back home?

Apparently the appraisal takes into account factors other than money, such as the psychological costs of being constantly surrounded by the environment of a depressed neighborhood. Although the migrants had experienced sizable economic gains, they had also lived through many of the undesirable aspects of ghetto residence. The change in the direction of being "much better off in Cleveland" between the two interviews is consistently higher among white than black migrants (Table 5.21). The upward shift in family income medians did not consistently produce positive self-appraisals of the migrants' own economic situation. In three of the eight comparison groups, the proportion who said that they were "much better off" in Cleveland than they would be back home was no greater at the time of the second interview, when aggregate incomes were higher, than at the time of the first interview. Black male latecomers, among whom median family income had risen by $3,100 over the time between the two interviews, was one of the groups in which there had been a slight downward shift in the real income appraisal. There is additional evidence that more than money is involved. At both times, white migrants were more likely than black migrants to evaluate their situation in Cleveland compared to what it would be back home in positive terms. Money aside, the urban milieu may also affect black and white men and women differently. At both times, white female migrants were consistently more likely than the men to evaluate their situation favorably. Among the black migrants, favorable evaluations tended to come more often from the men than the women. Perhaps the life space, even in poor neighborhoods, expands

for white women in the urban north while, relative to life in the
South, it contracts for black women. In either case, it seems that
the duration of experience in the new city is important; with only
two minor exceptions, the early arrivals were more likely than the
latecomers to say they were "much better off" in Cleveland than
back home.

These differing evaluations, and the attitudinal data presented
in the next chapter, provide some insight into the development of the
alienation that seems to overtake some black newcomers to the city.
Together they are indicators of feelings of dissatisfaction, alienation, or relative deprivation that emerge despite economic gains.

TABLE 5.21

Comparison of Real Income Between Cleveland and
Home Town: Percentage "Much Better Off"
in Cleveland

Type of Respondent	First Interview (T_1)	Reinterview (T_2)
White males		
Latecomers	47	55
	(116)	(117)
Early arrivals	54	54
	(143)	(143)
Black males		
Latecomers	34	32
	(80)	(79)
Early arrivals	42	46
	(78)	(77)
White females		
Latecomers	57	62
	(49)	(47)
Early arrivals	56	65
	(72)	(72)
Black females		
Latecomers	28	30
	(95)	(92)
Early arrivals	42	39
	(109)	(104)

NOTES

1. See Victor Fuchs, "Women's Earnings: Recent Trends and Long-Range Prospects," Monthly Labor Review 97, no. 5 (May 1974): 23-26. The ratio of women's to men's medians was also below similar ratios calculated by Fuchs.

2. See U.S. Bureau of the Census, Statistical Abstract of the United States, 93rd edition (Washington, D.C.: U.S. Government Printing Office, 1972), Table 372, p. 233.

3. This topic is the subject of several chapters in Cynthia B. Lloyd, ed., Sex Discrimination and the Divison of Labor (New York: Columbia University Press, 1975).

4. Larry H. Long discusses and documents the rising concern about migration from the South for the purpose of gaining access to higher welfare payments and provides data from the 1970 census that are counter to the popular argument in his paper "Poverty Status and Receipt of Welfare among Migrants and Nonmigrants in Large Cities," American Sociological Review 39, no. 1 (February 1974): 46-56.

6

EXPLORING THE HUMAN MEANING OF OCCUPATIONAL ADJUSTMENT AND MOBILITY

Previous chapters have dealt mainly with trends in objective aspects of the migrant's life space. In this chapter we describe trends and countertrends in the subjective aspects of the migrant's life space, but we will also from time to time introduce new data on some feature of our respondents' objective situation to provide a context for interpretation of the attitudinal data being presented.

Following the logic of the earlier analyses, we will continue to deal primarily with differences and similarities between the various groups in our study: men and women, blacks and whites, migrants and long-termers. However, the intent is not to provide an accounting of individual differences in subjective states or changes in them; rather, it is to set down alongside the earlier described trends in labor force participation, occupations, and earnings a series of trends and countertrends that highlight selected features of the human meaning of occupational adjustment and mobility among a low-income migrant population in a Northern industrial city.

The data presented in this chapter share with recent studies of perceived life quality a concern with measuring the human meaning of social change. The current effort differs from other recent related efforts, however, in one important respect. Our data were developed, not as a systematic set of descriptors of perceived life quality, but rather as a series of empirical probes into social and psychological dimensions that have not generally received attention in studies of migrants or of occupational adjustment consequent to migration.

In developing this more exploratory section of our research instruments, we sought to include topics from a wide diversity of measurement domains for which questionnaire items were available and whose repeated measurement was expected to help identify the

broader social and personal meaning of trends in labor force participation, occupational mobility, and earnings. In line with this objective, the research instruments were designed to provide information
on residential mobility and trends in place-related satisfactions,
work satisfaction, alienation, and perceptions of social progress in
the solution of social problems.

On the basis of analysis of the first round of interviews, it became clear that these diverse indicators did help us to identify sources
of satisfaction, as well as sources of frustration, in the lives of our
respondents. Nonetheless, it was extremely difficult to balance these
findings out so as to gauge what effect the move to and early years in
Cleveland had had on our respondents' overall sense of well-being.
To meet this need for a broad assessment of the quality of our respondents' lives, we decided that in our reinterviews we would let
the respondents themselves balance out their satisfactions and frustrations by reporting on their overall sense of well-being. These
self-reports on overall well-being were elicited through a modified
version of the Cantril self-anchoring striving scale (a series of items
dealing with personal hopes and fears, and ratings of self in relation
to those hopes and fears for the past, present, and future).

The organization of the present chapter reflects the development of our efforts to describe social and psychological trends con-
comitant to our respondents' experiences in the Cleveland labor market during the years covered by our study. First we present the results of our detailed probes into the social and psychological life
space of the study group. After that, we present a somewhat lengthier
analysis of our respondents' self-reports on life quality.

RESIDENTIAL MOBILITY AND PLACE-RELATED
SATISFACTIONS

Given the frequency with which the hope of a better standard of
living leads people to pick themselves up and travel to a distant city,
it is important to know to what extent these same people continue to
make local residential moves at their place of destination. Moreover, given the importance of an occupation in providing the economic
resources that make such local moves possible, it is important to determine the extent of trends in residential mobility that are correlative to occupational changes. For these reasons information was obtained in both rounds of interviewing on residential mobility, home
ownership, satisfaction with housing and neighborhood, and the prospects of future migration.

Residential Mobility

To some degree, residential mobility is a corollary of geographical mobility. Both types of movement share some of the same sources of motivation, access to or avoidance of desirable or undesirable aspects in the life space of the individuals concerned. In that regard, settling in also often entails moving about as the newcomers adjust their residences in view of changing employment and earnings statuses, the arrival of additional family members, or the formation of new households; or, on the avoidance side, to evade creditors. Apparently, the pattern of local mobility begins relatively soon after arrival in the city; more than two-fifths of all groups of those who had arrived most recently in Cleveland had moved at least once by the time of their first interview.* At that time, as in the later interview, a time-related aspect of local mobility was also relevant. Those who had lived in the city longest were most likely to have moved; in the time between the two interviews, levels of mobility tended to shift upwards (see Figure 6.1). The three instances in which the mobility reported in the second interview was lower than or equal to that reported in the first interview are interesting examples of recall error. Aside from the fact that the definition of neighborhood was left to the respondent, we have no other explanation for the lower levels of mobility reported in the second interview. In both interviews, however, mobility of black respondents was higher than that of whites, and levels of mobility within race were about equal for men and women.

To some extent, for the successful newcomers, settling in also entails moving out; in this sense, moving out of residences in the poorest neighborhoods, where the respondents were found for the first round of interviews, to neighborhoods located farther from the centers of poverty in the city. While the majority of respondents continued to live in the neighborhoods in which they were first found, the shift to neighborhoods on the fringes of the city and in the suburban communities was substantial (and, surprisingly in terms of earlier residential segregation in the city, about equal for blacks

---

*Levels of social mobility encountered by the interviewers in the neighborhood canvass to locate the original respondents were among the factors calling for modification of the original field procedures. Because so many of the newcomers moved soon after being located, we abandoned plans to use less skilled interviewers as canvassers, assigned more highly skilled interviewers to the task, and authorized them to complete the detailed personal interview immediately with persons who met the criteria for inclusion in the study.

FIGURE 6.1

Residential Mobility: Location of Residence at First
and Second Interviews (Male Respondents)

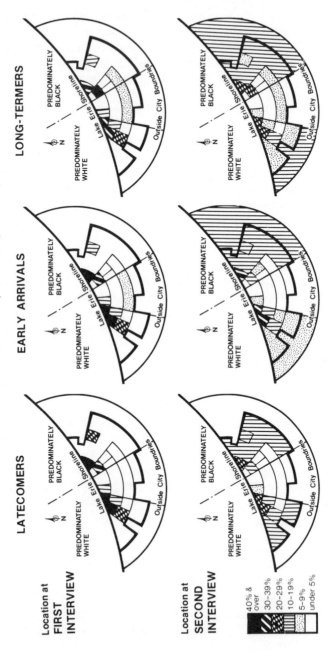

Note: Residential patterns for female respondents were virtually identical.

208

and whites). Except for the outward movement of the blacks on the
East Side, the respondents made little contribution toward the residential integration of Cleveland. Few in either group crossed the
river or district boundaries to move into areas predominantly inhabited by members of the other racial group.

Home Ownership

We observed on several occasions that the continued use of the
term "migrants" to designate the Southern newcomers had pejorative
connotations and was in fact a small exercise in labeling. By impli-
cation, one is led to expect instability and further movement; while,
in fact, the modal expectation of the newcomers was that the move to
Cleveland would be a permanent one. Informants who saw the first-
round data were surprised at the extent to which the newcomers had
acted on their inclination toward permanent residence in the city by
purchasing homes, and were particularly impressed by the finding
that the level of home purchase among the migrants was higher for
blacks than whites.

The more recent data show a general increase in home ownership or purchase. In assessing these data it is important to remem-
ber that these respondents are the survivors from earlier waves of
newcomers. At the same time, however, it is also important to re-
member that the original search for migrants and interviewing was
done in the city's poorest neighborhoods.

Residential ownership is clearly related to duration of residence. In every instance long-termers were more likely than migrants to be buying their own homes (as roughly half of the male
long-term residents were). But the rate of investment in their own
homes had gone up so that every group of later migrants stood at or
above the highest rate for earlier migrants in the 1968 data, while
the earlier migrants were approaching or had attained levels of home
ownership previously attained by the long-term residents.

Neighborhoods and Housing

Satisfaction with residential neighborhoods, which was low to
begin with, appears to have fallen off slightly. Given the choice,
somewhat fewer in 1972 than in 1968 would choose to live in the same
neighborhood. White migrants, male and female, were most likely
to choose suburban communities as a site for future residence.
Among black migrants the choice was more evenly balanced between
other areas in Cleveland and the desire to move outward to suburban

areas. Despite their inclination to move on to other neighborhoods, most who had moved felt that they had bettered their life surroundings. This amount of change or improvement was greater for migrants than for the long-term residents. As a result the 1972 data show the mobile migrants more likely than long-termers to rate their current neighborhood as better than their last. Though the differences are slight, in 1972 mobile white migrants were more likely than blacks to say that they had moved to a better neighborhood.

Prospects of Future Migration

Most of the migrants and long-term residents who were not native Clevelanders said they never experienced the desire to leave Cleveland and return home, or, if they did, the desire was an infrequent one occurring no more often than "once in a while." However, the number of those who felt differently was far from negligible. Nostalgia was most commonly experienced by the whites, whose longing for their home country is a major theme in bluegrass and mountain music. When first interviewed, between 19 and 35 percent of the whites and roughly twice as many as among the black respondents said they thought about leaving for home "some" or "most of the time."

By the time of the second interview, levels of nostalgia were generally higher. In three of the four race-sex groups the long-term residents were less likely than other migrants to express relatively frequent bouts with nostalgia, but there was no clear patterning as between earlier and more recent migrants. In 9 of the 12 comparison groups, the number expressing relatively frequent nostalgia was greater than observed in the first round of interviews with these same respondents; the level of this kind of expressed discontent was higher for all except white and black female long-term residents and for earlier white female migrants.

Parallel findings were obtained when we investigated the prospects for future migration, either to return home or to move to another city. To a degree, the desirability of Cleveland as a life site for the future had waned. In both rounds of interviews the respondents were asked what kind of work they would most like to do in the future and where they would like to exercise that occupation. In the first interviews Cleveland was the overwhelming choice for future residence in connection with a preferred occupation (for between 59 and 67 percent of the white male migrants). Women and black males were even more likely to name Cleveland as the preferred site (as 80 percent or more in each group did). Over time, however, the popularity of Cleveland fell in all but two groups. White males, especially among the migrants, were least likely to regard Cleveland

as the best setting for one's choice of work; they were closely followed by white females. Among black respondents the popularity of
Cleveland had sagged less than among whites. Here the long-term
residents were less likely than migrants to consider Cleveland an
ideal workplace (though at least 80 percent in each group did).

The proportion who said they had given no thought at all to leaving Cleveland and moving elsewhere had also fallen slightly. In the
first round at least 70 percent in each group had not been thinking
about moving from Cleveland. Four years later that proportion had
dropped in three groups (to a low of 56 percent among earlier white
male migrants).

Work Satisfaction

Work satisfaction was a second general area selected for prob-
ing in both interviews. Job satisfaction is a direct indicator of worker
well-being on the job, and an indirect indicator of worker well-being
off the job. Work satisfaction is also a dimension of worker well-
being that is directly and predominantly affected by qualities of a person's job rather than by personal or demographic characteristics.
Cross-sectional differences in job satisfaction between the sexes or
the races can be traced thereby to the kinds of jobs that prevail
among workers in each of these respective groupings. Similarly,
changes in job satisfaction may well reflect changes in occupations
held.

Self-evaluation of jobs in terms of work satisfaction tends to be
consistent with our own impressions of the kinds of jobs the respondents had. With only two exceptions, both in the second-round interviews, only among white workers did as many as half regard themselves as very satisfied with their jobs (Table 6.1). When the proportions "very satisfied" and "fairly satisfied" are combined, however, the overall levels of satisfaction are comparable to national
estimates for the same time periods, as are the differences that exist
between the race groups. Across time the level of job satisfaction
appears to have increased for black men and women but to have held
steady for white female workers and fallen slightly for the white
males. The main reason for this, at least for black males, probably
lies in the fact that they have made greater gains in occupational
status between the first and second interviews than have white males.*

_____

*Job satisfaction was measured in each interview by the fol-
lowing question: "Would you say that you are very satisfied, fairly
satisfied, or not satisfied?" As Quinn and his associates have pointed

TABLE 6.1

Satisfaction with Current Job at the Time of the First and
Second Interviews by Type of Respondent, Sex, and Race
(percentages)

Degree of Satisfaction	Type of Respondent					
	Latecomers		Early Arrivals		Long–Termers	
	Time of Interview					
	First	Second	First	Second	First	Second
White males						
Very satisfied	60 }94	55 }92	46 }88	45 }89	57 }91	47 }92
Somewhat satisfied	34	37	42	44	34	45
Not satisfied	6	8	11	11	9	7
Total percent	100	100	100	100	100	100
(N)	(108)	(98)	(134)	(120)	(99)	(84)
Black males						
Very satisfied	31 }75	43 }84	16 }79	36 }83	34 }82	51 }90
Somewhat satisfied	44	41	63	47	48	39
Not satisfied	24	16	20	18	18	10
Total percent	100	100	100	100	100	100
(N)	(70)	(63)	(73)	(62)	(56)	(51)
White females						
Very satisfied	52 }90	54 }92	48 }92	51 }91	65 }92	67 }94
Somewhat satisfied	38	38	44	40	27	27
Not satisfied	10	8	8	9	8	7
Total percent	100	100	100	100	100	100
(N)	(29)	(24)	(48)	(43)	(37)	(30)
Black females						
Very satisfied	28 }77	38 }88	22 }72	40 }95	30 }74	54 }96
Somewhat satisfied	49	50	50	55	44	42
Not satisfied	23	12	28	5	26	4
Total percent	100	100	100	100	100	100
(N)	(47)	(42)	(68)	(58)	(46)	(48)

By and large white males made their greatest change in occupational status upon entering the Cleveland work force.[2]

ALIENATION

Broad general agreement undoubtedly exists for the view that communities in which people trust one another, as well as their public officials, and in which the future is viewed with hope and a sense of personal control, are generally much better places to live in than are communities in which this is not the case. On the basis of this premise, respondents were asked both in 1968 and 1972 to state their agreement or disagreement with a series of statements designed to assess trust, faith in people, and general optimism (Table 6.2). The responses to these questions, which have been frequently used in studies to measure alienation, indicate a pervasive deterioration in trust, faith in people, and general optimism between the two time periods for persons in all race, sex, and duration-of-residence groups.

The first statement ("These days a person doesn't really know who he can count on") shows this growth of negative sentiments between the two interview periods less strongly simply because the percentage of agreements was already so high at the time of the first interview that a "ceiling effect" became operative. Table 6.3 takes these effects into account and shows the extent to which negative feelings increased between 1967-68 and 1972, in terms of both absolute and relative change. There is little evidence in these two sets of data that migrants generally hold more positive attitudes than long-term residents. In fact, among the white males, the opposite seems to be true. Only among black males does the response pattern suggest somewhat more positive initial attitude constellations; but by the time of the second interview--when migrants had between four and nine years of Cleveland residence--no residual differences remained and the responses of long-term residents and migrants looked very much alike. Among women, the initial responses of migrants and long-term residents were very similar; by the time of the second interview women migrants tended to be more alienated than long-term residents, thus lending additional credence to our findings about the negative labor force experiences of female migrants in Cleveland.

---

out, this particular question wording produces a conservative estimate of work dissatisfaction.[1] At the time these observations were made, surveys of U.S. workers using almost identical question wording were showing 90 percent of male workers to be "very satisfied" or "satisfied" with their jobs.

TABLE 6.2

Changes in Attitudinal Indicators of Social Alienation Between 1968 and 1972
(percentage agreeing)

Attitudinal Indicator*	Men						Women					
	White			Black			White			Black		
Years in Cleveland →	Late-comers	Early Arrivals	Long-Termers	Late-comers	Early Arrivals	Long-Termers	Late-comers	Early Arrivals	Long-Termers	Late-comers	Early Arrivals	Long-Termers
These days a person doesn't really know who he can count on.												
First interview	73	78	48	79	72	71	88	78	55	80	85	65
Second interview	81	77	70	77	81	75	90	85	64	77	82	76
Nowadays a person has to live pretty much for today and let tomorrow take care of itself.												
First interview	51	43	40	49	41	56	53	58	45	59	44	44
Second interview	59	50	51	56	55	69	50	67	55	70	70	63
It's hardly fair to bring children into the world with the way things look for the future.												
First interview	47	50	27	31	33	34	60	58	34	43	50	35
Second interview	70	63	55	60	53	41	79	76	54	57	61	50
There's little use writing or talking to public officials because they aren't interested in your problems.												
First interview	46	53	43	46	36	53	42	41	42	37	41	44
Second interview	61	67	56	63	57	57	55	65	51	63	70	57
In spite of what some people say, things are getting worse for the average man, not better												
First interview	51	53	37	38	42	37	50	44	40	33	30	28
Second interview	63	66	67	70	64	79	71	67	60	75	77	61
Minimum base for percentages	(112)	(141)	(102)	(79)	(77)	(60)	(48)	(68)	(50)	(94)	(108)	(79)

*These questions are from an index of social integration developed by Leo Srole (see his article, "Social Integration and Certain Corollaries," American Sociological Review 21, no. 4 [1956]: 709–16). All five questions are from the original index were asked.

TABLE 6.3

Absolute and Proportional Shifts in Responses to Attitudinal Indicators of Social Alienation*

(percentages)

Attitudinal Indicators	Men — White			Men — Black			Women — White			Women — Black		
Years in Cleveland	Late-comers	Early Arrivals	Long-Termers	Late-comers	Early Arrivals	Long-Termers	Late-comers	Early Arrivals	Long-Termers	Late-comers	Early Arrivals	Long-Termers
These days a person doesn't really know who he can count on.												
Absolute change	8	-1	22	-2	9	4	2	7	9	-3	-3	11
Proportional change	30	-1	42	-2	32	14	17	32	20	-4	-4	31
Nowadays a person has to live pretty much for today and let tomorrow take care of itself.												
Absolute change	8	7	11	7	14	13	-3	9	10	11	26	19
Proportional change	16	12	18	14	24	30	-6	21	18	27	46	34
It's hardly fair to bring children into the world with the way things look for the future.												
Absolute change	23	13	28	29	20	7	19	18	20	14	11	15
Proportional change	43	26	38	42	30	11	48	43	30	25	22	23
There's little use writing or talking to public officials because they aren't interested in your problems.												
Absolute change	15	14	13	17	21	4	13	24	9	26	29	13
Proportional change	28	30	23	32	33	8	22	41	16	41	49	23
In spite of what some people say, things are getting worse for the average man, not better												
Absolute change	12	13	30	32	22	42	21	23	20	43	47	33
Proportional change	24	28	48	52	38	67	42	41	33	64	67	46

*Data base is percentage agreeing with each attitudinal statement, shown in preceding table. Absolute shifts are signed differences in percentages agreeing with the statements in the first and in the second interview. Proportional changes are adjusted for ceiling and floor limitations on the amount of change possible, because many of the shifts were constrained by ceiling effects. Upward proportional shifts were computed by the Effectiveness Index $\frac{P_2-P_1}{100-P_1}$ proposed by Hoveland, Lumsdaine and Sheffield (see their Experiment in Mass Communications [Princeton, N.J.: Princeton University Press, 1949], pp. 284–89). Downward shifts were computed by the formula $\frac{P_2-P_1}{P_1}$ to adjust for floor effects.

In addition to being direct indicators of one important aspect of the quality of our respondents' lives, these same data raise an important issue about the aggregate impact of psychological variables, such as alienation, on the functioning of labor markets. The smooth functioning of labor markets assumes that workers are willing to take initiatives in searching for jobs that provide good job-worker matches. The willingness of workers to engage in such initiatives depends, however, on their belief that better job-worker matches are possible. and can be found through their personal efforts. Feelings of alienation, however, erode the foundations of these psychological prerequisites of labor market functioning. This issue, which data such as those presented here merely raise, needs to be addressed in future analyses of labor market functioning.

PERCEPTIONS OF SOCIAL PROBLEMS

The decline in general optimism that has just been described is also reflected in our respondents' perceptions of the extent to which progress had been made in the solution of various social problems impinging in important ways on their life histories. This was the final area that was probed in both interviews.

Views on Race Relations and Discrimination

Although most respondents were not optimistic about the racial situation in 1968, pessimism increased markedly between the two interview periods, especially among black study participants. In 1968, about 20 percent of the respondents or more perceived the racial situation in Cleveland as improving; and among the black long-termers almost 50 percent saw such improvements. Generally, at that time, more long-termers than migrants thought that the racial situation had got better and, within each duration-of-residence group, more whites than blacks saw improvement. By and large men saw improvement more often than did women.

Since the first interview, however, the proportion of respondents perceiving improvement in the racial situation had decreased in most groups. In several instances the decrease had been substantial. Among black female long-termers, for example, there was a downward shift of 33 percentage points; among black male long-termers, a downward shift of 21 percentage points; and among black female early arrivals and white male long-termers, downward shifts of 17 and 13 percentage points respectively.

Except for long-termers, men continued to make more positive assessments of the racial situation than did the women; within each sex group, more whites than blacks saw an improvement. Generally, migrants more than long-termers saw an overall improvement. However, the sizable changes among black respondents shown in Table 6.4 suggest that perceptions of heightened racial hostility may well have played a part in the attitude changes observed in this study.

TABLE 6.4

Trends in Racial Relations: Percentage Perceiving
Situation as Improving

Type of Respondent	First Interview (T_1)	Reinterview (T_2)
White males		
Latecomers	19	29
	(116)	(116)
Early arrivals	12	31
	(143)	(144)
Long-termers	32	18
	(104)	(104)
Black males		
Latecomers	28	22
	(80)	(80)
Early arrivals	22	20
	(78)	(77)
Long-termers	52	30
	(59)	(61)
White females		
Latecomers	22	20
	(49)	(49)
Early arrivals	9	22
	(69)	(71)
Long-termers	27	17
	(52)	(52)
Black females		
Latecomers	23	18
	(92)	(95)
Early arrivals	33	16
	(107)	(109)
Long-termers	48	15
	(79)	(80)

Blacks not only saw a deterioration in race relations; they also felt that it affected their own lives.* Even at the time of the first interview, blacks far more often than whites reported that discrimination had retarded their personal careers (Table 6.5). Among the men, for example, no more than 8 percent of the whites in any residence group reported that they had been held back in life due to discrimination, yet 46 percent of the blacks reported such personal hardship. Among the women, more than twice as many blacks as whites reported negative effects of discrimination on their personal careers. Finally, more black men than black women reported that they had been held back by discrimination.

Since the first interview there has been an upward trend in the proportion of respondents who identify discrimination as a source of personal setbacks in their lives. Although there are exceptions, this increase has generally been greater among blacks than among whites, and generally greater among women than among men. By the second interview, over two-fifths of the blacks reported that they had been held back personally in life due to discrimination; and among the blacks, the men continued to report this experience slightly more often than did the women. The earlier difference between blacks and whites in this regard persists; but among the white migrants, women now report being held back due to discrimination twice as often as men. These data do not suggest that white men were aware of the kind of reverse discrimination that, it is claimed, now exists in some work contexts, but women had clearly become more aware of the issue of discrimination.

Views on the Economic Situation and
Individual Life Chances

So far, we have found evidence in our data of some disenchantment with the quality of life in Cleveland, and some nostalgia for the premigration existence; we have also located some of the sources of dissatisfaction in feelings of increasing racial hostility and in greater awareness of the impact of racial and sex discrimination on one's personal life. The data we have shown are suggestive, but not dramatic. The findings dealing with respondents' attitudes in the economic sphere leave no doubt, however, that substantial changes took place between 1968 and 1972.

---

*The data reported here are broadly consistent with other data on deteriorating optimism, increasing militancy, and increased perception of white obstructionism reported by Howard Schuman and Shirley Hatchett.[3]

TABLE 6.5

Effects of Discrimination: Percentage Held Back
Personally in Life by Discrimination

Type of Respondent	First Interview (T_1)	Reinterview (T_2)
White males		
Latecomers	8	6
	(116)	(117)
Early arrivals	8	8
	(145)	(145)
Long-termers	1	2
	(105)	(105)
Black males		
Latecomers	45	50
	(80)	(80)
Early arrivals	45	58
	(78)	(78)
Long-termers	46	46
	(61)	(61)
White females		
Latecomers	8	12
	(49)	(49)
Early arrivals	7	19
	(72)	(72)
Long-termers	4	--
	(53)	(53)
Black females		
Latecomers	31	41
	(93)	(95)
Early arrivals	38	44
	(109)	(109)
Long-termers	30	45
	(80)	(80)

As one would expect in the light of a general downward turn in
the level of economic activity, there was a decline in the pervasive
optimism regarding the availability of jobs for "all of the people who
are moving to Cleveland" that was observed in the first round of interviews (Table 6.6). This decrease in optimism about the job situation was greater for men than women (except among the white

long-termers), was greater for blacks than whites, and was greater for migrants (except among white women) than long-termers. On the whole, however, while the earlier differences between men and women, between whites and blacks, and between migrants and long-termers persisted, there was a decrease in the distance between these groups attitudinally.

TABLE 6.6

Attitudes Toward Migrants: Percentage Agreeing That
There Is Plenty of Work for Everyone

Type of Respondent	First Interview (T$_1$)	Reinterview (T$_2$)
White males		
Latecomers	78	22
	(116)	(116)
Early arrivals	78	19
	(144)	(144)
Long-termers	61	15
	(104)	(103)
Black males		
Latecomers	65	14
	(79)	(79)
Early arrivals	56	12
	(77)	(78)
Long-termers	44	12
	(59)	(61)
White females		
Latecomers	61	12
	(46)	(49)
Early arrivals	69	21
	(68)	(68)
Long-termers	62	13
	(52)	(53)
Black females		
Latecomers	52	7
	(91)	(94)
Early arrivals	49	7
	(108)	(108)
Long-termers	31	2
	(77)	(79)

While relatively few respondents at either time agreed that something should be done to stop people from coming to Cleveland, there was also a general overall increase in the proportions of respondents, particularly among white women, who agreed that direct action to reduce migration should be taken. This, too, is consistent with the overall decline in optimism about jobs (Table 6.7).

TABLE 6.7

Attitudes Toward Migrants: Percentage Agreeing That Migrants Should Be Stopped from Coming to Cleveland

Type of Respondent	First Interview (T_1)	Reinterview (T_2)
White males		
Latecomers	8	12
	(116)	(144)
Early arrivals	14	16
	(144)	(144)
Long-termers	22	29
	(104)	(105)
Black males		
Latecomers	4	10
	(79)	(80)
Early arrivals	6	12
	(78)	(78)
Long-termers	20	10
	(60)	(61)
White females		
Latecomers	2	22
	(48)	(49)
Early arrivals	6	14
	(71)	(70)
Long-termers	19	33
	(53)	(52)
Black females		
Latecomers	4	8
	(95)	(95)
Early arrivals	6	11
	(108)	(109)
Long-termers	12	14
	(78)	(79)

A noteworthy consequence of the perceived deterioration in the larger environment is some erosion in the belief that the individual, through hard work and self-improvement, can control his destiny and improve his situation. When this low-income population was first interviewed in 1968, their responses conveyed a very high commitment to the work ethic and great faith in the individual's ability to succeed through his own efforts; in this respect, these Cleveland respondents were quite typical of poor people studied by other investigators, whose faith in the system had not been eroded by their personal difficulties. [4] But by 1972 important changes had taken place.

The way in which we investigated this dimension was to ask a broad open-ended question, "Why do you think some people are always poor?" The responses were recorded in detail for later coding. Because many of the answers included more than one reason, we developed a priority code. If any mention was made of "system working against people," that code was assigned. We then took out all mentions of lack of education or training. If neither of these was mentioned, we looked for statements indicating that individuals are responsible for their own failures. Finally, we coded those responses that mentioned only bad luck. In their first interviews, no fewer than 46 percent of the respondents in any of the comparison groups passed over systemic defects and training failures to focus on individual responsibility (Table 6.8). Only a minority, most often the white women latecomers (20 percent), blamed the system, but at most only 13 percent in any of the other groups.

Since the first interview, however, the perception of the system as a source of poverty has increased for every group except one. In nine of the groups there has been an increase of almost ten percentage points or better, and in four of the groups, an increase of almost 20 percentage points or better. Overall, the increase has been greater among the blacks than among the whites.

By the second interview, roughly a fifth or more of the respondents in all but one of the groups perceived the system as a cause of poverty. Except among the latecomers at this time, blacks were slightly more likely than whites to perceive the system as a source of poverty. Except for the black long-termers, men were slightly more likely than women to attribute poverty to systemic causes.

Conversely, there was a decline in the proportion of respondents who continued to adhere to the individualistic belief that poverty was the fault of the poor (Table 6.9). Although at least half of all respondents continued to hold this view, this represents a marked decline over the earlier period. Long-termers were especially likely to have changed their mind in this respect.

TABLE 6.8

Why Some People Are Always Poor: Percentage
Giving "System's Fault" as Reason

Type of Respondent	First Interview (T_1)	Reinterview (T_2)
White males		
Latecomers	11	23
	(117)	(117)
Early arrivals	12	21
	(142)	(145)
Long-termers	10	21
	(104)	(105)
Black males		
Latecomers	13	25
	(79)	(80)
Early arrivals	12	32
	(78)	(76)
Long-termers	12	35
	(60)	(60)
White females		
Latecomers	20	18
	(49)	(49)
Early arrivals	8	20
	(72)	(71)
Long-termers	8	15
	(53)	(53)
Black females		
Latecomers	10	18
	(94)	(92)
Early arrivals	6	25
	(108)	(108)
Long-termers	10	36
	(80)	(80)

TABLE 6.9

Why Some People Are Always Poor: Percentage Giving "Their Own Fault" as Reason

Type of Respondent	First Interview (T_1)	Reinterview (T_2)
White males		
Latecomers	68	50
	(117)	(117)
Early arrivals	63	51
	(142)	(145)
Long-termers	69	42
	(104)	(105)
Black males		
Latecomers	51	55
	(79)	(80)
Early arrivals	46	53
	(78)	(76)
Long-termers	63	47
	(60)	(60)
White females		
Latecomers	49	57
	(49)	(49)
Early arrivals	62	51
	(72)	(71)
Long-termers	79	51
	(53)	(53)
Black females		
Latecomers	67	51
	(94)	(92)
Early arrivals	65	50
	(108)	(108)
Long-termers	55	44
	(80)	(80)

SELF-REPORTS ON LIFE QUALITY

Using information on perceptions of social problems, alienation, work satisfaction, place-related satisfactions, and residential
mobility, it is difficult to assess our respondents' overall well-being
at the time they were last interviewed. For this reason, we sought
to develop from our second round of interviews a set of measurements that could be used to summarize our respondents' own perceptions of their progress and hopes for the future. Toward this end,
we included in our follow-up interviews a modified version of the
Cantril self-anchoring striving scale.[5]

In retrospect, the inclusion of the Cantril items in our follow-
up interviews was particularly fortuitous for two reasons: (1) recent
efforts to develop measures of perceived life quality have emphasized
the importance of taking respondents' values into account in an assessment of the meaning of such measurements; and (2) it is particularly
important to do this in the context of assessing occupational adjustment consequent to migration. One of the longstanding criticisms of
past research on the assimilation of in-migrants to Northern cities
has been that the criteria used to evaluate the extent of assimilation
have been biased in the direction of the values of the host community.[6]
The Cantril scale produces measures of perceived life quality and
achievement framed in terms of each subject's values and aspirations.

In the Cantril striving scale technique, the subjects are first
asked to describe what, for them, would be the best and worst possible life situation or condition. (The substance of the hopes and
fears mentioned is subsequently coded by major categories of concern.) After the respondent has described his best and worst possible life situation, he is shown a drawing of a ladder (similar to the
one shown in Figure 6.2) and asked to indicate where he currently
stands on this "ladder of life" if the top represents his best possible
life situation and the bottom the worst. He is also asked to indicate
where he stood in the past and where he thinks he will stand in the
future. The respondent thereby provides a verbal mapping of his
own idealized life space from its best and worst perspectives and a
series of ratings (present, past, and future) of his achievement and
aspirations in terms of the idealization.

Hopes and Fears

In articulating their hopes and fears for the future, the migrants are primarily concerned with those aspects of life whose
personal and familial impact is immediate--a better standard of

living, a good job, and continued or improved health. Aspects of
life beyond the family seldom enter into definitions of future personal happiness (Tables 6.10 and 6.11).

FIGURE 6.2

Ladder Drawing Used to Obtain Life Ratings

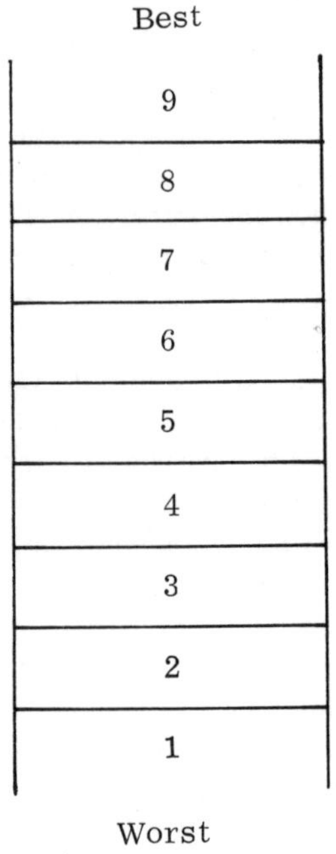

Best

9
8
7
6
5
4
3
2
1

Worst

     A better standard of living for self and family is the most wide-
ly expressed personal hope; in their hopes for the future, over 70
percent of the respondents in each group mention a better standard
of living for self and family (see Table 6.10). Among the blacks,
migrants were slightly more likely than long-term residents to have
hopes centered on an improved standard of living. The centrality of
standard of living concerns in the hopes of the respondents has its
corollary in their fears. Among the fears, general financial situations and jobs or work--key elements in standard of living improve-
ment--were mentioned far more often than other topics (see Table
6.11).

TABLE 6.10

Personal Hopes by Sex, Race, and Type of Respondent
(data shown are percentages of respondents
expressing hopes about each topic)

| | Males | | | | | | Females | | | | | |
| | White | | | Black | | | White | | | Black | | |
Topic of Concern	Late-comers	Early Arrivals	Long-Termers	Late-comers	Early Arrivals	Long-Termers	Late-comers	Early Arrivals	Long-Termers	Late-comers	Early Arrivals	Long-Termers
Hopes for self and family												
Better standard of living	80	76	75	80	87	72	82	76	79	82	83	71
Good job	41	48	48	54	46	31	35	28	43	54	39	34
Health	23	29	42	10	13	28	43	39	38	16	17	24
Education and training	18	22	18	19	27	28	22	21	11	38	35	27
Leave Cleveland	10	14	6	1	—	3	10	15	8	2	3	5
Own character development	6	5	4	6	8	10	8	6	6	6	12	5
Other hopes for family	15	10	10	15	13	5	14	17	15	10	8	9
Other hopes for children	9	8	8	2	1	10	22	20	9	8	6	14
Other hopes for self	28	26	37	24	18	36	21	31	49	23	23	19
Hopes for others, community, or nation												
Moral, aesthetic, or religious affairs	2	3	4	2	3	2	8	4	4	1	1	4
Political, economic, or social affairs	3	—	3	—	3	5	2	—	4	2	—	1
International affairs	2	1	2	—	—	2	2	1	4	—	1	3
Other hopes for others	3	2	4	6	5	—	2	1	8	5	5	4
(Minimum N)	(117)	(145)	(105)	(80)	(78)	(61)	(49)	(72)	(53)	(95)	(109)	(80)

227

TABLE 6.11

Personal Fears by Sex, Race, and Type of Respondent
(data shown are percentages of respondents
expressing fears about each topic)

Topic of Concern	Males						Females					
	White			Black			White			Black		
	Late-comers	Early Arrivals	Long-Termers	Late-comers	Early Arrivals	Long-Termers	Late-comers	Early Arrivals	Long-Termers	Late-comers	Early Arrivals	Long-Termers
Fears for self and family												
Job or work situation	45	58	60	62	59	51	47	40	38	40	51	28
Other financial worries	44	50	50	60	60	52	43	54	40	60	62	45
Health	32	32	43	28	31	46	37	25	51	36	44	31
Education	2	3	3	8	9	5	2	12	--	3	1	14
Death	9	9	13	1	1	5	8	15	13	3	7	8
Morals, crime, drugs, or alcohol	6	7	3	1	5	5	6	8	2	4	3	7
Other concerns about self or family	23	26	15	17	12	10	26	28	30	13	16	17
Fears for others, community, or nation												
Morals, crime, drugs, or alcohol	3	5	4	6	6	2	6	7	6	2	5	10
Political, economic, or social affairs	8	4	5	2	6	2	2	7	9	3	1	1
International affairs	8	7	4	--	--	3	8	11	13	3	1	4
Aesthetic, religious, or health concerns	2	3	3	2	--	2	--	3	--	1	--	--
Other fears for others	8	9	3	10	2	7	8	13	2	12	9	5
(Minimum N)	(117)	(145)	(105)	(80)	(78)	(61)	(49)	(72)	(53)	(95)	(109)	(80)

Jobs--one's own or those of family members--are the second most common topic in the hopes of all but two of the groups (health was mentioned more often than jobs by both groups of white female migrants). Among the blacks, higher proportions of migrants than long-termers expressed hopes focused on jobs. For the white women, however, the reverse is true. Among them, long-termers expressed hopes about jobs more often than the migrants did. With the exception of the white men, recent migrants were more likely than those who came earlier to express job-related hopes. Job-related fears were more often expressed by long-term residents than by migrants (except among the white males) and, with the exception of white migrants, males were more likely than females to have job-related anxieties.

Next most often mentioned are hopes about health, education, and training (see Table 6.10). Whites mention health concerns more often than they do concerns about education and training, while the reverse is true for blacks. Among all race-sex groups except white females, long-term residents (who tend to be older) express health concerns more often than do the migrants. Among women, those with longer durations of Cleveland residence are more likely than those who came later to mention education and training in their hopes. A somewhat similar pattern of health concerns is seen in the expression of health worries (see Table 6.11).

Women were more likely than men to express general hopes for children and, except among the long-term residents, these hopes were mentioned more often by whites than by blacks. In the variety of other hopes mentioned for self, own character development, and family, there is either little variation among the comparison groups or the variation that does appear is difficult to interpret. While the proportion mentioning miscellaneous concerns for self appears sizable, it is actually composed of small frequencies of a wide variety of concerns. Concerns such as recreation, travel, vacation, retirement, leisure time, hobbies, getting married, or staying single were all coded together. None was mentioned frequently enough to be singled out as a distinct topic. White migrants, perhaps because of their predominantly rural background, were more likely than long-termers to have expressed fears about morals, crime, and drugs.

There are differences among our respondents with regard to their hopes and fears for the future, but from a broad perspective the essential similarity of their hopes and fears and those of most Americans is apparent. In 1959, 1964, and again in 1971, national samples of Americans were asked the same questions as our respondents.[7] From their responses it is clear that most Americans are also generally concerned with those aspects of life whose personal and familial impact is immediate. But in their relative emphasis, the Clevelanders differed markedly from the national sample responding to the survey taken in 1971. [8] Hopes for a better standard of living were at least twice as important, and hopes for a good job were at least four times as important in the Cleveland responses as they were in the national sample. Hopes for peace and fear of war ranked third in the hopes and fears of the national sample, but armed conflict was not an important theme in the Cleveland responses. Also, the third-ranked prominence the black respondents in Cleveland gave to hopes for education and training was not sufficiently discernible in the responses of the national sample to warrant a specific category. Clearly, an overriding concern with their personal economic situation and a belief that they can utilize education and training to improve it distinguishes the migrants, and especially the black migrants, from their fellow-Americans, who see their lives somewhat more circumscribed by external events.

Perceived Status and Mobility

As we indicated, the second part of the Cantril technique involves the use of the "ladder of life," with the top representing the respondent's best possible life situation and the bottom the worst. He was also asked where he stood in the past and where he would stand in the future. (To turn the Cantril scale more directly toward the subject matter of the Cleveland study, the time reference of the past ladder rating was changed to obtain ratings for migrants just before the move and after they had been in Cleveland about a year. In addition, the respondents were also asked to indicate where their father, or father surrogate, stood on the ladder of life when he was about the respondent's age.)

Because they are quantitative, the ladder ratings provide convenient indications of respondents' perceptions of their current life situation. By comparing ratings for different time periods, we can also obtain an indication of perceptions of past mobility and aspirations for the future.*

---

*In the present study, the respondent's own mobility is indicated by comparing ladder ratings for the time before moving to Cleveland, one year after arrival, at the time of the second interview, and for a projection five years into the future. Intergenerational mobility was appraised by having each respondent indicate where his or her father (or father surrogate) was on the ladder when he was about the respondent's own age and comparing these ratings with the respondent's current ladder rating.

Since the top of the ladder represents the best personal future
for each individual and the bottom the worst, the median ratings
for current position suggest that the respondents are balanced
about halfway between what they conceive to be the best and
worst possible life situations, with about half in each group being
above the midpoint on the ladder and half below. With the exception
of white female latecomers, each group tended to place their fathers
lower on the ladder of life, indicating that in the aggregate they felt
that they had improved their lot over their recollections of what life
had been like when their fathers were about the same age. Generally, medians for the year before coming to Cleveland are lower than
those for ratings assigned to fathers. Even so, life was not as bleak
as it could have been, since the median for each group is above the
bottom third of the ladder. For all groups except the black female
early arrivals, ratings for the first anniversary in Cleveland are
higher than those for the time prior to migration. In their own eyes,
the future looks rosier still, with half or more in every group predicting that they would be on one of the top three steps of the ladder
in five years. The optimistic trend represented in these subjective
ratings is impressive. Over time and in comparison with their
fathers, these working-class respondents tended to place themselves
higher and higher on the ladder.

Comparing the median ladder ratings for the various time
periods is useful insofar as it highlights the optimistic overall trend
in the data. At the same time, however, the medians conceal a substantial minority of respondents who perceive either no improvement
or a downward movement on the ladder over time. As a case in
point, while the shift in median ratings for the pre-Cleveland situation and the first anniversary after the move was generally upward,
not everyone's ladder rating had changed (Table 6.12). A fifth or
more of the respondents in eight comparison groups gave the same
ladder rating to their first year in Cleveland as they did to their pre-
Cleveland days. Holding sex and length of residence constant, blacks
gave themselves identical ladder ratings at both times more often
than did whites. Within each racial group, long-termers located
themselves on the same rung more often than did the migrants.

There were also sizable proportions who viewed the move to
Cleveland as at least a temporary dip in their life position. Though
the proportion of respondents whose ladder position changed for the
better after a year in Cleveland is at least twice as great in each
group as the proportion whose ladder rating moved downward, at
least 10 percent in each group (and about 20 percent or more in four
groups) saw themselves as moving downward on the ladder. Again,
the black migrants were more likely than the whites to express negative feelings; among the long-termers, however, the reverse was true.

FIGURE 6.3

Median Personal Ladder Ratings by Sex, Race, and Duration of Residence

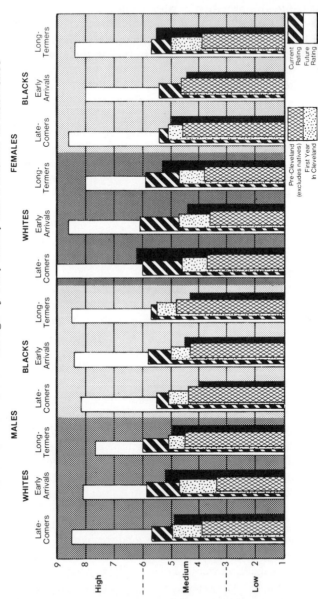

Note: Because there are nine intervals, the reader may wish to think of the bottom three intervals as equivalent to a verbal rating of "low," the middle three as "medium," and the top three as "high."

TABLE 6.12

Changes in Ladder Ratings: Position on First Anniversary
in Cleveland Compared with Situation Before the Move
(percentages)*

Sex, Race, and Type of Respondent	Direction of Move			Total	
	Downward	No Change	Upward	Percent	(N)
White males					
Migrants	11	22	67	100	(260)
Long-termers	20	29	51	100	(41)
Black males					
Migrants	15	24	62	100	(156)
Long-termers	12	47	41	100	(32)
White females					
Migrants	12	19	69	100	(121)
Long-termers	21	26	53	100	(19)
Black females					
Migrants	26	27	48	100	(204)
Long-termers	18	36	45	100	(44)

*Percentage basis for long-term residents excludes native Clevelanders.

Comparison of the ladder ratings for the current situation with the retrospective ratings for the period about a year after arriving in Cleveland shows a substantial upward trend in each group (ranging between 52 and 73 percent). Again, black respondents were least likely to give ratings that indicated a perceived advance in their personal situation and, with the exception of the white female long-term residents, were more likely than white respondents to indicate that their situation had deteriorated (Table 6.13).

Roughly three-fifths or more in every comparison group assigned higher ladder ratings to their present position than they had to their situation before moving to Cleveland (Table 6.14). Except for the male long-termers, whites were generally more likely than blacks to view their current situation as an improvement over their previous one. Among the two-fifths or fewer in each group for whom the present was no improvement over the past, about as many had stayed in roughly the same place on the ladder of life as had moved

TABLE 6.13

Changes in Ladder Ratings: Current Position Compared with
Position at First Anniversary of the Move to Cleveland
(percentages)

Sex, Race, and Type of Respondent	Direction of Move			Total	
	Downward	No Change	Upward	Percent	(N)
White males					
Migrants	16	22	62	100	(261)
Long-termers	15	17	68	100	(41)
Black males					
Migrants	24	24	52	100	(157)
Long-termers	27	21	52	100	(33)
White females					
Migrants	15	12	73	100	(121)
Long-termers	32	10	58	100	(19)
Black females					
Migrants	27	20	54	100	(204)
Long-termers	32	16	52	100	(44)

TABLE 6.14

Changes in Ladder Ratings: Current Position Compared with
Situation Before the Move to Cleveland
(percentages)

Sex, Race, and Type of Respondent	Direction of Move			Total	
	Downward	No Change	Upward	Percent	(N)
White males					
Migrants	12	14	74	100	(261)
Long-termers	16	23	60	100	(43)
Black males					
Migrants	19	19	62	100	(156)
Long-termers	16	22	62	100	(32)
White females					
Migrants	12	13	75	100	(121)
Long-termers	21	10	68	100	(19)
Black females					
Migrants	26	17	57	100	(204)
Long-termers	27	11	61	100	(44)

downward, except for the black female migrants and female long-
termers of both races, who were more likely to give ratings indicating a deterioration of position.

While upwards of half of the respondents rated themselves as
better off than their fathers were at about the same age, there were
still sizable proportions who saw themselves in a less favorable position; roughly a quarter or more in each group made judgments im-
plying that, relative to their fathers, they had been downwardly mobile (Table 6.15). In all groups, respondents who did not rate themselves as being better off than their fathers were more likely to as-
sign higher ratings to their fathers than to say that they and their
fathers were about equally well off. *

The data for expectations for the future reveal a sharp break
with what the respondents indicated they had experienced in the past.
Each of the past comparisons shows a small but substantial group
who gave themselves lower ladder ratings for a later period of time
than they had for some earlier time, thus acknowledging in effect
some deterioration in status. Looking toward the future, specific
optimism persisted despite these experiences. The overwhelming
majority in each group (about three-quarters or more) indicated that
in about five years they would be higher on the ladder of life than they
were when interviewed the second time in Cleveland (Table 6.16).
The proportion who expected their condition to deteriorate was minis-
cule. Generally, those who expected to remain about where they were
already saw themselves as being relatively close to realizing their
ideal life state. Moreover, as projected by the respondents, in the
next five years, in the aggregate each ladder position will have
gained only from lower positions and will have lost only to higher
positions--that is, in the balance, the aggregate expectation is for
a general net movement upward (Table 6.17). Similar present-to-
future ladder shifts are also found in national sample data only
among the youngest age groups. Since our study group is relatively
young, it would appear that the net upward movement in the ladder
ratings reflects the optimism of young adults, which the migratory
experience did not dampen.

---

*Generally, in the other comparisons we find that the propor-
tions in the "stable" category tend to be greater than the proportions
in the categories indicative of deterioration of personal position.
Significantly, these ratings are between children and parents, and
the progeny are, in a sense, telling us that when it is a close call,
Dad gets the nod. In the self-comparisons over time, when the call
is close, we tend to find an apparent reluctance to acknowledge skid-
ding downward in terms of one's own personal values.

TABLE 6.15

Intergenerational Mobility: Respondent's Current Position Compared with Father's Position at Same Age
(percentages)

Sex, Race, and Type of Respondent	Ladder Position Relative to Father			Total	
	Below	Same Level	Above	Percent	(N)
White males					
Migrants	28	18	54	100	(247)
Long-termers	29	19	52	100	(98)
Black males					
Migrants	23	13	64	100	(151)
Long-termers	23	15	62	100	(53)
White females					
Migrants	30	14	56	100	(117)
Long-termers	28	24	48	100	(46)
Black females					
Migrants	31	17	52	100	(193)
Long-termers	33	19	47	100	(72)

TABLE 6.16

Expected Change in Ladder Ratings: Expected Position in Five Years Compared with Current Position
(percentages)

Sex, Race, and Type of Respondent	Direction of Move			Total	
	Downward	No Change	Upward	Percent	(N)
White males					
Migrants	3	17	80	100	(256)
Long-termers	7	22	72	100	(102)
Black males					
Migrants	2	11	87	100	(157)
Long-termers	--	16	84	100	(58)
White females					
Migrants	4	11	85	100	(120)
Long-termers	2	19	79	100	(52)
Black females					
Migrants	*	10	90	100	(203)
Long-termers	5	22	72	100	(76)

* = 0.5 percent or less.

TABLE 6.17

Net Turnover on Current to Future Ladder Shifts
(percentages)

Ladder	Whites		Blacks	
Rating	Migrants	Long-Termers	Migrants	Long-Termers
Men				
1	-2	2	-2	-2
2	-2	-1	-7	-7
3	-4	-5	-6	-4
4	-10	-8	-14	-16
5	-26	-24	-23	-17
6	-12	-8	-7	-5
7	7	12	12	-5
8	17	11	15	22
9	31	22	32	33
(N)	(256)	(102)	(157)	(58)
Women				
1	-2	-2	-1	-3
2	-2	-8	-4	-1
3	-4	--	-8	-5
4	-2	-10	-16	-9
5	-27	-25	-25	-13
6	-16	-8	-6	-14
7	-2	12	5	--
8	14	17	16	16
9	42	23	39	30
(N)	(120)	(52)	(203)	(76)

Perceived life quality over time, as measured by the Cantril self-anchoring striving scale, points to a remarkable consistency between the migrants' assessment of progress and that obtained through our objective analyses of work experience. The majority are better off than they once were, but a substantial minority are not. Most are still hopeful about their own future, although, as we have seen, such hopes do not extend to the larger social environment.

NOTES

1. See Robert P. Quinn, Graham L. Staines, and Margaret R. McCullough, Job Satisfaction: Is There a Trend? (Washington, D.C.: U.S. Department of Labor, Manpower Administration, 1974).

2. For an analysis of the role of differential rates of mobility upon aggregate job satisfaction rates, see Kenneth Land, "Two Preliminary Models for the Analysis of Changes in a Social Indicator of Job Satisfaction," in Proceedings of the Social Statistics Section, 1974, American Statistical Association (Washington, D.C.: American Statistical Association, 1975).

3. See Howard Schuman and Shirley Hatchett, Black Racial Attitudes: Trends and Complexities (Ann Arbor, Mich.: Institute for Social Research, 1974).

4. See Leonard Goodwin, Do the Poor Want to Work? (Washington, D.C.: The Brookings Institute, 1972).

5. The scale was developed by Hadley Cantril and Lloyd A. Free in their studies of patterns of human aspiration in 18 different countries. See Hadley Cantril, The Pattern of Human Concerns (New Brunswick, N.J.: Rutgers University Press, 1965); Lloyd A. Free and Hadley Cantril, The Political Beliefs of Americans (New Brunswick, N.J.: Rutgers University Press, 1967); and F. P. Kilpatrick and Hadley Cantril, "Self-Anchoring Scaling: A Measure of Individuals' Unique Reality Worlds," Journal of Individual Psychology 16 (November 1960): 158-73.

6. See, for example, Lyle W. Shannon and Magdaline Shannon, "The Assimilation of Migrants to Cities: Anthropological and Sociological Contributions," in Urban Research and Policy Planning, Volume 1, ed. Leo F. Schnore and Henry Fagin (Beverly Hills, Calif.: Sage Publications Inc., 1967), pp. 53-55, 65-67.

7. The national data are reported by Albert H. Cantril and Charles W. Roll, Jr., The Hopes and Fears of the American People (Washington, D.C.: Potomac Associates, 1971).

8. Ibid., p. 19.

7

The detailed materials presented in the preceding chapters were assembled and analyzed to help us understand the respective parts played by migratory status, race, and sex in the economic, social, and personal fate of inner-city residents. We are now ready to speculate a little more freely about the troubling questions that prompted the initial undertaking of this study: What happens to low-income Southerners, black and white, who migrate to our cities? How vulnerable are they with respect to unemployment and social pathology? To what extent do they contribute to the dismal social statistics describing inner-city problems and to the rising Northern welfare rolls? Are the attitudes, hopes, and expectations of migrants different from those of long-term city residents, and do these sentiments change over time? A joint review of the situational and attitudinal changes experienced by our panel of respondents during the four-year period for which we collected this information sheds some light on these questions.

Before undertaking this review, however, it is useful to re-examine the underlying assumptions. The initial policy concerns that prompted the undertaking of this study and stimulated other research on internal migration stemmed from a widespread belief in the pervasive presence of problem migrants in Northern cities. Research findings have failed to support this assumption. Our preceding data have pointed to the favorable demographic profile presented by the migrant population, in particular their youth and high level of education. These findings were not unexpected. As would have been hypothesized by knowledgeable students of demographic processes and as has been convincingly demonstrated in much of the newer research and especially the recently published detailed analyses of 1970 census data, present-day low-income migrants, like

those who have preceded them in most countries and in most time
periods, are predominantly young, optimistic, eager to work, and
eager to succeed through their own efforts. Furthermore, white
and black Southerners who migrated during the 1960s, unlike those
who came to the Northern cities during the two preceding decades,
tended to be better educated and were more often of nonfarm origin.
Given their social background, they may even be better equipped, in
terms of basic educational skills, previous work experience, and
work motivation, than those city-born whites or blacks who have remained in inner-city ghettos for a generation or more.* However,
based on our data, broad generalizations about the superior attri-
butes of migrants are hardly warranted given the probability of residential moves out of ghetto areas on the part of the more successful
long-term inner-city residents. This is especially true of whites;
for blacks, who until recently had fewer residential alternatives,
such comparisons may be more soundly based. Recent census data
for blacks clearly point to higher labor market participation rates
for Southern migrants living in inner cities compared to Northern-
born blacks in the same age cohorts.[2] A similar conclusion was
reached by researchers who have analyzed data from the National
Longitudinal Surveys carried out at the Center for Human Resource
Research at Ohio State University.[3] Our Cleveland data also suggest that migrants are more likely to be marriage- and family-
oriented, although here again our own comparison group is not a
good one. Census information on this topic has not been published
to date.

    The information we have developed on labor force participa-
tion, unemployment, wages, and income points rather clearly in the
direction of "successful" outcomes for most groups of migrants, although there are obvious and very marked differences by race and
especially by sex. At the time of the first survey, in 1967-68, relatively few newcomers were unemployed. Most of them, however--

---

    *In relation to our own data, comparisons between recent mi-
grants and "old timers" are speculative. For one thing, our long-
term Cleveland resident comparison groups turned out to be older
than the migrant groups. Our "comparison group"--those who lived
in Cleveland ten years or longer--was also not designed to test the
question of the impact of Southern vs. Northern birth place or place
of education; our main focus was on length of residence in the city.
Detailed census data analyses have thrown better light on these issues than surveys with imperfectly matched samples, and they have
shown that especially in the case of blacks, a higher proportion of
migrants graduated from high school than was the case among
Northern-born blacks.[1]

and especially the women--worked at very low wages and in low-
status occupations, although industrial employment, which most of
these migrants were interested in obtaining, had been obtained by
white men and sizable numbers of black men as well. Sporadic
rather than chronic unemployment plagued many of these migrants,
increasingly so, as their longer residence period in Cleveland coin-
cided with a period of declining economic activity.

These findings are very much in line with the data of other researchers, which suggest that few migrants experience serious initial employment problems. For white migrants similar to those in
our survey, we have convincing data from the special surveys conducted at the University of Kentucky, showing that recent migrants
from eastern Kentucky to Lexington and to Cincinnati were success-
fully absorbed in both labor markets, experienced significant income
gains, and expressed satisfaction with many aspects of their life in
the city to which they had migrated.[4] For blacks, analysis of recent
census data suggests that although recent migrants have higher unemployment rates and are less likely to be in the labor force than whites
in comparable migration categories, migrants compare favorably
with Northern-born blacks.[5]

With the rediscovery of the "successful migrant" and the atten-
dant dismissal of migration as a source of urban pathology goes the
temptation to adopt a mirror-image view of urban problems from the
migration perspective. Thus, black migrants are "more successful,"
it is hypothesized by several of the researchers whose findings we
have quoted here, because Southern-born migrants are more persistent and goal oriented, more committed to the work ethic, more willing to accept low-paying jobs, and more interested in pay than in the
nature of the work required to obtain the pay. With respect to white
migrants, it is often claimed that long-term residents are more
problem-prone because of the disruptive effects of large city living,
culture shock, and disruption of cohesive family ties.

There is some danger in the ready acceptance of this mirror
image, which--like the earlier stereotype--tends to locate the source
of social problems in the characteristics and predispositions of individuals rather than in the social and economic system in which
these individuals operate. With the help of our data, we have tried
to throw some additional light on the issue of the development of social pathology, as evidenced by lack of attachment to the labor force,
deviant behavior, and personal and social alienation. We would like
to offer several ideas suggested by our data:

1. Almost all detailed analyses presented to date by researchers on migrant populations are restricted to men; yet women are a
very large segment of this population and, like all women, increasingly enter the labor force. Our data suggest that their work

experience is largely negative, both in terms of pay and the nature of the work available. Our data lead us to suspect that the "success" findings that characterized male black migrants would not be shown if large-scale data for black female migrants were to be analyzed. White women in our study, like other low-income white women who were recently observed in a large-scale study, sought to withdraw from the labor force over time.[6] Yet, given the need for female labor force participation if low-income groups are to attain more adequate living standards, female employment success is certainly as important a factor in predicting the emergence of social problems (in particular welfare dependency) as male employment success.

The data pertaining to women in Chapters 2, 4, and 5 are replete with indications of the difficulties women experienced in the Cleveland labor market over the four-year period. For example, the percentage of respondents unemployed at the time of the second interview was as follows (most recent migrants only):

Category	Percentage
White men	8 percent
Black men	16 percent
White women	17 percent
Black women	24 percent

Almost any other set of statistics shows the same rank order of race and sex. Severity of unemployment, as measured by longest period of unemployment in the two years preceding the second interview, averaged as follows (most recent migrants only):

Category	Length of Unemployment
White men	3 weeks
Black men	4 weeks
White women	6 weeks
Black women	6.6 weeks

The data on earnings show a narrowing of race but not of sex differentials, with women, at the time of the second interview, averaging lower wages than men four years earlier when the first interviews were conducted. Occupational mobility, as measured by skill and functional shifts, is more difficult to assess with our data, largely because so many women are in the heterogeneous service category, and because "leaving the labor force" has a different meaning for women than for men. Still, among women who were employed at both interview periods, it seems that there is a change for the better, with women more often employed at higher skill levels and in white-collar work at the time of the later interview. Quite a few among them declared themselves very satisfied with their jobs at the time of the second interview, although whites were more likely to do so than blacks, and this was true of the men as well. These improvements, however, affected only a small number of our respondents. The bulk of white and black women were working in jobs that provided little stability and little monetary or other incentive to remain in the labor market if adequate spouse's earnings, unemployment insurance, or welfare could be substituted for work.

2. In the case of the men, it may be misleading to look only at averages or gross distributions when examining social data of the type presented in this study. Obviously, summary measures of this type are a necessary first step to dealing with vast bodies of information, and it is certainly informative to know that most respondents are employed or have experienced wage gains or that more of them are satisfied with their jobs than are not. But the next step must be to look at the number of deviant cases, which on some issues was sizable. We know that social pathology does not require that all or even most participants in a social system show symptomatic evidence; the presence of a significant minority of persons with severe social problems is sufficient. In our data, we see enough indicators of individual difficulties--in particular with respect to unemployment or the opportunity to secure well-paid work--to shy away from over-optimistic interpretations of migration outcomes. Throughout Chapters 2, 3, and 5, ample evidence can be found of persistent clusters of male problem migrants.

The most important single statistic refers to unemployment. Over time, the unemployment rate among our respondents increased, no doubt as a result of changing economic conditions in Cleveland during the observation period. The men most seriously affected by this deterioration were the most vulnerable ones, those who had initially taken very marginal jobs, usually as common laborers, and had not secured a toehold in a primary labor market. Among the group of black men who at the time of the first interview had not landed "good" jobs and were working as common laborers, close to one-half were unemployed at the time of second interview. Most of the others had moved into better jobs as operators or craftsmen. Whites who were in such common-laborer jobs at the time of the first interview were more likely to have found better jobs, but one-fourth of them were also unemployed. Although we have not been able to refine our data to the point where we can confidently describe the least successful as moving toward a hard-core unemployed or "moving out of the labor force" subgroup, we have a strong hunch that they are in the process of doing so. We found that this phenomenon held true for recent and not-so-recent migrants. Among the long-term residents in our survey, unemployment also increased

markedly during the observation period, but it affected all job categories (although black men in factory jobs--operatives--were apparently slightly more immune). Thus, migrants who do not secure
factory jobs early may well be as likely as other disadvantaged inner-
city residents to join the pool of casual laborers who eventually re-
treat from the labor force.

A possible related problem is that of health. White migrants,
but especially long-term residents of both races, claimed that they
had trouble with their health at both interviewing periods. As migrants get older and spend more time in the labor force, all health
problems (including job-related ones) are likely to increase. Compared to other barriers to employment--such as alcoholism or
trouble with the law, which are usually believed to be major employment obstacles--health problems are much more serious, judging
from our data.

It would be useful to regroup and reanalyze some of our data
in order to introduce more refined comparisons between "successful" and "unsuccessful" migrants and study the characteristics and
attitudes associated with the two groups. Meanwhile, however, we
feel it important to bear in mind the significant number of deviant
cases and temper somewhat the current optimism about the successful integration of migrants into Northern labor markets.

3. The earlier studies cited here are based on census information or data from longitudinal surveys. For these studies attitudinal data were either not collected at all or were gathered only at
one point in time. The findings about higher labor force participation rates of migrants as compared to Northern-born black males
led to the speculation that this might be the consequence of some
erosion of the work ethic, the prevalence of different value systems
in the inner-city environment, the accumulation of negative experience such as job discrimination, negative feelings about education,
or the fact that Northern blacks are less willing than Southerners to
settle for menial and "dead end" jobs for the sake of good wages. In
their 1966 data Adams and Nestel found some attitudinal differences
between migrants and long-term residents, in particular concerning
schools and the importance of nonmonetary aspects of work. However, on the basis of the data that we have presented above as well
as nationwide opinion data collected in other surveys, we are more
inclined to believe that in recent years such attitudes have become
more common in all segments of the population, white as well as
black, migrant as well as nonmigrant.

4. Finally, we see a great deal of congruence between the
soft and hard data that we have examined in this study. For the
majority of migrants the move north or west to Cleveland has resulted in a significant improvement in their life situation, and it is

so perceived. Hopes for their personal future are high, and this despite considerable evidence of growing negative feelings about the
larger society. This is not an inconsistent finding; contradictory
feelings about one's own life and the situation in the larger society
can and do coexist at many times and in many groups.[7] But all
inner-city residents--both the more and the less successful--are
deeply affected by job-related concerns. Job insecurity, frequent
unemployment, and the perception of a shrinking of job opportunities
are the central issues that shape the lives and attitudes of this population. Their attitudes toward education or the work ethic are also
undergoing changes, but these, we suspect, are largely the result of
specific experiences and observations in the labor market rather than
the effect of some "urbanization" process that has weakened their
traditional belief structure. The frustrations and economic difficulties experienced by many of the women in this population are also
likely to contribute to the emergence of a climate of dissatisfaction
that is bound to affect the men with whom they interact. Obviously,
many complex psychological and social processes occur in the process of migration, but in view of the many similarities in the attitude
pattern and attitude changes among migrants and long-term residents,
we are inclined to minimize migration effects--positive or negative--
and see inadequacies in the job markets on which they are dependent
for their livelihood as the main source of continuing difficulties in
the lives of these inner-city residents.

One can only speculate on the effects of the economic recession
of the mid-1970s on the labor force participation of these workers.
Other data suggest that their vulnerability on the job may do much to
erase the modest gains they made in occupational positions and earnings and to erode the confidence with which they viewed themselves
and addressed the world. The differential vulnerability of white and
black workers and the competition for jobs of which black women
claim an increasing share suggests the development of levels of
racial tension far exceeding those observed in Cleveland during the
period of the study.

NOTES

1. See Manpower Report of the President (Washington, D.C.:
U.S. Government Printing Office, April 1974), p. 91.
2. Manpower Report of the President, pp. 90-99; also Larry
H. Long, "Poverty, Welfare and Migration," American Sociological
Review 39, no. 1 (February 1974): 46-56; and Larry H. Long and
Lynne R. Heltman, "Income Differences Between Blacks and Whites
Controlling for Education and Region of Birth" (paper prepared for

1974 Annual Meeting of the Population Association of America, New York City, April 18-20).

3. Avril V. Adams and Gilbert Nestel, "Interregional Migration, Education and Poverty in the Urban Ghetto" (unpublished report, Center for Human Resource Research, Ohio State University, Columbus, Ohio, September 1973).

4. Larry C. Morgan, "Economic Cost and Returns of Appalachian Out Migration" (paper presented at the Conference "Appalachians in Urban Areas," Academy of Contemporary Problems, Columbus, Ohio, March 27-29, 1974); Larry C. Morgan and A. Frank Bordeaux, Jr., "Urban Public Service Costs and Benefits of Rural to Urban Migration" (paper presented at the Sixth Annual Meeting of the Southern Agricultural Economics Association, Memphis, February 3-6, 1974).

5. Long and Heltman, "Income Differences Between Blacks and Whites," p. 9.

6. Harold W. Watts and Albert Rees, eds., Central Labor Supply Response, Part A; Part B, Chapters 1-4, Final Report of the New Jersey Graduated Work Incentive Experiment (Madison: Institute on Research on Poverty, University of Wisconsin).

7. Kenneth Land has developed the concept of individual "life space," which consists of three interacting domains: objective conditions, subjective well-being, and subjective values (see his "Social Indicator Models: An Overview," in Social Indicator Models, ed. Kenneth C. Land and Seymour Spilerman [New York: Russel Sage Foundation, 1975]). In Albert H. Cantril, Jr. and Charles W. Roll, Jr., Hopes and Fears of the American People (Washington, D.C.: Potomac Associates, 1974), the question on individual hopes yielded much higher ratings than questions pertaining to the future of the nation.

This section of the study deals with the selection procedures through which the original (1967-68) panel of study participants was chosen, the extent of success in reinterviewing panel members four years later, the differences in the characteristics between those panel members who were reinterviewed and those who were not (attrition biases), and the implications of these data for our study findings.

The original study design called for the identification of an unbiased cohort with specified characteristics and of sufficient size for the analytical procedures planned. This cohort was to include recent Southern newcomers to Cleveland and their long-term resident neighbors who, during the initial screening and interviewing from the spring of 1967 to the spring of 1968, were living in Cleveland's poorest inner-city neighborhoods. Consideration of the biases inherent in the identification of newcomers from public records (such as driver's license bureaus, school records, or the records of police or other public agencies) led to the initial decision to assemble the study population by canvassing low-income residential areas, so that newcomers would be included regardless of employment status, family situation, or needs or problems. The original target populations specified for the first round of interviews are shown in Table A.1. Our goal for the second round of interviews was, of course, to reinterview the largest possible number of original subjects still residing in Cleveland at the time of the second round. However, because of the well-known difficulties of maintaining panels of low-income respondents over a period of several years, we did not anticipate locating for reinterview in Cleveland more than two-thirds of the original study participants. As will be shown, our success in this respect exceeded our expectations.

TABLE A.1

Study Target Population by Race and Duration of Residence

	Duration of Residence			
Race	Less Than 2 Years	2 to 5 Years	10 Years or More	All Durations
White	400	400	200	1,000
Black	400	400	200	1,000
Both races	800	800	400	2,000

SELECTION OF RESPONDENTS AND COMPLETION
OF THE FIRST INTERVIEWS

To be eligible for inclusion in the study, migrants were required to have lived less than five full years in Cleveland and less than six months in any other non-Southern place (excluding time in the armed forces). No duration of residence restriction, other than a minimum of ten years of residence in Cleveland, was placed on the long-term residents. The analytic focus of the study also led us to exclude persons who were neither white nor black, or who usually spoke a language other than English in their homes. Since the emphasis of this research was on adjustment of workers in their prime years, we also excluded persons who were younger than 18 years of age or who had attained their fiftieth birthday. Males were included only if they were members of the labor force as usually defined or were not working or not looking for work because they believed no work to be available for them (that is, were "discouraged workers"). Females who met these same criteria were also included, as were female heads of house irrespective of labor force status. A brief household screening questionnaire was used to determine whether household members met the study criteria. Detailed personal interviews were conducted with migrants and long-term residents located and selected through the screening process.

Locating special-characteristics populations for whom no register exists is never easy, but the task of uncovering specific categories of recent in-migrants proved to be exceptionally difficult. We had originally hoped to assemble our target population by screening a sample of households in selected low-income census tracts that local informants had described as predominantly inhabited by recent arrivals from Appalachia (on Cleveland's East Side) and the Deep South (on the predominately black West Side). However, presurvey tests of early versions of the questionnaire indicated that recent Southern migrants to Cleveland were not nearly so abundant nor so concentrated residentially as imagined by those concerned with the so-called problems and burdens brought to their city by these newcomers. Accordingly, we abandoned plans to locate migrants through a sample of dwelling units and made preparations for a systematic house-by-house canvass of low-income neighborhoods.

A total of 60 census tracts, of which 39 were predominantly white and 21 predominantly black, were selected on the basis of 1960 census information, using income and influx of Southern in-migrants between 1955 and 1960 as the principal criteria (see

Figure A.1).* All black and all but two white tracts were in the three lowest income deciles for the Cleveland SMSA. The exact distribution is shown in Table A.2.

TABLE A.2

Tracts Selected for Screening by Race
and Family Income Decile[a]

Income Decile	Number of Tracts Within Decile		Number of Tracts Entered for Screening		Percentage of Tracts Entered for Screening	
	White	Black	White[b]	Black	White	Black
Lowest	21	34	9	12	43	35
Second	26	15	17	6	65	40
Third	32	6	11	3	31	50

[a]Upper limits for the four lowest deciles of family income for Cuyahoga County in 1960 were, respectively, $4,836, $5,679, $6,105, and $6,482. (Source: "A Sheet-A-Week Founded by Howard Whipple Green," 31, no. 41 [June 1964], issued by Real Property Inventory of Metropolitan Cleveland.)
[b]In addition to the 37 tracts shown here, two tracts in low-income neighborhoods in the next highest income decile were also entered for screening, because they reportedly contained exceptionally high numbers of recent in-migrants.

Under a block abandonment procedure, a block was considered to have been completely screened when contacts with at least 70 percent of the households on the block revealed no household containing a Southern in-migrant. If any migrant was found on the block, screening was continued until all households had been contacted or until the required number of call-backs had been made at hard-to-reach households. We required at least three call-backs, of which two were to be on days of the week and hours other than those of the first attempt.

---

*Data on the race composition and completeness of screening in census tracts are based on hand tallies of the results of contacts with individual households from the block fieldwork records in 60 of the 70 census tracts entered.

FIGURE A.1

Cleveland Residential Areas Canvassed in 1967–68 to Locate Southern In–Migrants

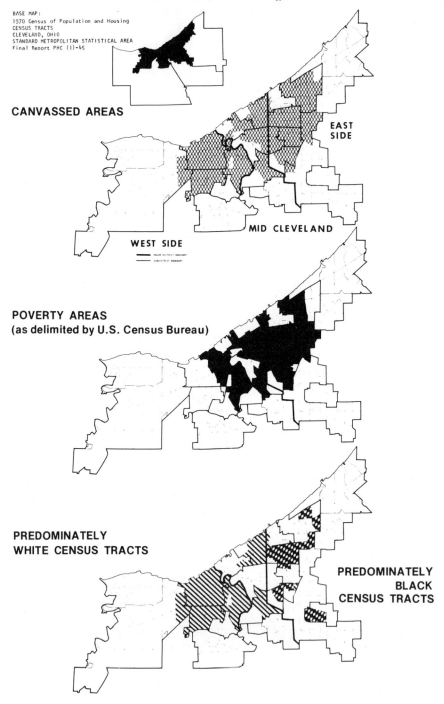

BASE MAP:
1970 Census of Population and Housing
CENSUS TRACTS
CLEVELAND, OHIO
STANDARD METROPOLITAN STATISTICAL AREA
Final Report PHC (1)-45

CANVASSED AREAS

EAST SIDE

MID CLEVELAND

WEST SIDE

MAJOR DISTRICT BOUNDARY
SUBDISTRICT BOUNDARY

POVERTY AREAS
(as delimited by U.S. Census Bureau)

PREDOMINATELY
WHITE CENSUS TRACTS

PREDOMINATELY
BLACK
CENSUS TRACTS

The 60 low-income census tracts in Cleveland entered by the
interviewers were estimated to contain about 87,000 households
(Table A.3). By the time the designated numbers of migrants and
long-term residents had been found, nearly 68,000 households had
been screened. The proportion of migrant households varied greatly
among tracts (from 1 in 19 to 1 in 195 households in white neighborhoods and 1 in 20 to 1 in 107 in black neighborhoods) but over the
entire group of tracts screened, the proportion of migrant households
in white and in black neighborhoods was nearly identical (1 in 50).

TABLE A.3

Neighborhood Screening Record

	White Neighbor-hoods	Black Neighbor-hoods	All Neighbor-hoods
A. Tracts			
Number of census tracts entered for screening	39	21	60
Number of tracts completely screened	33	6	39
B. Households			
Estimated number of households in tracts entered[a]	50,913	36,486	87,399
Households screened	38,855	28,949	67,804
Percent of households screened	76	79	77
C. Migrant households			
Number of migrant households located[b]	814	601	1,415
Migrant households per 1,000 households	20.9	20.8	20.9

[a]Real Property Inventory of Metropolitan Cleveland, 1966.
[b]Households containing at least one Southern in-migrant as
defined for this study.

Note: Not included in these calculations are results from
screening in two predominantly white fourth family-income decile
tracts, chosen for screening because they were thought to contain
exceptional numbers of fairly recent Southern in-migrants.

Fieldwork records for each city block were combed to appraise
the amount and direction of bias resulting from the screening procedures used. Two variables were used to establish priorities for
entering tracts for screening; the same two variables--relative
poverty and expected number of recent Southern migrants--were
used as criterion variables to judge the representativeness of the
sample.

Biases in the ultimate panel of migrants entered at two main
points. First, the initial selection of tracts to be screened favored
the inclusion of some tracts over others. In black neighborhoods,
and to a lesser extent in white areas, the initial tract selection was
biased upward in the three lowest family-income deciles (see Table
A.4). Second, the screeners met with differential levels of success
in screening households once they had actually begun the fieldwork.
This response to screening attempts further increased the considerable upward bias in black neighborhoods and enlarged the cluster at
the middle of the low-income range in white neighborhoods (see
Table A.4).

TABLE A.4

Percentage of Living Units Screened by Family-Income Decile and Predominant Race of Tract's Inhabitants

Family Income Decile	Number of Living Units Screened Within Decile		Percentage of Living Units Screened Within Family-Income Decile*	
	White Tracts	Black Tracts	White Tracts	Black Tracts
Lowest	2,960	8,394	23	22
Second	10,318	8,192	49	30
Third	8,904	4,061	23	44

*Percentage base is the estimated number of living units within
the decile for the entire city proper of Cleveland.

Obviously we need to be most concerned with the bias in the
selection of black respondents, which should be kept in mind in
evaluating the findings presented in this study. These data provide
clear evidence that systematic surveys, no matter how carefully
structured, encounter the greatest problems in the very poorest
neighborhoods, a fact brought out in earlier studies conducted by
other investigators.

Between May 1967 and March 1968, the actual period for field-work in the first round, a total of 77 interviewers (45 women and 32 men) were recruited, trained, and employed for work either in screening or interviewing or both. By and large, white interviewers worked in white neighborhoods and black interviewers were employed in black areas; however, there was some crossover of white interviewers into black residential areas, primarily because of the severe difficulties encountered in the recruitment of black staff. Almost all interviews were conducted in the respondent's home.

In the last stages of the project, when the work became increasingly difficult because of fewer daylight hours in the fall and winter, we began to experiment with office interviews. The field-work supervisor arranged for space in his downtown office building where interviews could be conducted and began making incentive payments to respondents who came there to be interviewed ($5.00) or kept appointments for interviews in their own home ($2.00). It is his opinion that progress on the study would have been greatly facilitated by establishing storefront interviewing centers in the neighborhoods, but he is still ambivalent about the incentive payments (a procedure that has gained much favor, largely as a result of militant pressures, but that many survey researchers feel is fraught with the danger of introducing response biases), even though he admits that the cost is more than offset by savings in time and travel.

The final sample of 1,713 persons--1,299 migrants and 414 long-term residents (see Table A.5)--fell below the numbers originally specified.

TABLE A.5

Distribution of Respondents by Race, Sex, and Duration
of Residence in Cleveland

	Duration of Cleveland Residence			
Race and Sex	Less than 2 Years	2 to 5 Years	0 to 5 Years	10 Years or More
White				
Males	269	245	514	143
Females	103	93	196	63
Both sexes	372	338	710	206
Black				
Males	144	123	267	87
Females	163	159	322	121
Both sexes	307	282	589	208
Total	679	620	1,299	414

As can be seen, the categories in which the number of respondents is farthest off the target are the black migrant groups, but the white migrant group, too, fell below target. Basically, the reason for the lower-than-specified quotas must be sought in our difficulties in locating migrants despite the extensive household screening. Furthermore, it should be noted that in addition to the 1,713 respondents whose interviews were usable for purposes of the survey, another 596 individuals (419 migrants and 177 long-term residents) had originally been slated for interviews, but did not participate for a variety of reasons. Refusals constituted only a small group (81 migrants and 46 long-term residents). The more important categories were those who moved and could not be located between screening and interview (110 migrants and 60 long-term residents), and those not found at home despite three or more call-backs (76 migrants, 58 long-term residents).

FOLLOW-UP PROCEDURES AND COMPLETION OF THE SECOND INTERVIEW

The 1,713 respondents interviewed in 1967-68 were assigned for reinterview in 1971. The basic instrument for the second round interviews was a modified version of the questionnaires used in the first round of interviewing. In 1967-68 two forms were used, one for the Southern in-migrants and a shorter form for the long-term residents. In the second round these were combined into a single form. In this modified version, the earlier questions measuring current occupational and social adjustment were retained, as were the items measuring the use of services and public dependency. Additional questions were inserted primarily to cover employment experiences since the time of the first interviews.

Production interviewing in Cleveland began in early July 1971 and continued until the end of June 1972. During the fieldwork, 67 persons were recruited, trained, and employed as interviewers. As in the earlier survey, black respondents were generally assigned to black interviewers and white respondents to white interviewers. Cooperation of the respondents was sought in several ways. A "dear friend" letter identifying the study and mentioning that a Special Surveys Company Interviewer had called and would be calling again was left for respondents who were not at home when the interviewer first called. Respondents who doubted the legitimacy of the study or its sponsorship were shown a copy of a clipping from a local newspaper announcing the study and identifying the Special Surveys Company. In still further efforts to have respondents cooperate, interviewers were stationed in two storefront offices, one on each side of town, located near shopping centers at the intersection of major transportation routes. Respondents were urged to come to one of these offices for an interview and were offered $5.00 as an incentive for doing so.

Because four years had elapsed since the first interviews with these mobile respondents, a substantial amount of time and effort was devoted to locating respondents and establishing that they were the persons to be interviewed. One indication of the effort that was expended is the variety of procedures that were employed to locate respondents for reinterview (Table A.6). The most frequently used means were the most accessible ones: the post office, the phone book, and control card information from the first interview. Personal sources of information were next most frequently used: persons given as permanent contact in the first interview, neighbors, building owners, relatives, and tradesmen.

In terms of the fields staff's ability to accurately locate persons assigned for reinterview, the most successful method of locating long-termers was information close at hand, the address on the control card from the first interview (see Figure A.2). Permanent contacts proved to be the most successful means of locating the survey migrants. More generally, personal sources of information proved to be more successful retrieval procedures than various types of record data. For the migrants, however, school records and the post office also proved to be fairly productive sources of information.

As a result of these retrieval efforts, a surprisingly high proportion of study participants--81 percent of the migrants and 86 percent of the long-term residents--were located (Table A.7). In each race-sex group the success in locating respondents tended to be better for long-termers than for migrants and better for white than black respondents of the same sex.

Not all of those located, however, were eligible to be reinterviewed in Cleveland. This was particularly the case with the newcomers. While 91 percent of the long-term residents were eligible for reinterview in Cleveland, only 73 percent of the newcomers were eligible (Table A.8). Among the newcomers, black women and men were eligible for reinterview more often than were white women and men. Migration out of Cleveland was the major reason for the differences between newcomers and long-termers with regard to their reinterview-in-Cleveland eligibility status (Table A.9). While 52 percent of the long-term residents who were ineligible for reinterview in Cleveland had moved from Cleveland, 90 percent of the

TABLE A.6

Procedures Used to Locate Respondents During Round Two of
the Cleveland Southern In-Migrant Study: All Respondents

Procedure	Number of Times Used
Post office	1,713
Phone book	1,697
Address given on control card	1,691
Phone number on control card	1,032
Permanent contact	848
Neighbors	684
New occupants	393
Building owner	343
Relative	236
Tradesman	207
Board of elections	158
City directory	156
Crisscross directory	105
Long-distance information operator	79
Tax records	72
Other	60
Metropolitan General Hospital	29
Employer	28
Local information operator	26
Marriage bureau	11
Vital statistics	7
Cleveland Job Training Center	5
Address from Washington	3
Electric company	2
Gas company	1
PEACE Skill Center	1

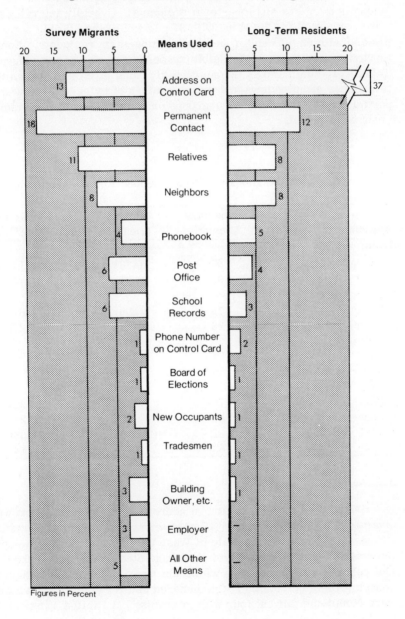

FIGURE A.2

Comparison of Successful Means Used to Locate
Long-Term Residents and the Survey Migrants

Survey Migrants	Means Used	Long-Term Residents
13	Address on Control Card	37
18	Permanent Contact	12
11	Relatives	8
8	Neighbors	8
4	Phonebook	5
6	Post Office	4
6	School Records	3
1	Phone Number on Control Card	2
1	Board of Elections	1
2	New Occupants	1
1	Tradesmen	1
3	Building Owner, etc.	1
3	Employer	–
5	All Other Means	–

Figures in Percent

ineligible newcomers had moved..* As shown in Table A.8, after
removal of ineligibles, the number of study participants located and
eligible for interview was reduced to 1,095. The completion of interviews with these eligible respondents located was exceptional both
among newcomers and long-term residents. Overall, interviews
were completed in Cleveland with 97 percent of the eligible newcomers and with 92 percent of the eligible long-term residents. Nonin-
terviews in each group of eligible respondents were due to refusals.
Table A.10 summarizes the sources for panel attrition between the
two rounds of interviews and the percentage of twice-interviewed
participants in the various subgroups on which the analyses in this
study were based.

TABLE A.7

Locating Original Respondents for Second Round of Interviews

Type of Respondent	Percentage Located	Number Located	Number in Original Group
White males			
Migrants	85	(436)	(514)
Long-termers	92	(131)	(143)
Black males			
Migrants	74	(198)	(267)
Long-termers	83	(72)	(87)
White females			
Migrants	91	(179)	(196)
Long-termers	90	(57)	(63)
Black females			
Migrants	76	(245)	(322)
Long-termers	80	(97)	(121)
All migrants	81	(1,058)	(1,299)
All long-termers	86	(357)	(414)

---

*Reasonably well-confirmed addresses outside Cleveland were
obtained for 276 respondents (17 long-termers and 259 migrants).
Of these, 115 were in the state of West Virginia. Brief follow-up
interviews were attempted with these and other members of the original cohort living in clusters within the reach of available field personnel across the country. One hundred and forty-four interviews
were completed (all but four with migrants). A limited range of
tabulations were made from these data; but, due to the thinness of
the data base when disaggregated by race, sex, and duration of residence, none of the resultant data were included in this study.

TABLE A.8

Eligibility of Located Respondents for Reinterview in Cleveland by Sex, Race, and Type of Respondent: Located Respondents Only

Sex/Race/Type of Respondent	Eligible		Ineligible		All Located Respondents	
	Percent	(f)	Percent	(f)	Percent	(N)
White males						
Migrants	62	(269)	38	(167)	100	(436)
Long-termers	89	(117)	11	(14)	100	(131)
Black males						
Migrants	82	(163)	18	(35)	100	(198)
Long-termers	92	(66)	8	(6)	100	(72)
White females						
Migrants	68	(122)	32	(57)	100	(179)
Long-termers	96	(55)	4	(2)	100	(57)
Black females						
Migrants	89	(217)	11	(28)	100	(245)
Long-termers	89	(86)	11	(11)	100	(97)
All migrants	73	(771)	27	(287)	100	(1,058)
All long-termers	91	(324)	9	(33)	100	(357)

TABLE A.9

Reasons Why Respondents Were Ineligible for Reinterview in Cleveland
by Sex, Race, and Type of Respondent
(percentages)

Type of Respondent	Reason for Ineligibility for Reinterview in Cleveland				All Ineligibles	
	Respondent Moved from Cleveland	Deceased	Institutionalized	In Military Service	Percent	(N)
White males						
Migrants	92	4	3	2	100	(167)
Long-termers	57	36	7	--	100	(14)
Black males						
Migrants	68	17	3	11	100	(35)
Long-termers	16	67	17	--	100	(6)
White females						
Migrants	100	--	--	--	100	(57)
Long-termers	50	50	--	--	100	(2)
Black females						
Migrants	89	11	--	--	100	(28)
Long-termers	64	36	--	--	100	(11)
All migrants	90	5	2	2	100	(287)
All long-termers	52	42	6	--	100	(33)

TABLE A.10

Distribution of Respondents by Sex, Race, and
Duration of Cleveland Residence
(frequencies)

Type of	Male		Female	
Respondent*	White	Black	White	Black
Latecomers	117	80	49	95
Early arrivals	145	78	72	109
Long-termers	105	61	53	80

*Because of our interest in the process of adjustment, tabulations of the Cleveland data were routinely made for three duration-of-residence groups, as well as separately for each race-sex combination. Newcomers with less than two years of residence in Cleveland when first interviewed are called "latecomers" in the text, those with two to five years of residence then are called "early arrivals," while respondents who had lived in the city ten years or more are called "long-termers." When first interviewed all respondents were living in low-income Cleveland neighborhoods; most were residents of the poverty area as delimited by the U.S. Bureau of the Census.

PANEL ATTRITION AND BIAS

The loss of original study participants for reasons other than service in the armed forces, death, or institutionalization is one of the main drawbacks in longitudinal designs. Panel mortality or the failure to recover the entire original cohort raises the question of whether those recovered differ substantially from members of the study population who are lost. In one incontrovertible sense the missing panel members do of course differ. The most important source of panel mortality in the Cleveland study was the loss of members of the original cohort who had moved to other locations, most commonly back to points of origin but also on to other states in the Northeast and on the West Coast. By their mobility, these members of the original panel had demonstrated that they were different from those who remained in Cleveland. Similarly, the small group who refused to be interviewed a second time demonstrated by their refusals their hostility to the study and the interviewers and thus, perhaps, their alienation.

From the point of view of the basic aim of this study--to assess the economic and social adjustment of migrants over time--the study actually encountered minimal attrition problems. The vast majority of respondents "lost" to the study were persons who had moved and thus were not part of the study population as originally defined; that is, persons living in Cleveland at both points in time. Only the small proportion of refusers or those who could not be located are of concern with respect to the biasing effect contributed by their attrition from the panel population. However, since the data were at hand, we chose to compare three groups: those interviewed in Cleveland, those interviewed elsewhere during the second round of interviews, and those who were not interviewed at all the second time (Tables A.11 through A.13). It is this last group, the original members of the panel who were not recovered in the second round, who are of greatest concern for their possible biasing effect on the conclusions drawn from the study. (In these comparisons the uninterviewed population excludes those deleted from the panel by reason of being deceased, institutionalized, or in the armed forces.)

In terms of their characteristics at the time of the first interview, relative to the group of respondents interviewed twice in Cleveland, those not reinterviewed among both migrants and long-term residents were more often found to be unemployed or outside the labor force, to be at the lower end of the income scale, to have stated that they were giving serious thought to leaving Cleveland, and to be agreed that, in general, things were getting worse for the common man. Among the migrants, both white and black, more of those not reinterviewed had not completed high school; but among long-termers, blacks not reinterviewed tended to be better educated than those interviewed twice. In sum, from a variety of indications in the data collected during the first round of interviews, the study participants who were not interviewed a second time appear to have already demonstrated lower levels of integration into the labor force and somewhat greater social alienation. Unless one is willing to argue that these respondents were likely to have made up the difference in the interval between the two rounds of interviewing, the failure to reinterview them probably tends to make the general picture of migrant adjustment and integration into the economy more favorable than it would have been if interviews had been conducted with all study participants. Ultimately, to reduce the unknown bias posed by the inability to locate and reinterview all or almost all of the original study subjects who had remained in Cleveland, the analysis in this study was confined to comparisons among the study participants for whom data were collected in Cleveland in 1967-68 and again in 1971-72.

TABLE A.11

Panel Attrition by Residency Status, Sex, and Race

	Type of Respondent							
	Males				Females			
	White		Black		White		Black	
	Migrants	Long-Termers	Migrants	Long-Termers	Migrants	Long-Termers	Migrants	Long-Termers
Number interviewed in 1967–68	514	143	267	87	196	63	322	121
Number eligible for reinterview in Cleveland*	269	117	163	66	122	55	217	86
Percentage of original cohort	52	82	61	76	62	87	67	71
Number interviewed in Cleveland, 1971–72	262	105	158	61	121	53	204	80
Percentage of original cohort	51	73	59	70	62	84	63	66
Percentage of number eligible for interview in Cleveland	97	90	97	92	99	96	94	93

*Excludes persons known to be deceased, institutionalized, in the armed forces, or living outside the Cleveland area.

263

TABLE A.12

Comparison of Respondents and Nonrespondents by Race and Selected Characteristics of Study Population at the Time of the First Interview: Migrants Only (percentages)

	White Participants in Study			Black Participants in Study		
	Interviewed in Cleveland	Not Interviewed*	Interviewed Outside Cleveland	Interviewed in Cleveland	Not Interviewed*	Interviewed Outside Cleveland
Sex						
Male	68	80	70	44	47	45
Female	32	20	30	56	53	55
Total percent	100	100	100	100	100	100
(N)	(383)	(178)	(122)	(362)	(173)	(20)
Education						
Less than high school	64	78	57	39	49	50
High school or greater	36	22	43	61	51	50
Total percent	100	100	100	100	100	100
(N)	(382)	(178)	(122)	(362)	(172)	(20)
Migration support						
Kin and friends urged respondent to come	12	12	9	13	12	10
Kin urged respondent to come	38	44	39	45	42	50
Friends urged respondent to come	10	10	10	6	9	--
Kin and friends were present	12	9	12	9	10	15
Kin or friends were present	22	17	23	23	24	15
All other	6	8	7	4	3	10
Total percent	100	100	100	100	100	100
(N)	(383)	(178)	(122)	(362)	(173)	(20)
Marital status						
Single	19	25	25	29	40	65
Married	76	71	73	63	55	35
Widowed	1	2	--	2	1	--
Divorced	3	2	2	4	4	--
Total percent	100	100	100	100	100	100
(N)	(382)	(178)	(122)	(362)	(173)	(20)

Total annual family income						
Less than $3,000	7	16	8	12	15	15
$3,000 to $4,999	23	24	18	27	28	35
$5,000 to $7,499	34	36	47	24	26	25
$7,500 to $9,999	28	15	20	22	16	20
$10,000 or more	7	7	7	10	7	--
Don't know	1	1	--	5	6	--
Total percent	100	100	100	100	100	100
(N)	(380)	(176)	(122)	(362)	(170)	(20)
Labor force status						
Employed full-time	81	74	85	65	62	80
Other employed	2	3	5	7	2	5
Unemployed	11	16	8	15	24	10
All other	6	7	2	13	12	5
Total percent	100	100	100	100	100	100
(N)	(383)	(178)	(122)	(362)	(173)	(20)
Skill level of current occupation						
High	14	19	22	14	15	9
Medium	68	62	68	54	48	36
Low	19	20	11	33	37	54
Total percent	100	100	100	100	100	100
(N)	(207)	(86)	(74)	(159)	(65)	(11)
Thinking about moving from Cleveland						
Not thinking about leaving	72	69	57	77	72	75
Thinking about leaving but not at all sure	11	9	16	9	12	15
Thinking about leaving but not too sure	12	12	16	11	13	5
Thinking about leaving and pretty sure about it	5	10	9	2	3	5
Total percent	100	100	100	100	100	100
(N)	(382)	(178)	(122)	(362)	(173)	(20)

*This group excludes those known to be deceased, in the armed forces, or in institutions.

Comparison of Respondents and Nonrespondents by Race and Selected Attitudinal Characteristics of the Study Population at the Time of the First Interview: Migrants Only[a]

Attitude Statement	White Participants in Study						Black Participants in Study					
	Interviewed in Cleveland %	(N)	Not Interviewed[b] %	(N)	Interviewed Outside Cleveland %	(N)	Interviewed in Cleveland %	(N)	Not Interviewed[b] %	(N)	Interviewed Outside Cleveland %	(N)
Getting ahead here on earth isn't nearly as important as preparing for the next world	58	(372)	50	(171)	56	(119)	37	(357)	50	(170)	50	(20)
Don't expect too much out of life and be content with what comes your way	66	(380)	70	(177)	55	(122)	32	(359)	37	(171)	25	(20)
Planning only makes a person unhappy, since your plans hardly ever work out	50	(381)	60	(177)	46	(121)	47	(360)	46	(172)	40	(20)
There's little use writing or talking to public officials because often they aren't interested in your problem	47	(373)	47	(175)	46	(117)	40	(359)	43	(169)	30	(20)
Nowadays a person has to live pretty much for today and let tomorrow take care of itself	50	(382)	53	(178)	50	(122)	48	(361)	50	(173)	40	(20)
In spite of what some people say, things are getting worse, not better, for the average man	50	(375)	53	(176)	48	(118)	35	(354)	42	(168)	25	(20)
It's hardly fair to bring children into the world with the way things look for the future	52	(379)	57	(173)	44	(122)	40	(360)	39	(171)	30	(20)

[a] Data shown are the proportion of respondents who agreed with each statement at the time of the first interview.
[b] This group excludes those known to be deceased, in the armed forces, or in institutions.

TABLE A.14

Comparison of Respondents and Nonrespondents by Race and
Selected Characteristics of Study Population at the Time
of the First Interview: Long-Term Residents Only
(percentages)

Characteristic	White Participants in Study		Black Participants in Study	
	Interviewed in Cleveland	Not Interviewed*	Interviewed in Cleveland	Not Interviewed*
Sex				
Male	66	79	43	36
Female	34	21	57	64
Total percent	100	100	100	100
(N)	(160)	(24)	(143)	(45)
Education				
Less than high school	64	66	65	58
High school or greater	37	34	35	42
Total percent	100	100	100	100
(N)	(160)	(24)	(143)	(45)
Marital status				
Single	21	17	14	13
Married	65	75	67	75
Widowed	1	--	6	4
Divorced	13	8	13	7
Total percent	100	100	100	100
(N)	(160)	(24)	(143)	(45)
Total Annual Family Income				
Less than $3,000	8	12	15	18
$3,000 to $4,999	15	21	19	20
$5,000 to $7,499	24	29	31	25
$7,500 to $9,999	32	25	18	16
$10,000 or more	19	12	10	9
Don't know	2	--	7	11
Total percent	100	100	100	100
(N)	(158)	(24)	(141)	(44)
Labor force status				
Employed full-time	83	67	67	51
Other employed	4	8	7	6
Unemployed	5	12	10	20
All other	8	13	16	23
Total percent	100	100	100	100
(N)	(160)	(24)	(143)	(45)
Skill level of current occupation				
High	29	11	9	12
Medium	58	72	58	46
Low	13	17	33	42
Total percent	100	100	100	100
(N)	(138)	(18)	(105)	(24)
Thinking about moving from Cleveland				
Not thinking about leaving	75	50	79	50
Thinking about leaving but not at all sure	13	17	10	17
Thinking about leaving but not too sure	8	8	7	1
Thinking about leaving and pretty sure about it	4	25	4	23
Total percent	100	100	100	100
(N)	(160)	(24)	(143)	(45)

*This group excludes those known to be deceased, in the armed forces, or in institutions.

TABLE A.15

Comparison of Respondents and Nonrespondents by Race and Selected Attitudinal Characteristics of the Study Population at the Time of the First Interview: Long-Term Residents Only[a]

Attitude Statement	White Participants in Study				Black Participants in Study			
	Interviewed in Cleveland		Not Interviewed[b]		Interviewed in Cleveland		Not Interviewed[b]	
	%	(N)	%	(N)	%	(N)	%	(N)
Getting ahead here on earth isn't nearly as important as preparing for the next world	43	(150)	48	(23)	34	(143)	25	(44)
Don't expect too much out of life and be content with what comes your way	51	(158)	54	(24)	27	(142)	24	(45)
Planning only makes a person unhappy, since your plans hardly ever work out	34	(158)	38	(24)	39	(142)	33	(45)
There's little use writing or talking to public officials because often they aren't interested in your problem	43	(157)	52	(23)	48	(142)	55	(42)
Nowadays a person has to live pretty much for today and let tomorrow take care of itself	42	(160)	50	(24)	49	(142)	44	(45)
In spite of what some people say, things are getting worse, not better, for the average man	38	(157)	56	(23)	32	(141)	47	(45)
It's hardly fair to bring children into the world with the way things look for the future	30	(158)	50	(24)	35	(143)	40	(45)

[a] Data shown are the proportion of respondents who agreed with each statement at the time of the first interview.
[b] This group excludes those known to be deceased, in the armed forces, or in institutions.

As we have shown, despite our careful instructions and monitoring, the cohort that we originally assembled for this study was probably slightly biased in the direction of including a lower proportion of the very poorest migrants and long-termers than were present in the poorest Cleveland census tracts in 1967-68. The panel losses that occurred between the two interviews also tended to affect the least successful segment of our study population the most, although the variations in retrieval success are primarily related to the study participant's sex and race, and to a lesser extent to other characteristics. We suspect that our data are better for women than for men, and that they are strongest for white females. Insofar as caution is needed in interpreting our findings, it is because they may convey an overly favorable image of the social and economic situation of a population of low-income in-migrants and residents. Given the high incidence of unemployment alienation that we have documented, as well as the economic marginality of the women in this population, it is disturbing to think that these data may represent an understatement of inner-city conditions in 1971-72.

GENE B. PETERSEN is a sociologist and was a research associate at the Bureau of Social Science Research from 1963 to 1976. Prior to that time he was assistant professor and chair of the Department of Sociology at the American University of Beirut. His interest in occupations and manpower began at Columbia University under Kingsley Davis, with whom he later worked on the International Urban Resources project at the University of California at Berkeley. A Ford Foundation Foreign Area Training Fellowship provided the opportunity to work in Egypt for two years on a study of the reasons for and consequences of migration from Delta area villages to Cairo. His work at the BSSR was concentrated primarily in manpower areas ranging from the utilization of training by former participants in Agency for International Development Training Programs to that of participants in programs sponsored by the U.S. Department of Labor.

LAURE M. SHARP is a sociologist and has been a research associate at the Bureau of Social Science Research for the past 20 years where she is responsible for the execution of many large-scale surveys in social problem areas. Most of her work has been in the field of manpower and education; among her publications are Education and Employment, the Early Careers of College Graduates (Johns Hopkins Press, 1970) and numerous journal articles and monographs. She has served as consultant and task force member on survey methodology, manpower, and education problems for many private and public organizations, including the National Institute of Health, the National Academy of Arts and Sciences, and the National Society of Professional Engineers.

THOMAS F. DRURY, formerly with the Bureau of Social Science Research, is now a health statistician at the Division of Health Interview Statistics, National Center for Health Statistics. He is the coeditor (with Albert D. Biderman) of Measuring Work Quality for Social Reporting (Halsted Press, 1976). Work, health, and organizations are his main interests. He is a Ph.D. candidate in sociology at the Catholic University of America.

ABOUT THE BUREAU OF
SOCIAL SCIENCE RESEARCH

The Bureau of Social Science Research, Inc. is an independent, nonprofit organization in Washington, D.C., devoted to the development of social science knowledge about contemporary social problems. The Bureau was founded in 1950 as a division of the American University, but was separately incorporated in 1956.

The Bureau pursues a multidisciplinary research program, concentrating in survey research and program evaluation. Sociology and social psychology are the disciplines most heavily represented in the professional staff, which also includes specialists in the other social sciences, statistics, and law. The major portion of its work is sponsored by public agencies through contracts and grants. Diversified research support has prevailed throughout the Bureau's history, however, and many of its projects have been sponsored by foundations and other nonprofit institutions, as well as by research, business, and industrial firms.

COMPREHENSIVE SERVICES TO RURAL
POOR FAMILIES: An Evaluation of the
Arizona Job Colleges Program
> Keith Baker, Myfanway Glasso, Don
> Goyette, and C. Freemont Sprague

DEPRIVED URBAN YOUTH: An Economic and
Cross-Cultural Analysis of the United States, Colombia,
and Peru
> John P. Walter, William H. Leahy,
> and Arthur G. Dobbelaere

THE EFFECTS OF URBAN GROWTH: A Population
Impact Analysis
> Richard P. Appelbaum, Jennifer
> Bigelow, Henry P. Kramer,
> Harvey L. Molotch, and Paul M. Relis

POLITICIZING THE POOR: The Legacy of the War on
Poverty in a Mexican American Community
> Biliana C. S. Ambrecht

PROBLEM TENANTS IN PUBLIC HOUSING: Who,
Where, and Why Are They?
> Richard S. Scobie

A SURVEY OF PUERTO RICANS ON THE U.S.
MAINLAND IN THE 1970s
> Kal Wagenheim

URBAN NONGROWTH: City Planning for People
> Earl Finkler, William J. Toner,
> and Frank J. Popper